SWANSEA AND THE SECOND WORLD WAR

*Dedicated to All Those Who Lived in Swansea
During the Second World War*

SWANSEA AND THE SECOND WORLD WAR

BERNARD LEWIS

First impression: 2024

© Copyright Bernard Lewis and Y Lolfa Cyf., 2024

The contents of this book are subject to copyright, and may
not be reproduced by any means, mechanical or electronic,
without the prior, written consent of the publishers.

The publishers wish to acknowledge
the support of the Books Council of Wales.

Cover design: Sion Ilar
Front cover image: The Ben Evans store, February 1941
West Glamorgan Archive Service, P/PR 95/4/27

ISBN: 978-1-80099-440-9

Published and printed in Wales
on paper from well-maintained forests by
Y Lolfa Cyf., Talybont, Ceredigion SY24 5HE
website www.ylolfa.com
e-mail ylolfa@ylolfa.com
tel 01970 832 304

Sir John Hodsoll, Inspector General
of Air Raid Precautions, in March 1941:
'Probably no town in the country, and certainly
no town in south Wales, has been subjected to
such severe raiding as Swansea.'

~o~

Winston S Churchill, on a visit
to a bomb-ravaged Swansea in April 1941:
'Are we downhearted?'
Onlooking Swansea citizens:
'No! Not likely!'

Contents

Acknowledgements

I AM VERY grateful to my wife, Elizabeth (Lib), who assisted me in copying material at the West Glamorgan Archive Service. Her efforts considerably speeded up my research and eased the burden on myself. Kim Collis, the recently retired County Archivist, and his colleagues at the West Glamorgan Archive Service provided the excellent service and advice that I have become accustomed to over the last 20 years, and I am very grateful to all concerned.

I would also like to thank others who have assisted me in a number of ways, including the Books Council of Wales (which provided financial support to my publisher), Glenn Booker, Andy Chatterton, the Commonwealth War Graves Commission, Liz Courtney, Louise Davies, Michael Edmunds, Mair Norris Ellery, Lyndon Elsey, Pippa Ettore, Dr Neil Evans, John Fitzjohn, Henry and Judy Foner, Gerald Gabb, Trevor Harkin, John Hayward, Richard Huws, Dr Hazel Kent, Chris Kolonko-Weet, Mike Lewis, Steve Littlejohns, David Lloyd, Gareth Lovering (photography), Gareth Madge and Jake McDonald (South Wales Police Heritage Centre), Jessica Madge, Jeff Manning and Ian Rogerson (Swanseadocks.co.uk), John and Carol Powell (A History of Mumbles), Daniel Richards, Lee Richards at Arcre.co.uk (for record copying at the National Archives at Kew), Rogers Jones Auctioneers, Commodore Nick Stanley RN (Retd), Jeff Stewart, Ceri Thomas, John A Thomas, Peter Wakelin and Peter Webster.

My sincere thanks are due to Lefi Gruffudd and the team at Y Lolfa and especially to Carolyn Hodges who championed my work while it was still an incomplete jumble and guided it through the Books Council of Wales grant process. I must also thank my editor at Y Lolfa, Eirian Jones, whose expertise and eagle eyes vastly improved my manuscript.

Finally, I would like to offer special thanks to Dr John R Alban (formerly City Archivist at Swansea City Council and latterly County Archivist of Norfolk), my inspirational course tutor when I studied part-time for a Diploma in Local History at Swansea University between 1993 and 1995. He encouraged his students to keep researching and offered this sage advice: 'Have a plan. Try and get your research published. Before you die...'

Seven books later, I am still dutifully following his advice...

A Note on the Coinage of 1939–45

£1 consisted of 240 pennies.

A shilling consisted of 12 pennies and, consequently, there were 20 shillings to £1.

It was customary to show prices in £s, shillings and pence, £10 5*s.* 6*d.*

Comparative Money Value 1939 and 2024

According to the Bank of England website the sum of £10 in 1939 would be worth £541 in February 2024.

Measurements

One foot = 0.305 metres (30.48cm)

CHAPTER 1

Swansea on the Eve of War

ON 18 MARCH 1941, Howell L Lang-Coath, the Town Clerk at the Swansea County Borough Council, was preparing himself for an important and potentially difficult meeting. Swansea had suffered heavily in both human casualties and material damage during the German air raids of the nights of 19–21 February 1941, and it seemed that some borough councillors felt that they should have been consulted during that ordeal before certain important decisions had been personally taken by the Town Clerk in his role as the unpaid Air Raid Precautions Controller for Swansea. The council meeting of 18 March would give the disgruntled councillors a chance to express their concerns to Lang-Coath himself.

Lang-Coath was 66 years old and had been Town Clerk of Swansea for almost 30 years, having been appointed to the post as far back as 1911. He lived in Mumbles with his wife; their only child, a grown-up son, having been killed in an accident in 1935. It was noted in February 1941 that there were nine Town Clerks and three deputy Town Clerks in other parts of Britain who had earlier served under him in Swansea.[1] He was a strong character, as was shown in May 1938 when he became involved in a disagreement with W T Mainwaring Hughes, a councillor who was often a thorn in the side of his political opponents and many officials at the council. When Mainwaring Hughes contested the accuracy of one of Lang-Coath's minutes and could not be persuaded as to its correctness, the Town Clerk promptly removed his jacket and suggested that the issue be settled outside. Happily, the situation was swiftly defused by other council members – one helpfully suggesting that the matter be referred to the mental health committee – before blood had been shed.[2]

Before starting to explain his actions to councillors at their March 1941 meeting, Lang-Coath requested that the members of the press who were present did not record his remarks, as he regarded what he was about to say as being essentially private (though shorthand notes were taken by an official). He said:

> ... in view of the observations which have been made by some members of the council in regard to the officials acting and carrying on during these dreadful times, and no committees being called, I am compelled to indicate how wrong and unfair those observations are... What did we find on that Saturday morning? [22 February 1941] Roads damaged and impassable. Sewers damaged. Electric cables and equipment damaged. Fifteen schools destroyed or seriously damaged. Telephonic communication cut off. A casualty list, fortunately and providentially, not as large as might be expected. Over 6,500 people without a home to be dealt with... The town's shopping centre wiped out, including the market. Shops rendered useless by being destroyed by bombs or being burned out, or by having delayed action bombs in front of them... 171 food shops gone – 64 grocers, 61 butchers, 12 bakers and 34 hotels restaurants and cafés gone.

He added that gas and water supplies had been damaged in many areas, resulting in difficulties in the cooking of food, while St Mary's Church in the town centre and several other places of worship had also been destroyed. Dangerous buildings abounded and had to be cordoned off and made safe, the injured treated and the bodies of the dead recovered, identified and buried. After recounting how the Guildhall control room and its staff had managed during the crisis, he outlined his frustration at the way that some council members had viewed his actions, saying:

… it is very discouraging, when one has done one's best, and when one has been told by experts that things are satisfactory, to have it suggested, that on Saturday morning at 9 o'clock, with all that was facing me, and having gone through the responsibility of those terrible three nights, when you think of all the damage, and all the deaths, and all that is falling in the trail of those bombers, to have it suggested that I should have taken instructions in regard to calling a committee. What for? What could they have done? I carried out my instructions to act in an emergency, and if there had been any committee or any interruption, I can tell you, quite frankly, I could not have acted. I was too over-wrought – I had to keep a cool head and do my best, and my work has been approved by the powers that be and all concerned.

Unsurprisingly, in the light of Lang-Coath's forceful and heartfelt explanation, his actions were duly endorsed by council members.[3]

But why had Swansea been the target of such a sustained and deadly onslaught by Hitler's Luftwaffe over three consecutive nights in February 1941? Had the town been as well prepared as possible before the bombing attacks came in? What would have happened if a Nazi invasion of Britain had ensued shortly after the raids had taken place, with Swansea being targeted as a possible landing place? And how did the war affect the town and its people outside of the all too frequent air raids?

To begin to understand just how ready the town of Swansea was for all-out war and how its people were affected, it is necessary to go back to the mid-1930s and the darkening political situation on mainland Europe.

In any new war involving Britain, a European enemy's modern airpower would undoubtedly be ranged against Swansea, a town of some importance to the British economy that contained a number of tempting targets. The Swansea of the 1930s had a relatively large population and was the home to a wide range of works, factories and other businesses. Indeed, the estimated population of the borough of Swansea in 1937 was around 169,000, of which over 10,000 people worked in the metal processing industries, with a further 10,000 involved in transport and communications. Another 10,000 people were employed in non-clerical roles in finance, insurance and other commercial activities, while the work of that and other sectors of the local economy was underpinned by around 4,000 individuals who performed clerical, administrative or typing tasks. There were 4,000 people working in domestic service, an indication that Swansea possessed a sizeable number of middle- and upper-class families, typically living in substantial homes, who needed many of their day-to-day needs attended to by others and had the money available to pay for those services.

In the 1930s Swansea could lay claim to being the nearest of the large Bristol Channel ports to the sea-borne trade routes that traversed the Atlantic Ocean, and within 20 miles of the town there were around 500 works and collieries, all keen to get their products into the market place, whether that be in the local area or the wider world. As such, the town and its port were well placed for facilitating trade with the dominions and colonies of the British Empire, as well as Europe, the countries of Canada, America and those of South America. If a new conflict was to arise, Swansea would clearly have a significant role to play in the manufacture of products for domestic and war related purposes, as well as in importing and exporting a wide range of equipment and materials that would be important to Britain's economy at a time of war.[4]

Despite its convenient position on the south Wales coast, Swansea had not been particularly prompt in the construction of effective port facilities until the arrival of the Victorian era, though, by the 1930s, the docks infrastructure had become extensive and well developed. It was thus able to efficiently deal with the considerable quantities of coal, iron, steel, oil and other commodities that arrived at or left the harbour each year, with items being dispatched to all corners of the wider world. The deep-water area contained within the docks ran to 270 acres, with the quaysides having a length of 32,000 feet. Transit sheds provided storage space of almost 817,000 square feet, while there were 21 coal-handling devices on the dockside and 102 cranes, with the weight-carrying capacity of the strongest cranes (of which there were 24) being an impressive 70 tons. The Queen's Dock was the largest dock, being 150 acres in size, and it was used primarily by the National Oil Refineries, a subsidiary of the Anglo-Iranian Oil Company, for unloading crude oil for processing at the Llandarcy Refinery near Skewen. The King's Dock, Prince of Wales Dock and South Dock completed the docks complex (the North Dock had closed to traffic in 1930). The principal exports were coal, coke, steel rails, ironwork and tinplate. Other exports included processed oil, grain, flour and cement, among other materials. The main imports consisted of oil, wood for mining purposes, grain, flour, copper and other ores, iron, steel and building sand.[5]

The tonnages handled by the port were impressive. The total imports in 1939 amounted to 1,351,000 tons, made up largely of oil (513,000 tons), iron and steel (297,000 tons), mining wood (110,000 tons), and copper (102,000 tons). On the export side, a staggering 3,409,000 tons of coal were exported during 1939, as well as 330,000 tons of oil and 273,000 tons of tinplate in a total export figure of 4,235,000 tons.

Beyond the docks another key target for an enemy during wartime would undoubtedly be Llandarcy Oil Refinery on the fringe of the town. The refinery was one of the largest in Great Britain and received its raw material from the Queen's Dock via a four-mile-long pipeline. The refining process involved the crude oil being separated into various grades of petrol, kerosene, vaporizing-oil, gas-oil, diesel engine oil and paraffin wax, all of which had an important role to play in both civilian and military activities. Output from the refinery had in fact already peaked in 1925 when it reached almost 90 million gallons.

The export trade emanating from Llandarcy Oil Refinery had then declined from the mid-1920s onwards after a decision by the company owners to refine the crude oil nearer to the oil fields themselves, essentially at a huge refinery at Abadan Island in what was then the Persian Gulf. Despite this contraction in trade, the refinery was still of significant economic importance to Swansea and Britain as a whole and, as such, would probably be a priority target for enemy attacks.[6]

Metal processing was another significant factor in Swansea's economic jigsaw. Even if the days when Swansea was the copper-smelting centre of the world were long behind it, there were still a number of companies around the town that worked with metals and would potentially have an important part to play in Britain's armaments industry during any future conflict. In 1929 the American International Nickel Company amalgamated with the Mond Nickel Company which had a long-established nickel plant in Clydach on the outskirts of Swansea. Nickel had been used extensively for naval armament purposes during the Great War, and the deteriorating international situation of the 1930s saw an increased demand for the product as weapons production received greater attention than had been the case in recent years.

Inasmuch as the industries of Swansea provided tempting targets for an adversary, the town centre and its suburbs also had a certain value to an enemy at a time of war. The bombing of Guernica in 1937 during the Spanish Civil War had shown that air raids could have a material effect in spreading terror, while also disrupting the defensive plans, communications and economic activity of a town or city to the benefit of an attacker. There was also the question of how well the morale of people under attack from the air would survive the shock of potentially suffering close personal loss, as well as seeing the possible destruction of their homes and familiar landmarks within their town.

It was entirely possible that a new enemy would attempt to demoralise the people of Swansea (as well as other towns and cities) by an immediate campaign of terror attacks from the air. That had occurred during the war of 1914–18, though the primitive aircraft of those days were unable to inflict major casualties or damage on their targets. It was obvious that the improved aircraft of a coming war, with their greater range and bomb-carrying capacity, could bring the conflict to the very doorsteps of the people with potentially disastrous results. This had been acknowledged as far back as November 1932, when Stanley Baldwin had advised the House of Commons that, 'I think it is well also for the man in the street to realise that there is no power on earth that can protect him from being bombed. Whatever people may tell him, the bomber will always get through...'[7]

When the bomber did get through to Swansea, apart from its important economic targets, what would its deadly cargo be likely to hit, whether by accident or design? There were large areas of old and closely-packed domestic housing within Swansea and a number of newer housing estates that had been constructed in the aftermath of the war of 1914–18. It was a constant fear for those in authority in Swansea that bombs dropped on those areas could not fail to inflict heavy civilian casualties, while also undermining morale and causing substantial physical damage to domestic properties, rendering many people homeless and producing a flood of refugees. Beyond the housing areas there was the new Guildhall of course, opened in 1934 and the proud centre of civic administration with its lofty and striking clock tower. The building provided a home to the British Empire Panels, the work of the eminent artist Frank Brangwyn. There were also the impressive offices of the Swansea Harbour Trust, which had been taken over by the Great Western Railway (GWR) company, and the nearby grand building that housed the Swansea Metal Exchange on Adelaide Street. There was a smattering of comfortable hotels in the town, including the Grand and the Metropole, all much-loved Swansea landmarks. The town had around 25 theatres, cinemas and public halls, including the popular Albert Hall, Plaza and Regal, as well as the Empire. The Grand Theatre had been opened in 1897 by the world-famous opera singer Madame Adelina Patti, who had also purchased an impressive home in the Swansea Valley. The stage at the Grand had been graced on more than one occasion by the doyen of British theatre, Sir Henry Irving, who brought along his business manager, one Bram Stoker, who is better known today as the author of the novel *Dracula*. There were over 120 places of worship in the town, including St Mary's Church which stood in the shadow of the town's Norman castle, as well as a Jewish synagogue. Other religious communities claimed membership numbers that ranged from 5,000 people (Congregational, Henrietta Street) to just 64 (Bethel Baptist, Waunarlwydd). A large public library and an important art gallery, as well as the oldest museum in Wales, all added to the aura of Swansea being a prominent town that had embraced industry, art and knowledge in its long and varied history.[8]

The best-known town-centre business was probably the Ben Evans department store on Castle Street, which proudly described itself in 1938 as 'The Shopping Centre of Wales' and 'The Establishment for Value and Modern Merchandise'. The store had been expanded over the years from its earliest incarnation by the gradual acquisition of adjoining properties, so that by the 1930s it was a large, attractive building that was hemmed in by Goat Street, Caer Street, Castle Bailey Street and Temple Street. The shopping experience was spread over three floors and the items offered for sale included carpets, rugs, mattings, cabinet furniture, bedsteads, cots and bedding, gentlemen's boots, shoes, hats and caps, together with a linoleum display area. That was merely the ground floor; the first floor was where customers would find soft furnishings, curtains, woollens, aprons, pocket handkerchiefs, dress materials and household linen. Space was also found for gloves, umbrellas, silks and velvets, hosiery, haberdashery and general ironmongery and – somewhat optimistically given the prevailing Swansea weather – sunshades. If that was not enough for that floor, there was also a display of bric-a-brac.

The second floor offered women's boots, shoes, cloaks, jackets, capes, corsets, blouses, millinery, tea gowns, silk shirts, flowers and feathers, mantles, engravings, paintings and travelling requisites. There was also a dining room where customers could rest their aching feet, a refreshment area and a library. It is hard to imagine many of the varied needs of much of Swansea's population not being met by a visit to 'Ben's' in the 1930s, and a trip to the store must have been keenly anticipated for those with the money available to spend on its undoubted attractions.

If the Ben Evans store could lay claim to being the most prestigious shop in Swansea, then its near neighbour, the Kardomah Café on Castle Street, held the title of Swansea's most influential premises for light refreshments. Though originally located on High Street, it had been in Castle Street since 1908, and during the 1930s it attracted a number of talented local writers, painters and artists who became known as the 'Kardomah Gang' and included Dylan Thomas, Vernon Watkins and Alfred Janes. There were several other cafés that were run by mainly Italian immigrant families that are still active in the Swansea of today, such as those run by the Cascarinis and Rabaiottis.

Beyond those high-profile examples, the town could boast of an abundance of butchers and bakers (though possibly no candlestick makers), as well as suppliers of just about every necessity that a Swansea inhabitant might require. If an enemy could inflict serious damage on the civilian and commercial infrastructure of the town by way of aerial attack, then the result was likely to be a substantial number of deaths and injuries, a terrorised population, wrecked docks, blocked roads, damaged water and gas mains as well as a significant loss of production in support of the British war effort. A shattered Swansea would be a fine result for a morally bankrupt enemy, and the town could expect to receive its murderous attention sooner or later at a time of war.

Indeed, that is precisely what did happen after Britain declared war on Nazi Germany following its invasion of Poland in September 1939. During the Great War of 1914–18, Swansea had sent its young men abroad to fight against an aggressor so that names like Mametz Wood, Pilckem Ridge and Gallipoli became well known locally through the heavy sacrifices made at those places by its gallant sons. In the new conflict the names of Dunkirk, El Alamein and Normandy, among a host of others, would soon become household words, while tragic losses were also sustained by those of its citizens who served elsewhere in the struggle to control the sea and the sky against a determined enemy.

For the people of Swansea who remained at home, the Second World War would not be experienced only through the stories told by relatives returning from action, newspaper reports or what was heard via broadcasts on the radio. Modern aircraft would bring the terror of war to the doorsteps of the people of the town itself, at Teilo Crescent, Brynsifi Terrace, Russell Street, Grafog Street and elsewhere. The town would be repeatedly attacked from the air and, for a period, would live under the threat of invasion, with almost 400 of its citizens dying within the town itself, with a large swathe of the town centre and much of its housing damaged or destroyed. The war's front line would no longer be in some distant and obscure part of the world; it would potentially be just outside the door of every building in Swansea. The horror of war would be faced by Swansea's pensioners, housewives and school children. It would be a searing and painful experience that would leave an indelible mark on the town's long history and, indeed, on the fabric of the town itself.

CHAPTER 2

Preparing for Disaster

IF TOWNS LIKE Swansea were likely to be targets in a new war, then what could be done to best prepare them for the trials that might lie ahead? During the 1930s the government had begun to encourage local authorities to put in hand preparations for a possible war though, given the straitened financial circumstances of the time following the Great Depression, it proved hard to nudge those bodies in the right direction without some element of legislative instruction. Swansea did finally proceed at a measured pace, and the building chosen to house its planned civil defence control room was the Guildhall, often affectionately referred to by the local population as 'the Civic' (centre).

The Guildhall had opened in 1934 and was (and still is) an imposing feature of the Swansea landscape, not least because its most prominent feature is a clock tower reaching to around 160 feet. Designed by Sir Percy Thomas, it was completed in white Portland stone in a neoclassical style. It was, given its prominence, perhaps a risky choice for an important wartime communications centre but, with cost always an important factor in the pre-war years, it had the advantage of already accommodating a number of key officials and their staffs, all of whom would be required to perform important roles in civil defence should war eventually come. It also occupied a site close to the foreshore but potentially away from the main centres of industry and population in the town, locations that would probably be the prime targets for enemy bombers.

As a future communications hub for the civil defence

services, the Guildhall was positioned between the eastern and western parts of the borough, a convenient location should it become necessary to pass messages by vehicle, motorbike or even bicycle when telephone or radio communication had been disrupted by an air raid. Modest steps were taken to improve the safety of those who worked within the building, given its important role in the embryonic civil defence structure and its striking appearance which made it easily identifiable from the air. A ground-floor room adjacent to the Guildhall garage was strengthened so that it could act as an air raid shelter for at least some of the staff, while in an emergency there was a small number of existing rooms in the basement that could provide staff members with some form of protection during a raid. Sandbags were placed around external doors, and windows were taped to reduce the danger from flying glass, while throughout the building provision was made for the probability of the staff having to deal with incendiary bombs and fires during or after a raid. To that end, stirrup pumps, buckets of water, scuttles containing sand, as well as scoops and rakes were provided in corridors and other areas. Several types of fire extinguisher were also placed in key locations within the building.[1]

The council had created an Air Raid Precautions Committee in February 1938 and it proceeded to appoint Town Clerk Howell L Lang-Coath to the important, but unpaid, role of Air Raid Precautions Controller, and Captain E B Backhouse to the paid post of Air Raid Precautions Officer during 1939. Ellis Brockman Backhouse was a retired Army officer in his early forties who had seen service with the East Kent Regiment during the Great War. He took lodgings on Bryn Road, conveniently close to the Guildhall, though his time there was destined to be short-lived as he was recalled for military service early in the war. At that time he did not head off to the War Office in London and a cushy desk job; in May 1940 he and several comrades commandeered a yacht at Dunkirk and were later picked up by a destroyer while attempting to escape the grasp of the advancing Nazis and return to Britain.[2] Backhouse was succeeded in the post during March 1940 by Mr E J Brayley, who had hitherto been employed in the Town Clerk's department.

During the time he was in Swansea, Captain Backhouse proved to be an energetic organiser, which was just as well since at a meeting held on 31 March 1939 it was stated that, 'Captain Backhouse's department is hopelessly inadequately staffed. It is not sufficient to co-ordinate the different services and he frankly states that if a single member of his existing staff went sick there would be chaos in a crisis.' Captain Backhouse was paid a salary of £400 per annum and in 1939 could only call on the services of two other dedicated staff members within his department, namely a clerk and a typist.[3]

The scale of the organisation that he nevertheless helped build up from almost nothing was indeed impressive. He was responsible for the enrolment of first aid parties, the staff of first aid posts, ambulance drivers, drivers who dealt with 'sitting' casualties, rescue parties, demolition and decontamination squads, as well as the personnel of numerous local report centres. He also provided gas training courses for a number of teams and that was a significant task in its own right. The use of gas by an unscrupulous enemy was widely anticipated and feared, given the history of gas attacks during the Great War. The course offered by Captain Backhouse gave attendees information on mustard, phosgene, chlorine and several other types of gas that could possibly be deployed from the air. Also discussed was the type of injury or effect inflicted by each gas type (typically blistering, choking with irritation of the lungs, nose and eyes causing tears), as well as how persistent they were in remaining in the atmosphere or on the ground.

Mustard gas was considered to be the most dangerous weapon of its type as it was very persistent, could soak into the skin, was difficult to destroy, could penetrate porous or semi-porous materials, and was almost odour free. Indeed, a gas mask could only protect the eyes and lungs while leaving the rest of an unprotected body vulnerable to its effects. It was noted that while metal, glass and glazed china were effective in keeping the gas off the skin, they were also impractical materials for everyday use. Oilskin outfits could provide protection for considerable periods though, but given the rise in body temperature and heart rate occasioned by wearing such a suit, it was only practical to work in such an outfit for perhaps three periods of time, each not exceeding an hour's duration, within 24 hours if physical collapse was to be avoided. During the course instruction was even given in the precise order in which oilskin suits should be donned and later taken off. Hurriedly putting on the garments in the wrong order during an emergency could have dire consequences if the need to overlap particular elements of the clothing was not strictly observed.[4]

The course also explained how refuge rooms could be created in domestic properties by sealing up every gap, whether it be a crack, ventilator, fireplace and so on to keep the gas at bay. Explanations were also given on how to decontaminate a room, building, clothing or outside areas in the aftermath of an attack. Typically, this would involve hosing, mopping, using solvents, burning, boiling or simple weathering – where an infected area could be left to the vagaries of the wind and rain. It was all the stuff of nightmares though, thankfully, gas weapons were never subsequently deployed during the Second World War. Other specialised training for Captain Backhouse's subordinates was given by the Medical Officer of Health as well as the Borough Engineer and Surveyor.[5]

During 1939 there was a concern over the numbers coming forward for civil defence duties in Swansea and it was noted that, at one training course arranged by the Medical Officer of Health, 30 of the 40 initial attendees had dropped out. Captain Backhouse believed that this was due to the Medical Officer of

Health requiring the voluntary course attendees to sit a formal examination on what they had been taught, though this was disputed. The Medical Officer of Health was adamant that he needed people who knew what they were doing, and an examination provided firm evidence of the standard achieved by an individual. Nevertheless, as an example, the rescue, demolition and decontamination squads were still well under strength in 1939, though, as many of the men who would form the teams were already employed on a day-to-day basis by the Borough Engineer's department, Captain Backhouse was quite satisfied as to their likely quality. Their availability in a real crisis, when faced with competing priorities between their daily duties and sudden emergencies, was, however, a cause for concern. It was agreed that more efforts would be made to encourage further volunteers. The numbers involved in the civil defence services on 1 April 1939 are shown in the following table:

Number of volunteers on 1 April 1939.[6]

Service	Men	Women	Total Enrolled/ (Requirement – including reserves)
Air Raid Wardens	1,252	89	1,341 / (2,525)
First aid parties	292	0	292 / (825)
First aid posts	109	866	975 / (737)
Ambulance drivers and attendants	29	288	317 / (615)
Car drivers (sitting casualties)	0	59	59 / (206)
Rescue parties	255	0	255 / (555)
Decontamination squads	76	0	76 / (210)
Report centres	76	51	127 / (180)
Messengers	5	0	5 / (0)
Miscellaneous duties	118	326	444 / (113)
Total	2,212	1,679	3,891 / (5,966)

Though the figures appear to show a shortfall in the requirements, it is apparent that the number of volunteers coming forward was still increasing as 1939 proceeded. Indeed, in the three months to 1 April 1939, 2,018 had been enrolled and, assuming that pattern was followed between April 1939 and the (as then unknown) date of the outbreak of war, the required numbers would probably be achieved.

While all of the roles shown above had an important part to play in the civil defence arrangements, it was the role of air raid warden that underpinned the system and employed the most personnel. The modern reader may well base their knowledge of the work of an air raid warden on actor Bill Pertwee's depiction of chief air raid warden Hodges in the television series *Dad's Army*. Hodges' main duties seemed to be regularly shouting 'Put that light out!' while interfering in the daily routine of the local Home Guard unit and insulting its commanding officer. In the reality of 1939, a warden needed to be 'a responsible and reliable member of the public who will undertake to advise and help his fellow-citizens, in the sector to which he is allotted, in all the risks and calamities which might follow from air attack, and will form a link between them and the authorities for reporting air raid damage and calling aid when required.' Once trained, an identity card would be issued to a warden, as well as a badge and a special armlet in recognition of his (or her) role.[7]

Even in the run-up to war, a warden could be active in advising neighbours on how to take precautions within their homes so as to reduce the risk from bomb blast, in addition to showing them how to use gas masks, stirrup pumps and other small items of civil defence equipment. During wartime, he could help calm and reassure the people in his sector and report bomb damage to the control centre. He could summon (though not instruct) policemen, first aid parties, fire patrols and decontamination squads, updating them on the situation before guiding them to the incident location. In his sector, a warden needed to be well acquainted with the local people, the location of local air raid shelters, fire hydrants and telephones, as well as details of those premises on his 'patch' that carried specific risks, such as petrol stores or timber yards. In the event of an alarm, a warden was required to clear the streets of pedestrians, sending to their home shelter those who were within a five-minute walk of it or, if their home was too far away, directing them to the nearest public shelter. Motorists would be told to safely park and leave their cars at the roadside before seeking shelter, while also ensuring that emergency vehicles could still pass by unhindered.

Based on the central guidance, the presumed basic air raid precautions organisational structure in Swansea was likely to have looked something like this, using Division 1 as an example:

CHIEF WARDEN
(Covering Swansea's 160,000+
civilians in two divisions)
|
DIVISION 1 (of 2)
(Divisional warden covering around
80,000+ civilians in ten groups)
|
GROUPS
(Ten groups each covering around 8,000 civilians,
each group with a head warden in charge)
|
POSTS
(Sixteen ARP posts within each group, each post covering around
500 civilians and under the control of a senior warden)

Division 2 would broadly follow the same structure for the other half of the borough.

In Swansea the chief warden had under his control two 'divisions', each one headed by a divisional (or head) warden.

Division 1 concerned itself with that area north of the Landore Viaduct and the Great Western Railway line that ran through Cockett, while Division 2 covered the centre of the town as well as St Thomas and the western parts of the borough.

Though unique circumstances in some areas might require a deviation from the norm, the guidance suggested that one ARP sector post should be provided for every 500 citizens and, for a town of Swansea's size, that suggested around 320 posts would be required across the borough. With the required number of air raid wardens for Swansea being set locally at around 2,500, that does seem to roughly fit, since at least six wardens were needed to cover each post. Posts were to be established in any room or building that was conveniently situated within a defined sector, and the premises chosen should be easily visible to the public. It could be in a warden's home, a shop, a garage or a school building among other possibilities, and the selected building should have access to or be near a telephone. Where necessary, powers of requisition could be used to take control of a suitable property. For example, in September 1939, a vacant property on Neath Road was taken over for use as a warden's post and, at the war's end, over £68 in compensation for damage caused was paid to the property owner.[8] Blocks of flats, hotels, factories and other premises containing more than 100 people would usually be expected to provide their own air raid warden service.

At each sector post, at least three wardens would be required to attend during an air raid and, to cover for absences due to work commitments or ill health etc., a further three to five wardens should be available to step in as required. At each post one warden was to be designated as the senior warden while a post of second warden should also be filled, with that person acting in the absence of the senior warden. In Swansea, for example, a surviving ARP identity card shows that post number nine was located at 148 High Street, in what seems to have been the home of senior warden Walter Corney, a draper and outfitter in the town (reporting to Haydn Hughes, divisional warden in command of Division 2), while the second warden was Oswald Roy, who ran a grocery and provisions store at New Orchard Street. There were 13 other wardens available for turns of duty at the post. The sector covered by the post and its team was broadly comprised of Prince of Wales Road, the Hafod Bridge area, the Palace, Thomas Row, High Street, Croft Street, Dyfatty Street, Willow Place, Howell Street, Greenhill Street, Chapel Street, Green Row, Prospect Place and Evans Court.[9]

The duties of the head wardens and divisional wardens were primarily administrative; they would be involved in recruitment, training and duty rota setting, as well as dealing with routine queries from those under their control. During an air raid emergency, however, it was vital that reports from the more junior wardens on the ground were sent directly to the control centre at the Guildhall, rather than up the warden's chain of command where delay would almost inevitably occur. Additionally, during an air raid one warden was always expected to remain at his designated post, as it would be to the post, in pursuit of information, that the police, fire parties and other specialist teams would first report in a crisis.

As well as the personnel needed to operate efficient civil defence services, there was also a requirement to provide the necessary equipment and infrastructure on which those services would depend. Every citizen would need a gas mask and that amounted to almost 170,000 masks in the case of Swansea, a total that posed immediate problems of storage. Premises were acquired at Adelaide Street, St Thomas, Sketty and Morriston to cope with the volumes involved. Gas decontamination centres were established at four locations across the town, while fixed first aid posts (typically to be used for dealing with the walking wounded after an attack) were set up in 15 places, including church halls, former police stations and schoolrooms. Eventually, there would be over 30 buildings in use for casualty and first aid purposes, including the British Legion building in Llansamlet, a church hall in Dunvant, the Ravenhill garage, the Oddfellows Hall in Mumbles, and the old tramway offices on St Helen's Road. Over 40 static water tanks were initially constructed around the town (the number increased greatly over time) to provide a source of water in emergency situations where supply pipes had been damaged by bombing. When local supplies proved to be difficult to obtain, the Home Office provided Swansea with 500,000 sandbags for the protection of buildings from the effects of bomb blast. Additionally, the Chief Constable of Swansea, F J May, fully expected to use new powers of requisition that would enable him to commandeer suitable civilian vehicles for conversion and use as ambulances during wartime.[10]

Even as preparations were being made for the possibility of war, the plans to mitigate its likely effects were being tested in readiness. One of the all-embracing requirements of civil defence planning was the need to impose a blackout at night so as to make towns like Swansea hard to see from the air. Switching street, house and business lights off, covering windows and door glass with blackout material, and shielding car lights, were all important elements of the plan. To test the arrangements it was announced that on 15 June 1939 at 11.30pm in Swansea and several other adjoining local authorities, all street lights were to be put out for two hours, while civilians were asked to remain indoors wherever possible while also switching off or screening internal lights. Local businesses were asked to do likewise. At the Guildhall control room it was noted that, '... fires, wrecked buildings and "casualties" were reported from various parts of the town and fire squads, ambulances, decontamination squads, rescue and repair parties moved over the district at the instructions of control.'[11]

The exercise was judged to be reasonably successful, despite it taking place in bad weather. The lighting restrictions were generally well observed, with building and street lights being extinguished according to the plan, while cars that were on the road due to unavoidable needs were seen to be driving with only their side-lights visible. Nevertheless, it was noted that in some properties, although blinds or curtains had been deployed, light was still visible through them. In one retail property within the town, neon lights remained illuminated and would have been an obvious marker for any enemy aircraft. With the matter being subsequently discussed with the offenders, it was hoped that in future the blackout restrictions would be more fully observed. Some 6,000 volunteers had taken part in the exercise that had covered an area from Swansea to Bridgend, with the civil defence air raid wardens and the rescue and demolition squads being active, together with several other services. The time of the daily blackout would vary depending on the seasons; by way of example, on 12–13 April 1941 it extended from 8.37pm to 5.55am.[12]

In a similar vein, air raid sirens had been placed at the Guildhall and Cefn Coed Hospital, as well as at a number of other buildings, in order that air raid alarms could be heard throughout the borough. Indeed, on Sunday, 3 December 1939, three months after the outbreak of war, Swansea staged an exercise that had the air raid sirens throughout the borough sounded, including those at the Mond Nickel works and the Baldwins Tinplate Works in Swansea Docks. Whistles and rattles added to the cacophony of alarms, though members of the public were still free to complete their Sunday worship, while those who could do so were asked to seek shelter as they would do during a real raid rather than merely stand and gawp as the civil defence personnel went about their business.[13]

The sort of actions illustrated above, along with a host of others, all needed careful coordination and direction from a central control point. At Swansea's Guildhall the civil defence 'report and control centre' had been established in and around the Green Room, a suite of rooms that was usually used for dressing and rest purposes by visiting artistes who were appearing at the Brangwyn Hall. One wartime visitor to the control centre, in a light-hearted account, described the controller's room as featuring a communication device of variable temperament that was nicknamed 'Clarence', the use of which involved much dial-twiddling and loud speaking as contact was attempted to be made with the more remote outposts of the Swansea civil defence network. There was also a telephone room where it was apparently the practice for the male staff who happened to be on duty to serenade the female team members with a moving rendition of 'Goodnight, Ladies' at the end of a shift, a much-appreciated gesture, since apparently most other staff members did not refer to them as 'ladies'. The operations room, as well as being generously supplied with a range of documents that contained often confusing civil defence acronyms, was also the home of 'Rolly' (Rowley) Davies, a man who kept a tight grip on any incoming incident report forms.[14]

If the civil defence service had needed building up largely from scratch, important elements of it were already in existence. In 1939 Swansea already had a combined and well-established police force and fire brigade service. The authorised strength of the police element of the force stood at 200, comprising the Chief Constable F J May, three superintendents, 11 inspectors, 29 sergeants and 156 constables, and there was an additional post that dealt with the inspection of hackney carriages. Based on the population of the borough as recorded in the census of 1931, there was one police constable for every 824 people. The fire brigade also came under the command of the Chief Constable, and it consisted of one inspector, one sergeant and nine firemen. A further 26 men served as auxiliary fire-fighters, making a total of 37 men being available for fire-fighting duties in the borough.

In due course, the advent of war saw an understandable increase in the manpower resources available to the Chief

Constable in Swansea. On 31 December 1939, there were 120 police auxiliary officers available for duty, a useful back-up force for when emergencies arose. Members of the First Police Reserve, a small body made up of retired police officers, had also been mobilised, yielding 28 enrolled recruits by the end of 1939. The Police War Reserve consisted of men who, for reasons of age or physical impairment, were not suitable for service in the armed forces, and that unit provided 92 enrolled men by 31 December 1939. These recruits were given a few weeks of basic training in policing duties before commencing duty in the town. Additionally, the Special Constabulary was also mobilized for emergency duty, and that added another 132 men to the roster of available manpower. Some of those men were available for full-time employment on policing duties and they worked eight hours a day on six days a week, while those only available on a part-time basis typically worked from 7pm to 10.30pm on a number of evenings each week. They had almost all been trained in routine police duties, air raid precaution measures, anti-gas attack procedures and first aid.

Between 26 August 1939 and 31 December 1939, the full-time members of the police auxiliary service in Swansea worked over 39,000 hours, while their part-time colleagues contributed over 17,000 hours, a useful addition to policing in the town. The members of the First Police Reserve and the Police War Reserve helped fill the gaps as regular officers were called up for military service after war had been declared. In October 1941, women were appointed to the force for the first time in a policing role, serving as auxiliary constables, though they tended to be employed in administrative and communication roles, thus freeing up men for street patrol duties.[15]

The experience of the Spanish Civil War (1936–39) had shown that, in addition to the danger posed by gas and high-explosive bombs, the humble incendiary device could also be the cause of major problems. Given that incendiary bombs were often dropped in large numbers, it was envisaged that during an attack fires could break out over a wide area of a town, possibly overwhelming the resources of the local fire services, and it would therefore be necessary to spread the fire-fighting workload beyond the remit of the dedicated fire-fighting teams. The Civil Defence Act of 1939 (2 & 3 Geo. 6 Ch.31) placed an obligation on the owners of commercial premises, in which more than 50 people worked, to ensure 'that a suitable proportion of those people are trained and equipped to give first-aid treatment, to deal with the effects of gas and to fight fires'. It was hoped that minor blazes could then be tackled by trained teams of onsite employees, leaving fire service personnel to deal with more serious fires. The issue of proactive fire-watching was addressed in an order of 1940 that required at least one person to be present at all times in premises that employed more than 30 people, as well as in warehouses of more than 50,000 cubic feet, or in saw-mills and timber yards that contained more than 50,000 cubic feet of timber.[16]

The role required the on-duty fire-watcher to detect fire and quickly summon assistance. The measure proved to be unequal to the size of the fire risk, since a great many premises did not come within its control as they were too small; while in many areas later experience showed that it was common for commercial and domestic premises to be left totally unoccupied for a period following earlier raids, the employees having been evacuated, thus having no one on site to observe developing threats. Additionally, the fire-watching work proved to be unpopular and it was often hard to fill the posts. By February 1941 it proved necessary to require any available males, aged between 16 and 60, to register for fire precaution work, with such work to be performed in the business and industrial areas close to their homes.[17] Even the potentially inflammable contents of domestic lofts came under scrutiny.

In July 1940 the Minister for Home Security issued an order that required all uninhabited loft spaces in domestic dwellings (which, oddly, included the lofts of hotels and hospitals) to be cleared of all articles stored therein, lest they provide extra material for an incendiary bomb to set ablaze.[18]

In addition to the preceding arrangements, during 1938 the Home Office had required many local authorities to form an Auxiliary Fire Service (AFS) so that plentiful assistance would be available to the regular local brigade in the aftermath of a bombing raid. In Swansea the Chief Fire Officer had thought that perhaps 500 auxiliary firemen would be required, a substantial number, as the threat of extensive fires following aerial attacks posed a considerable risk. In the event, it was reported in late September 1939 that the Home Office had recently agreed to an actual establishment of almost 1,500 persons for the new AFS unit in Swansea. In addition to more than a hundred management and administrative positions, there would also be a need for 162 leading firemen, 648 auxiliary firemen, 184 drivers and 296 messengers. The equipment would include 63 light trailer pumps, 15 heavy pumps and 82 lorries.

Recruitment to the new organisation proved to be somewhat slow, however, and after a month of operational duty the numbers working in the AFS in Swansea at the end of September 1939 amounted to just over 200 whole-time (paid) and 220 part-time (unpaid) members. Auxiliary fire stations were dotted across the borough at ten locations, including the Guildhall, Sketty (Potts Garage), Townhill (the Gwent Hall), St Thomas (Potter's Garage, Delhi Street) and Fisher Street (Alun Davies Motors). The shortfall in recruits was reflected in the number of patrols that could be carried out each day. Each patrol consisted of a leading fireman, five auxiliary firemen and two messengers.

For AFS members, patrolling one's 'patch' on a daily basis was an important part of the job. Patrol area No. 1 covered the town centre, with an overall street length of almost 5.5 miles, subdivided into seven beats. It was essentially a repetitive footslog through the town, with the patrol schedule clearly defining the route to be taken, assisted by the insertion of an 'L' or an 'R' after a street name indicating the direction of travel to be followed. Patrols were required to report back on anything unusual or in need of attention to one of a number of local auxiliary fire stations. Other patrols covered the streets of St Thomas, Morriston and Llansamlet among others. The shortfall in firemen numbers meant that the reality in September 1939 was that, although it was desirable to complete 22 patrols in the Guildhall area in a 24-hour period, only four patrols were actually being completed. Fisher Street was pencilled in for 24 patrols in a 24-hour period, though only three were able to be completed due to staffing issues. This was clearly a worrying situation and it could only be hoped that the numbers of serving AFS personnel could be ratcheted up before enemy raids became a regular occurrence.[19] As it happened, the lack of early offensive action from the air by the enemy soon caused the Home Office to reconsider the numbers of AFS personnel required in Swansea, and in October 1939 it proved necessary for the Chief Fire Officer to prepare a scheme that resulted in around a 50 per cent reduction from the original establishment of 1,500 or so personnel. As many posts remained unfilled at that time, it was unlikely to have a major effect on the service, at least until the first raids took place.[20]

Within the Division A area of the Auxiliary Fire Service in Swansea, there were 23 (it had been hoped to provide 51) buildings that were denoted as 'action stations' posts that could be used as focal points in an emergency. Most of them had or were located in close proximity to a telephone, thus having access to a means of instant communication. Indeed, some of the action stations consisted only of a police box with a telephone inside it, providing a simple but efficient local 'control centre' which could be used to send and receive messages in an emergency, as well as providing a gathering point for those reporting for duty at short notice during a crisis. Other action stations, some of which included onsite billeting arrangements, were located in the Masonic Hall on Caer Street, various post offices, several commercial garages, the Round Top School in Mayhill, the Unit Superheaters works and the King's Head Inn at Treboeth.[21]

The pace and scale of Swansea's civil defence preparations had gradually increased as the 1930s drew to a close, and that came at a cost. For the year ending 31 March 1940, the council spent almost £11,000 (equivalent to around £600,000 in 2023 terms) on civil defence preparations, with £10,027 going towards general precautions against air raids and a modest £625 on air raid fire precaution, though, happily for the council, government grants covered all but £3,200 of the expenditure incurred, though that still represented a considerable sum to be found from local funds.[22]

One idea that did not eventually result in any civil defence expenditure had concerned the Guildhall. After the German successes in France during May and June 1940 had brought the Luftwaffe even closer to Britain, concern was expressed within the council about the striking appearance of the Guildhall, a key building in Swansea's civil defence set-up, making it an obvious target for the enemy. Some thought was given to the possibility of somehow camouflaging its appearance so as to reduce its prominence in the urban landscape. In September 1940 the Borough Architect, Ernest Morgan, asked the civil defence camouflage establishment at the Ministry of Home Security for advice on what steps might sensibly be taken to make the building less conspicuous. The ministry proved to be lukewarm to the idea, stating that it did not require the Guildhall to be camouflaged in the national interest and, that being the case, any funding for such a scheme would have to come from the council's own resources. The ministry had suggested that a building such as the Guildhall could, if thought essential by the local authority, be painted in a single, plain colour, with brown, green or grey being suitable, though it still thought that the benefits of such an approach in Swansea were likely to be limited, as the building was just too prominent. The Borough Architect updated Alderman Percy Morris, the chairman of the council's Air Raid Precautions Committee, on the views of the ministry, adding in his own objection to the desirability of painting stonework and brickwork, while pointing out that any gain was, in any event, likely to be minimal, though expensive, for the council. In due course, the Town Clerk confirmed that Percy Morris did not wish the scheme to proceed.[23]

CHAPTER 3

Arrivals

EVEN AS THE preparatory work in creating an efficient and all-embracing civil defence organisation had been underway, the effects of events on the Continent began to become evident in the town. During the Great War, Swansea had seen an influx of refugees from the Continent after Germany's invasion of Belgium and France in August 1914. At that time several hundred Belgian refugees had reached the town, some arriving on Belgian fishing trawlers, as they strove to avoid living in a war zone that was partly under German control. Similarly, 80 children from the Basque area of Spain had arrived in Swansea in 1937, fleeing the civil war in their home country. Even before the Second World War had begun, Swansea received a small number of children who were fleeing Nazi oppression in Germany. The Kindertransport (Children's Transport) initiative, backed by the British Government, saw around 10,000 unaccompanied children (most of them Jewish) arrive in Britain between 1938 and 1939, and several of those children ended up in Swansea.

Heinz Lichtwitz had been born in Berlin in June 1932 and was the only son of Max and Ilse Lichtwitz. Max was a lawyer and Heinz's paternal grandfather owned a printing business in Berlin, while another family member owned a large apartment block in the Charlottenburg area of the city. The family were comfortably settled, though tragedy was not a stranger to it. In August 1937, Heinz's mother Ilse committed suicide, leaving her young son to be brought up by his father Max and his grandmother, assisted by a nursemaid. The family faced another problem that was becoming increasingly serious as the 1930s rolled by: it had the misfortune to be Jewish in Hitler's Germany.

In the shadow of the Kristallnacht pogrom against Jewish interests in November 1938, Max Lichtwitz must have decided that to remain in Germany exposed his family to grave danger. Max and little Heinz had actually seen Adolf Hitler being imperiously driven through Berlin in an open car and, in common with the other onlookers (though with no enthusiasm), they had both given a Nazi salute and shouted 'Heil Hitler!' as the Führer sped by. It was sensible not to draw attention to yourself in the Berlin of the 1930s if you were of Jewish origin.

Getting out of Germany was beset with bureaucratic hurdles, though a chance presented itself when the British Government decided to relax the immigration rules in respect of certain categories of Jewish refugees. Under pressure from British public opinion and the activities of several committees that had been set up to advance the cause of Jewish refugees, Britain agreed to accept up to 10,000 unaccompanied children who were under the age of 17, provided that those arriving should not be a burden on the public purse and that they should seek to return to their families once the crisis was over. Now referred to as the 'Kindertransport scheme', the first Jewish children arrived in Harwich on 2 December 1938.

On 3 February 1939, Heinz Lichtwitz arrived in Britain at the age of six and a half years. He was unaccompanied, and his father had undertaken the heart-breaking task of sending his only son to a country far away with no real idea of how or if they would ever meet again. Max Lichtwitz had already lost a beloved wife; in February 1939 he had to send away his son. During the train journey out of Germany, Heinz and the other children were body-searched by Nazi officials who also examined their suitcases in case any attempt to smuggle cash or valuables out of the country was being made. Once in

Britain, his group was taken from the port of Harwich by train to London where they were assembled in groups in a large hall. A member of the Jewish community in Swansea, Mrs Selina Levy, escorted Heinz and a number of other children to the town by train.

He was placed in the care of Morris and Winifred Foner of Swansea (who did not know his father) and, given the unpopularity of Germany in Great Britain at that time, he was sensibly given the new name of Henry Foner. Morris Foner owned a jewellery business that was situated in the High Street Arcade in Swansea, and Winifred worked in the shop while also busying herself with good works, particularly for the Swansea General and Eye Hospital. Another family member ran the famous Foner women's clothing shop on High Street in Swansea, a business that survives to this day, though at a different premises. The Foners were what Henry would later describe as 'Five days a year Jews', only attending at the synagogue on special occasions. Indeed, Henry is uncertain if he ever visited the synagogue at Goat Street in Swansea, though it is possible.

The first difficulty encountered after Henry (as he was now known) arrived in Swansea was overcome with patience, practice and time. He spoke only German, while the Foners spoke English and Yiddish. The upsets he had endured in leaving his father and arriving in a strange new country also had an effect on him: for his first three days with the Foners, he did not eat. His English soon developed, however, and when his father made a carefully arranged long-distance telephone call to Henry from Germany on the occasion of his seventh birthday in June 1939, it was realised that, in the relatively short time he had been in Swansea, he had lost his fluency in German.

As Henry's father and other family members were still at liberty in Germany, even if their freedoms had been further curtailed, they were still able to send him postcards to provide him with news and to confirm that he was generally happy in his new situation. The cards were typically illustrated with cute animals and characters, as befitting for a young child. They expressed the hope that he had arrived in Britain safely and was settling into his new home and, after it was realised that Henry had lost his understanding of the German language, the cards were written in English. Early difficulties with British food were soon overcome, and Henry's Jewish heritage was reinforced in Swansea by observing the faith's more important religious rituals and events. Numerous presents and treats were sent from Germany and Henry responded in letters which have regrettably not survived.

He did tell his family that he was happy in 'England' and had a number of pet animals as well as local friends, and he was visited by his father's former secretary, a woman who had managed to escape the grip of the Nazi regime. It seems that Max, Henry's father, was secretly trying to assist other Jews to flee from Germany, though he himself was unwilling to do so, still having his mother to care for in Berlin. He certainly travelled to the port of Hamburg, an exit route from Germany to Denmark or Sweden and a key escape route for those in fear for their safety in Germany. The last postcard from Max was dated 31 August 1939, the day before Germany invaded Poland. Once Britain had declared war on Germany two days later, routine postal communication between the two countries ceased.

A further communication from his father, dated 12 August 1942, did however reach Henry at his then address, Vivian Road, Sketty, Swansea. It was a pro forma item transmitted via the German Red Cross organisation that only allowed the sender to add no more than 25 words. Max stated that he was pleased about Henry's good health and the progress he was making in Swansea. He added a sobering line regarding his own situation: 'Our destiny is quite uncertain.' By this time it seems that Max had remarried, so he then had his mother and a new bride to worry about in Berlin as the Nazi regime tried to resolve, in ever more barbaric ways, what it saw as the 'Jewish problem'. Henry never heard directly from his father again and he, his second wife and stepdaughter were murdered by the Nazis at Auschwitz in 1942.

Henry referred to his new guardians as Uncle Morris and Auntie Winnie and they were always keen that Henry should remember that he had a father and that, perhaps, one day they would be reunited. Though they didn't know what had become of Max Lichtwitz in Germany, it was hoped that the end of the war would provide opportunities for contact to be resumed.

Within days of his arrival in Swansea, Henry started elementary school in Sketty, despite the problem of his distinct lack of English. The Foner's family dog, Tim, followed the young lad to school on his first day and, when the teachers failed to persuade the dog to go home, Henry had to leave school for a brief period in order to take him back. He found his new classmates to be welcoming and settled in well. Indeed, his welcome in Swansea could not have been warmer, and on his next birthday he received birthday cards from various neighbours as well as the local postmistress. Henry Foner would remain in Swansea until well after the war had ended.[1]

Henry was not the only Kindertransport arrival in Swansea, and his happy experiences with his new family were not to be the lot of all such arrivals. Kärry Wertheim had been born in 1929 in the village of Hoof, near Kassel in northern Hesse, central Germany. Her Jewish ancestors had lived in the town since 1760 but that lineage counted for nothing as Nazi Germany's oppression of the Jews gathered pace. The family was eventually evicted from their home during 1937 and had to move into what Kärry described as 'a hovel'. After cleaning and making the best of their new dwelling they were summarily evicted yet again, finding shelter in the schoolroom at the rear of the village synagogue where mattresses were spread on the floor for their use. In December 1937 Kärry remembered the synagogue being set alight by members of the Hitler Youth who were well aware that the Wertheim family were living on the premises. They fled the inferno and were given a night's shelter by a sympathetic German family who lived in a substantial house in the village.

The following morning the family was split up and Kärry and her four young siblings were sent to a Jewish orphanage in Kassel. Kärry was entrusted with the task of occasionally shopping for food in the town though, on a couple of visits, she suffered beatings at the hands of Hitler Youth members. She received dental treatment from a sadistic German who roughly dealt with the problem tooth while telling her that he was always happy to have Jewish blood running over his boots. On 7 November 1938, two days before Kristallnacht, a Kassel synagogue was set ablaze and the violence continued over several days with the orphanage also being attacked, though it proved possible to put out the minor fires that had been started there.

In June 1939, after her father (who still had limited freedom) had pursued options to try and get his family out of Germany, Kärry was taken from the orphanage alone and placed on a train to Hamburg, assisted by adults who were unknown to her. In Hamburg she boarded a ship for Britain and travelled there thanks to the Kindertransport scheme. She brought little with her except for a change of clothes and a treasured photograph of her family who were now all lost to her. On arrival at the railway station in Swansea it seems that Kärry was met by the mayor of the town, who was wearing his large ('pretty' to her) ceremonial chain. The pair shook hands, an incident that made no real sense to the confused youngster. She was in a strange town far from her home, surrounded by strange people who spoke in a language she did not understand. Happily, a young man approached her speaking clear German and explained that the man who had

SWANSEA AND THE SECOND WORLD WAR

travelled with her on the train, Mr Feigenbaum, was to be her new 'father' while his wife would be her new 'mother'.

She was taken to the family home in Northampton Place, enduring the usual difficulties over communicating with her new family and eating their strange food. It must be said that the placement, unlike that of Henry Foner, was not a happy one. Though Kärry found Mr Feigenbaum to be a very kind man whom she grew to love, her relationship with Mrs Feigenbaum was very difficult. Corporal punishment for minor offences was commonplace and she was given the new name of Ellen (which will be used from here onwards). Her entry into the Terrace Road School was not without its problems and the issue of young boys taunting her with shouts of 'Nazi' had to be addressed by the headmaster of the boys' school. She was aware of fellow arrival Henry Foner also being in the town, though there was no chance of friendship as she believed that he had been placed with a family of higher social standing than hers. She felt that the class divide was simply too large to bridge.

News of her family in Germany slowly filtered through and she learnt that her mother had given birth to another child while, in a surprising turn of events, a postcard arrived from the Isle of Wight where her father, powerless to protect his family in his homeland, had been interned as an enemy alien following his arrival in Britain. After a brief reunion in Swansea, Ellen's father was sent to Australia as an internee. In December 1941 she was notified that her mother and her five other children had been sent to Riga in Latvia where they were all subsequently murdered by the Nazis. Ellen received much sympathy from her adoptive father, less so from his wife and, in February 1941, the Feigenbaum's house was destroyed in an air raid.

Ellen endured an unhappy post-war marriage that was nevertheless blessed with children (a son and daughter) and, following the earlier death of Mr Feigenbaum, relations with

Mrs Feigenbaum did eventually thaw. Ellen and her husband eventually divorced and she found a new life and happiness with her second husband, Colin. Though things eventually turned out well, the striking contrast between Kärry/Ellen's and Henry's experiences of living in Britain after arriving on the Kindertransport clearly shows that even if a life was saved by a journey to Britain, happiness was not guaranteed, at least in the short term.[2]

Following the declaration of war in September 1939, over 500 English children arrived in Swansea before the end of the month. They had been voluntarily evacuated by their parents to stay with relatives or friends in Swansea and the Director of Education in Swansea, T J Rees, noted that they had only been assigned school places with some difficulty. The subsequent German invasion of Belgium and Holland in May 1940 prompted the council to establish a committee to deal with refugees who were expected to soon arrive from the Continent.[3] Other evacuees would soon flow into Wales from those areas of England that were expected to receive the enemy's bombing attacks. Some 7,000 arrived in Llanelli, Pyle and Porthcawl among other Welsh towns.

In Swansea there were 40 at Llanmorlais, 50 at Llanrhidian and 20 at Reynoldston, while Penclawdd took in 256. In all over 600 youngsters had made the journey and been sent to various villages on Gower and to Killay.[4] In the months to come it was noted that many of the new arrivals, coming into contact with Welsh-speaking locals, were soon picking up words and phrases from the language, an aptitude that aided integration. Indeed, in November 1944, when evacuated children were filtering back to their homes in England as the risk of heavy German bombing raids receded, it was noted that some of them did so having forgotten their English but being fluent in Welsh, a situation that must have been somewhat perplexing for their families.[5]

CHAPTER 4

Blood, Toil, Tears and Sweat

ROUTINE LIFE CONTINUED almost as normal in Swansea during the period September 1939 to June 1940 when little happened to disturb the lives of those who remained in the town, despite the country being on a war footing. That said, the *South Wales Evening Post* editions of September 1939 contained numerous advertisements and notices relating to some aspect of the approach and arrival of war and how it might affect the people of Swansea. The day after Britain declared war on Germany, a Swansea company was offering for sale asbestos cloth fire-proof curtains that would apparently reduce the risk from fire as well as meeting the requirements of the ARP anti-glare regulations – the blackout obligations. Luckwell's of Oxford Street could supply blackout paint and blackout paper, while stocks of blue lacquer paint (for use on light bulbs), as well as luminous paint to aid visibility in the dark, were expected to be in stock soon.[1] Even if your gas mask was not yet to hand, Bernstein's of Park Street could supply you with a gas mask carrier that would protect the important apparatus as it swung around on your shoulder as you went about your daily business. The carrier was waterproof, fleece-lined and available in a range of colours and a bargain at just under two shillings.[2]

Other public notices were of a far more formal nature. They included the publication in the *South Wales Evening Post* of proclamations by the King stating that, in the current situation, the Army reserve could be called out by a designated Secretary of State in the event that Parliament might not be sitting on particular days. Similarly, another proclamation allowed for the retention of men in the Army who would otherwise have completed their term of service and been transferred to the Army reserve.[3] Swansea Council was busy in inviting tenders for the supply of Auxiliary Fire Service uniforms (including axes),[4] as well as asking those who were prepared to accept evacuated children into their homes to get in touch.[5] Though schools in the town had remained closed after the summer holidays as a precautionary measure, on 15 September the *South Wales Evening Post* included a notice that indicated that all schools (except for infants' schools) would reopen on 18 September 1939. The Chief Constable posted a notice requiring those of German nationality to report at once to the aliens registration office at the central police station, and this included a number of those (typically) Swansea women who had earlier 'lost' their nationality by marrying German men.[6] Clearly, there was much to be done at short notice.

Given the advent of the blackout, Swansea's Chamber of Trade recommended that shops should in future close early so as to minimise any problems regarding lighting during the blackout.[7] Urgent meetings were called by the Transport and General Workers' Union, the Associated Road Operators and the Swansea and District Fish Fryers Association among others, all intended to investigate what would be the likely implications of the war for the members of each organisation.[8] At the Swansea Museum, the Royal Institution of South Wales reported that 'rare books, documents and specimens in the institution's library and museum' had been removed to a place of safety. The museum would consequently be temporarily closed until, presumably, less important items could be brought out of reserve to fill the empty display cabinets.[9]

Sporting and other leisure pursuits remained open to many and Swansea Town AFC played a small number of fixtures to begin the 1939–40 season before the Football League decided to abandon the programme. Even then, as sport was considered important for morale purposes, a number of regionalised leagues (reducing the petrol-consuming travel requirements) were established in which 'the Swans' took part, though attendances were limited in case a surprise attack from the air should strike those in a packed stadium. The league established in October 1939 saw the Swans competing with Cardiff, Newport, the two Bristol teams, Swindon, Torquay and Plymouth. Matters were not helped on the footballing front when the military requisitioned the Vetch Field, the home of the Swans, resulting in any football games that were played taking place at the St Helen's Ground, home to the local rugby and cricket teams. The Football League programme did not resume until 1946–47.[10]

Rugby union was of course amateur in status and less rigidly organised than football, and it proved possible for some games to be played, such as when the Neath team visited the famous 'All Whites' of Swansea Rugby Club and returned home victorious in March 1940.[11] Matches were frequently played for fund-raising purposes and a match between a South Wales XV and an RAF team, played during April 1941, raised almost £800 for the mayor's air raid distress fund.[12] Minor rugby was also reported as taking place during October 1939, while boxing, billiards and greyhound racing, among other sporting activities, were also available for the enjoyment of spectators.

Amusement could be sought in one of a plethora of establishments. These included the Plaza, the Albert Hall, the Rialto, the Castle and the Tivoli. The Picture House on High Street was also open, though a German bomb would demolish it during the course of the war. Chapel and church services were plentiful in the town though, like the ill-fated Picture House, a number of them would fall victim to bomb damage. In December 1939 the Rev. Leon Atkin posed the question 'Is Western Civilisation Worth Fighting For' to his congregation at St Paul's Church near the Guildhall, while the Rev. Rees

Howells of the Bible College of Wales predicted the 'doom of the Nazis' in a new book.[13]

The statistics of the war years show that, despite the ever-present danger and uncertainty, the usual significant milestones of pre-war life were still very much in evidence. The average annual number of marriages in Swansea during the period 1936–38 was 1,387, and during the period 1939–45 the average yearly number of marriages increased to a figure of 1,484, with the busiest year being 1940 when 1,908 marriages took place.

The number of wartime births did not stray very far from the average of around 2,500 per annum, though the year 1941 saw a dip to 2,085. The town did see an upturn in the number of illegitimate births during the war. During the period 1936–38 the average number of illegitimate births registered in the County Borough of Swansea (excluding Gower) averaged 60 per year. That average was exceeded in every year of the war, with 170 illegitimate births being recorded in 1944, while 1945 saw 127 such instances. Both 1942 and 1943 saw a figure in the high 90s being reached for such births. It is impossible to say how many of these illegitimate births resulted from casual sex between comparative strangers, or from within settled courtships where the enlistment of the male partner saw him moved away from home for military service, with only limited periods of leave, thus preventing a marriage until perhaps the end of the war.[14]

One family's story may not be typical but Walter and Leah Incledon lived in rented accommodation on Cradock Street and, by 1940, already had one daughter. Walter worked as a finance clerk at Swansea Council and was also the organist at the Argyle Chapel on St Helen's Road. A second daughter was born in January 1940 and, as was common at a time before the advent of the National Health Service, it was a home birth that was complicated by it being a breech delivery. By February 1941 Walter was in the Army and working in the

Pay Corps. Despite the obvious risks that attended living in a bomb-ravaged Swansea, another daughter was born in August 1942, the birth once again taking place in the home. It seems that despite all the difficulties involved in living in a time of war, the attraction of completing a family was still a very powerful urge. Times were understandably tough during the war for the Incledons with the eldest daughter, Elizabeth (Betty), for a time having only one acceptable outfit to wear – her school uniform. Rationing was also a strain aggravated by the fact that a relative had links to the farming community and often had a plentiful supply of butter conspicuously on display at home though – family or not – none was ever shared with other relatives. The family was at least able to move away from the town centre as the war progressed – to the Sketty area – so that the level of risk from enemy bombing was reduced for the growing family.[15]

As regards deaths within the town, the average number per year in the period 1936–38 had been 2,013, and that figure was only exceeded in 1940 and 1941 when 2,164 and 2,405 deaths were recorded respectively. Those years would, of course, be the worst years for deaths from air raids, even though the fatal casualty figures would thankfully still be in the low hundreds. In fact, the annual death figures for the period 1942–45 were consistently two or three hundred less than the pre-war average.

The Swansea of 1939 was already familiar with crime in most of its forms of course, ranging from murder (one case during 1939), manslaughter or infanticide etc. (one), rape and other offences against females (17), burglary (20), shop-breaking (87), robbery (four), forgery (four), receiving stolen goods (nine), fraud (three) and attempted suicide (12) which, at that time, was treated as a crime.[16] One serious wartime crime that remained unsolved was the murder of three-year-old Giustina Macari of Dillwyn Street in May 1941. Despite extensive police enquiries and the questioning of several suspects, a resultant trial collapsed without a conviction. The case sadly remains unsolved. Two other suspected murders took place in wartime Swansea – both in 1943. One involved a Liverpool seaman who became involved in an altercation with an American soldier in December 1943 which resulted in the death of the serviceman. The defendant claimed that he was acting in self-defence and the jury delivered a not guilty verdict to the charge of manslaughter. The other case concerned the murder of a young woman at Rhyddings Park Road on 18 November 1943. Evidence suggested the involvement of an American soldier but no charges were ever brought and the case remains unsolved.[17]

During 1939, 76 bicycles were stolen in Swansea while thefts from shops, vehicles and gas payment meters amounted to 359 cases. Other minor thefts of personal property totalled almost 500 cases. There were 159 convictions for drunkenness, the lowest figure since 1931, while there were also 114 cases where those accused were subsequently discharged. Perhaps unsurprisingly, seamen made up a large proportion of those charged with drunkenness during 1939 (there were 105 cases involving seamen), though some would possibly have been found not guilty after defending themselves against the charges.

Juvenile crime was always a matter of concern, and in 1939 proceedings were taken against 224 juveniles for more serious offences such as theft and house-breaking. Over 100 of the offenders were under 14 years of age, with nine of that number being girls. There were 68 cases of a less serious nature in 1939, including offences on the railway (22 cases), causing malicious damage (16), and stealing fruit or plants (seven). The coming of war saw an increase in juvenile crime so that in 1941 the number of more serious offences committed by youngsters amounted to 305, a rise of 73 per cent since 1939. The Chief Constable was of the opinion that many of the crimes showed evidence of careful planning, despite the youth of the culprits.

Furthermore, the lack of interest exhibited by some parents in what their children were up to when out of the house was also a factor, as was the frequent absence from the home of fathers who were away on active service and thus unable to assist their wives in controlling their errant children.

Under war conditions, much police work involved ensuring that the public observed the rules regarding the blackout, as well as the carrying and wearing of gas masks, as was appropriate. Gas mask carrying was certainly not universal, though it tended to improve soon after a bombing raid. The prevention of looting from damaged premises and the detection of black-market activities also occupied the police, as did the apprehension of those who attempted to avoid conscription or who had deserted from the military. Constables were also used to guard important infrastructure such as bridges and other 'vulnerable points' in the town and, in a stark departure from normal policing, those officers were armed lest they should encounter any determined enemy agents set on carrying out sabotage activities.[18]

The Swansea crime statistics for the war years seem not to highlight offences against the new and extensive defence regulations. Presumably the figures were simply lumped in with other minor (non-indictable) offences, of which there were 1,357 in 1939. In 1940 there were 2,424 non-indictable offences, though the figure fell back to 1,923 in 1941 and to 1,714 in 1942. In the last full years of the war the figures were 1,470 (1943) and 1,501 (1944).

At the national level for England and Wales, it is known that in 1940 – the first full year of war and a time when offences against the new defence regulations were commonplace – there were over 299,000 lighting offences and over 5,000 cases involving the central governmental control of the workforce and industry. Although it is not clear what the detailed situation in Swansea was regarding offences against the defence regulations, it clearly would have resulted in extra work for the hard-pressed Swansea constabulary, as was apparent from the numerous press reports.[19]

For example, in September 1940, Dominic Pelosi was managing his brother's café in Cradock Street when he was asked to extinguish a light that was visible from outside of the premises. After being spoken to by an air raid warden, he was subsequently summonsed for the offence. Although he called several witnesses in his defence, he was found guilty and fined with costs.[20] On a single day in September 1940, seven offenders were fined for offences against the lighting regulations, with Benjamin Thomas having the misfortune to be fined for merely striking a match during the hours of blackout on a road in Langland.[21]

There was a concern that the imposition of blackout restrictions would lead to a sharp increase in the number of road accidents, though that does not seem to be entirely borne out by the figures that are available. Getting knocked down by a motor vehicle was not an offence against the defence regulations, but the blackout conditions led to darkened streets which, coupled with the shading of vehicle lights, inevitably led to problems regarding the visibility of pedestrians and bicycle users. These difficulties were offset somewhat by petrol rationing reducing the number of journeys able to be undertaken. The position can be summarised as:

Year	Vehicle Accidents	Total deaths / deaths during darkness
1939	1,597	22 / Not available
1940	1,318	35 / 20
1941	1,306	24 / 10
1942	1,001	18 / 11
1943	717	24 / 12
1944	865	21 / 6
1945	783	12/ 4

The Chief Constable bemoaned the fact that far too many Swansea citizens had a habit of walking in the road rather than on the pavement, a risky undertaking during the hours of blackout. Many of these jaywalkers were apparently often trying to flag down passing vehicles in the hope of getting a lift. He recognised that most vehicle drivers had modified their behaviour by proceeding carefully during the imposed darkness, but their efforts were being undermined by those pedestrians who, after coming into contact with a vehicle and sustaining injuries, were found to be drunk. Some people were leaving buildings that were well lit internally (though also having blacked-out windows and doors) and were then failing to pause while their eyes adjusted to the darkness outside. Often setting off at a brisk pace and attempting to quickly cross a road without pause, they frequently came into contact with a vehicle due almost entirely to their carelessness, coupled with a driver's difficulty in seeing them in the gloom.

As Swansea was packed with soldiers, sailors and airmen, it was almost inevitable that some of them would break the law in some manner. Some offences were more serious than others and, in September 1940, with the threat of invasion still at a high level, a soldier inexplicably fired his rifle while inside a public air raid shelter in which were several members of the public. Though the bullet was aimed at a wall, the resultant splinters struck two children, one of whom was the accused's own daughter, though luckily the injuries were not serious. The soldier was found to be drunk and was fined £2.[22] A soldier of the Auxiliary Military Pioneer Corps fired a gun five times on High Street for no obvious reason. Upon questioning he seemed to be under the influence of alcohol, and his defence that he had fired 'at a light' was not accepted by the court. He was also fined £2.[23]

Even some of those in positions of authority were not averse to a spot of criminal activity, such as minor pilfering at a time of rationed food and shortages of other items. Such a case was that of a special constable who worked at the docks in Swansea who was fined £5 in September 1944 after being found guilty of receiving six dressed chickens, 5lbs of bacon, and a quantity of tea from a cook on an American ship. Two other docks special constables were also fined £5 each for stealing 14 packets of margarine from the port, having no doubt intended to sell them at a profit on the black market.[24] Another special constable of the docks police was charged with stealing 30 women's vests and six dusters from a bomb-damaged warehouse in Burrows Place. He was remanded in custody for one week, pending further enquiries.[25]

Prostitution remained a problem throughout the war. The presence of various elements of the military in the town and its surrounds and the regular arrival of seamen at the port presented plenty of opportunities for immoral conduct and a possible increase in sexually transmitted diseases – bad news for a nation that needed every man (and woman) it could get in support of the war effort. At the outbreak of war the town already had a clinic based at the Swansea General and Eye Hospital, St Helen's Road, that was dedicated to the treatment of the disease. During the war, records were kept on the number of new cases among servicemen in the town (excluding the general population) and, in 1941, there were 210 such cases, and in the succeeding years the figures were 250 (1942), 202 (1943), and 119 (1944). The number of unreported cases remains unknown, of course. It should be noted that the figures for 1943 onwards appear to include sailors as well as servicemen, though there is no mention whatsoever of infected servicewomen, of whom it must be possible that there were some. Within the general male civilian population of Swansea (excluding service personnel), there were 132 new instances of sexually transmitted disease cases in 1941 and then there were 145 (1942), 193 (1943) and 197 (1944), numbers that, although relatively low when set against the population size, nevertheless show an upsurge year-on-year. It is possible that civilians would usually remain within the town due to their employment and would naturally seek treatment locally, whereas an infected serviceman would possibly only need treatment after leaving the town due to a move to a new location, thus not appearing in the figures.

During 1941 Swansea's police force took active measures to suppress the problem of brothel use, though only four cases were instigated in the courts, with action being taken against 14 women and two men. Five of the women involved were imprisoned (typically for a month), three received fines, while a further five were placed on probation. One woman was acquitted of all charges, though while one of the males was acquitted of any offence the other was convicted and received a fine. A 1944 case involved a Morriston man who had persuaded a 21-year-old woman to consort with black (presumably American) soldiers after which she shared the money received with the defendant. He was convicted of living in part off immoral earnings.[26]

In May 1944 three women were charged with unlawfully keeping a disorderly house in the Waun Wen area of the town. While the house was under police observation, several men had been seen entering it in the company of the defendants, and when the property had been entered by police constables it was obvious that prostitution was taking place. In a sign of the changing times regarding the compulsory employment of females, and with war production being of paramount importance, one of the accused, a 26-year-old woman, gave her normal occupation as that of 'welder'.[27]

After the declaration of war on 3 September 1939, the British government had been only too well aware of the colossal effort that had proven necessary in mobilising the manpower and material that was needed to emerge victorious in the Great War. There was no doubt that a similar effort would need to be made in a new conflict and that anything – whether manpower or material – that might advance the cause should be made readily available for use by the state. It would have to be a total war if victory was to be achieved over Nazi Germany. The government therefore took early steps to ensure that it would have the requisite manpower available to it to conduct an all-out war, should war come. As early as May 1939 it had guided through Parliament the Military Training Act which applied to single men between the ages of 20 and 22 years of age, and required those affected to undertake six months of military training. It resulted in some 240,000 young men of military age being registered and potentially available for military service in a future crisis.

This move was designed to remove the uncertainties regarding the availability of manpower that had occurred after the government of the day had at the start depended on voluntary enlistments during the First World War. The declaration of war against Germany and her allies in 1914 had initially seen recruiting stations being often overrun by patriotic volunteers, though the torrent had dwindled to a trickle by the end of 1915. In March 1916 legislation that allowed the conscription of men into the military was enacted in Britain for the first time. To avoid similar recruitment problems in a new conflict, Parliament passed the National Service (Armed Forces) Act[28] on 3 September 1939, the day that war was declared, in order to give what was now the wartime government firm control over the recruitment process from the outset. This was no longer a simple requirement for those of a defined age to be trained in military routines; it was a measure that would compulsorily transfer men to the fighting forces as and when required.

The Act required men aged between 18 and 41 to serve in the military and, on 1 October 1939, a Royal Proclamation was issued that necessitated men then aged 20 or 21 to register at a local office of the Ministry of Labour. Successive age groups were captured by subsequent proclamations so that, by June 1941, all men up to the age of 40 had been required to register.

Notice of the need to register for particular age groups was publicised via the BBC and the local press, and in 1939 around 727,000 men were so registered and the process then continued into 1940. For 1940 the number of men registered was 4.1 million, and for 1941 it was 2.2 million, giving a total of just over seven million to date.[29]

On presenting himself for registration at an employment exchange, a man was required to provide information about his address, occupation, employer and the type of industry in which he was engaged. This would subsequently be checked with the man's employer regarding the accuracy of the information provided, and also helped to determine whether the work he was involved in was likely to preclude his future transfer to the military for some reason – such as his job being important to the war effort. The potential recruit was also asked if he had a preference for a particular service, though no guarantees could be given in that respect. People not required to register under the Act included existing members of the armed forces, men in holy orders, those undergoing training at certain military colleges, and anyone subject to the Lunacy and Mental Treatment Acts. The staggered approach of calling in men by age group assisted the hard-pressed military depots in coping with large influxes of new recruits in a short time period. After the registration formalities had been completed, a man could carry on with his normal affairs and simply await the arrival of his call-up papers, which would be issued at a time that was convenient to the military. However, three possible obstacles still needed to be cleared by the military before it could firmly clasp a potential and much-needed recruit to its bosom.

Firstly, in certain cases it might be possible for a man to request a postponement of his call-up. Postponements for no more than six months, in the first instance, could be granted where the man's absence could be shown to have a detrimental effect on his domestic arrangements or business interests. Other exceptional or unusual difficulties might also qualify a man for postponement for a period that would be subject to review, with each case being judged on its merits. Secondly, each recruit would, as a matter of course, be given six days notice of a medical board examination, and after being examined he would be placed in one of four grades of fitness, with only the lowest grade deeming him to be unfit for any type of military service. Finally, a man could apply at the time of registration to be placed on a register of conscientious objectors and this would initially be done on a provisional basis, though he would then need to apply to a local tribunal (within 14 days) to have the merits (or otherwise) of his case considered.

A request from an employer for the deferment of a call-up to the armed forces of an employee whose work was deemed vital to a business was viewed seriously. When Swansea Council requested a deferment for a man named Webber of the Brooklands Hotel in Swansea, since he was working on important council contracts, officials in Cardiff were quick to request additional information. They desired to have confirmation that the man himself was indeed employed by a contractor who was involved in the construction of communal or domestic air raid shelters for the council, and that he was engaged in work for that specific purpose. Additional questions asked as to whether he could simply be replaced in his current job by another man and, if not, then for how long a deferment was required. They reiterated that under the National Service (Armed Forces) Act, deferment of a call-up could only be granted in exceptional circumstances and for a defined period. There was no question of total exemption, only a period of postponement in which an employer would have to make other arrangements in the knowledge that the man had to be released for national service.[30]

Similarly, a self-employed man of Bernard Street was said by the council to be working full-time for them on electrical installation work in air raid shelters. Indeed, he had been doing this for 18 months and had had no spare time whatsoever to perform any other type of work. The Borough Engineer and Surveyor stated, in June 1941, that he had 260 air raid shelters that required electrical wiring work and, were the man to be called up, he would be unable to replace him due to a shortage of electricians. Regrettably, the file does not note the decision reached.[31]

As regards conscientious objection, tribunals that looked into such requests would be keen to ascertain whether a man's conscience had only appeared once he was asked to register for military service, or whether it was actually grounded in some genuine and long-standing belief. Clearly, a man who was in holy orders would have no difficulty, if he so chose, in having his status as a conscientious objector unconditionally confirmed in the register. Other cases would not be so clear-cut, and it was possible that a man might be conditionally registered as a conscientious objector but would then be required to perform specified work of a civilian character and under civilian direction that supported the war effort. In some cases a man might be prepared to work under military direction but only in a strictly non-combatant role. If a man's application for recognition of his status as a conscientious objector failed, then his name would be removed from the register and he would be subject to enlistment in the armed forces at a future date without further ado. During the war there were some 59,000 applications for registration as a conscientious objector, of which 12,000 applications were refused.[32]

During the First World War, the military service tribunals that were set up to hear the applications of conscientious objectors typically gave those appearing before them a difficult time. Recognizing this, in the Second World War the tribunal members were picked on the basis that they would give a firm but sympathetic hearing to applicants, thus minimising the controversy that had flared up in the earlier war over the seemingly harsh treatment of many genuine conscientious objectors. Hearings in Swansea were typically held at the Guildhall and, as might be expected, there were numerous contretemps despite the supposedly more relaxed regime.[33]

Swansea Council itself became entangled in a controversy over the position of members of its staff who held or expressed anti-war sentiments. In June 1940, a request that had been signed by over 200 members of staff was placed before the Parliamentary and General Purposes Committee asking that the committee should dispense with the services of those council officers who could not fully support the prosecution of the war. After a sometimes heated debate, it was agreed that the letter from the staff should merely be allowed 'to lie on the table'. That decision unleashed a torrent of criticism within the town, with noisy protest meetings and numerous letters to the local newspaper.[34]

An editorial piece in the *South Wales Evening Post* derided the views of many councillors, hinting that there would be those within the council who opposed the war but were nevertheless fully aware of many sensitive defence arrangements within the town, given the nature of their roles. It observed: '… the terrible revelation in the debate that councillors themselves, in their academic wordy theorising, showed no realisation that the council is an integral and important part of a vast war machine, because of its control of the ARP, AFS, food and fuel, and all the secret knowledge of any defence movements…'[35]

At a special meeting of the council, held on 28 June 1940, it was agreed by 33 votes to 12 that all staff should be given the opportunity to express in writing their unswerving support for the war effort. Those who were unable to do so for reasons of conscience were liable to be suspended from their employment.[36] This was a controversial move, since the apparatus of military conscription that had been established in law during the First World War allowed for those with sincere conscientious beliefs to be excused from military service after examination, often being able to carry on with their civilian lives almost as normal. The council decision interfered with that process and, as was pointed out by several sympathetic Swansea councillors, it ignored the existence of the tribunals that had been set up to specifically consider matters of individual conscience. Unsurprisingly, the Swansea decision – if undoubtedly popular at the local level – was viewed askance by those at the centre of government.

As the *South Wales Evening Post* reported in October, the Home Secretary and the Minister of Home Security duly issued a circular to local authorities explaining that no one in Britain should be penalised for simply holding an opinion that was different to the majority of people. It requested that the Swansea decision be rescinded and certain councillors, suitably chastened, ultimately agreed that the council's previous decision should indeed be overturned, though Councillor Dan Jones still felt 'that anybody who attempted to sell his country should be put up against a wall'.[37] It was stated that in Swansea ten women and nine men had been suspended from their jobs with the council before the situation was clarified by the Home Office.[38] By way of comparison, by late August 1940 it had been noted that Cardiff Council had decided to dismiss any staff members who gained unconditional registration as a conscientious objector, while in Merthyr one member of staff had voluntarily left to work on the land. Breconshire and Newport councils seemed to be in the presumably happy position of having no conscientious objectors in their employ.[39]

Rosalind Bevan (later Rusbridge) of Raglan Road, Sketty, was employed by the council as a teacher at Glanmor School, and her unqualified support of the war effort was in doubt due to her presumed views or her possible membership of the pacifist organisation, the Peace Pledge Union (PPU). On 1 July 1940, a letter signed by Howell L Lang-Coath, Town Clerk, informed her that she was suspended from her duties.[40] With some difficulty she found alternative employment in Chester, and did not return to Swansea when the original decision to suspend staff members was rescinded. Rosalind had earlier been involved in running a 'peace stall' in the market, from where anti-war literature was available. Following complaints to the council and the apparent threat of violent action against the stall, her tenancy for the market stall was summarily terminated in early June 1940 by the council's estate agent.[41]

Another council worker in Swansea who found himself caught up in the controversy was Bernard Owen of Sketty, a man who had been employed as a clerk at the council for over a decade. In the aftermath of the council's decision on conscientious objectors, Owen had indeed been suspended and had subsequently commenced new employment in forestry work. He attended a tribunal in Aberystwyth in August 1940 to claim registration as a conscientious objector. He told the chairman, Sir Thomas Jones KC, that he had been required by the council to sign a declaration confirming that he was not a conscientious objector or a member of the PPU, and that he did not hold views that were in conflict with the country's war aims. He was also asked to sign a document indicating that he supported the vigorous prosecution of the war.

Given his sincerely-held beliefs, Owen had declined the opportunity to sign the documents proffered to him by the council and that had led to his suspension. Sir Thomas Jones was clearly unimpressed by the actions of Owen's employers, stating that, in his view, there was no justification for it to issue such documents to its employees. He added that the idea, expressed by some at the council, that conscientious objectors were potentially 'fifth columnists' was 'sheer nonsense'. He asked Owen to forward the documents he had been given to the Ministry of Labour for its consideration. Owen was then granted conditional registration as a conscientious objector, provided he remained in forestry work.[42]

The local tribunal in Swansea soon began hearing cases and it became apparent that the members of the PPU who were sitting in the public gallery during some sessions, were declining to stand up as a mark of respect as tribunal members entered the room, and were also pointedly taking shorthand notes during the proceedings.[43] One case involved PPU member William Gammon of Llwynderw. After listening to the representations made, the tribunal chairman, the Honourable Judge Frank Davies, pointed out that Gammon's membership of the PPU did not come with an automatic exemption from military service and his name was placed on the register on condition that he undertake agricultural or constructional work.[44]

John Williams, a colliery rider of Clydach, did not impress the tribunal chairman with the sincerity of his conscience, the chairman stating: 'Your conscience now is the same as your convenience. It is nice for you to go on with your work while other young men are joining the forces. Show us something where your conscience has operated to something disagreeable and not to your comfort.' Williams had no real answer and was registered for non-combatant work.[45]

Being a member of a religious group such as the Christadelphians or Jehovah's Witnesses did not routinely mean that the applicant would be automatically excused from any form of service. In a hearing at the Guildhall in June 1940, several such men were registered as conscientious objectors but were nevertheless required to undertake mining or other non-combatant duties. Evan Williams, an unemployed librarian, succeeded in his claim for registration as a conscientious objector as he was able to demonstrate that he was opposed to all forms of military service and had previously been the secretary of the No War Movement before that body had merged with the PPU. He was duly granted unconditional registration.[46]

One case concerned an Italian café owner who had lived

in Wales for a number of years and had become a naturalised British citizen in 1936. Some years prior to that, while living in Swansea, he had refused to serve in the Italian Army as he was opposed to war in all its forms. He was asked whether he had returned to Italy to lodge his objection and whether, had he done so, he would have got away with it. He replied 'no' to both questions and was essentially told that he wouldn't get away with it in Britain, either. He was removed from the register of conscientious objectors.[47] Another unusual case involved 15 missionary students who were training at the Bible College in Swansea. The gist of their argument was that they had given up their previous employments after being called by God to become his missionaries overseas. They were spending three days a week on maintaining the Bible College grounds in Swansea, though they were not prepared to do similar work outside of its confines as to do so would possibly free up other men for military service. Judge Frank Davies, presiding, took a dim view of their request, as was reported in the *Western Mail*:

> The majority of the students who had appeared before the tribunal had been at the college for four years and more. Their student days were over, and now they were merely marking time until the war was over, when it was their intention, apparently, to go abroad to the mission fields.
>
> They were filling in time at such works as forestry and gardening which was entirely unconnected with their theological studies...

The tribunal chairman added that, in his view, their description of their college gardening work as being of 'national importance' was intended as a mere 'sop' to persuade the tribunal to leave them alone. The sop was not accepted and they were registered for work on the land or in full-time civil defence duties.[48]

Simple non-attendance at a tribunal was not an option.

When William Moss and George Rust, both of Swansea, failed to appear to present their cases, their names were promptly removed from the register of conscientious objectors, rendering them liable for military service once they were apprehended by the police.[49]

Garfield Morgan of Morriston worked as a shop assistant and told the tribunal that he would do nothing to assist the prosecution of the war, while admitting that he happily sold items over the shop counter to those who worked in war-related industries. Tribunal member Oliver Harries advised Morgan that, in his view, 'The only logical thing for people like you to do is to commit suicide.' The decision in his case is unclear as it was not noted in the press report.[50]

The arrival of war in September 1939 had brought with it the disheartening prospect of food rationing having to be introduced at some point, as had happened during the 1914–18 conflict. As early as 4 September 1939, Swansea Council established a Food Control Committee on which sat ten councillors as well as a three co-opted members to represent the town's bakers, butchers and Co-operative Society members. The committee was administered by the Town Clerk in his role as food controller, though a lesser official would be the committee's main point of practical support. It was chaired by Councillor W J F Webber and had offices at the Rutland Street schools.[51] On 12 September 1939, it was reported that certain traders in the town were imposing unreasonable conditions on customers before they would sell them certain food items. This practice had been seen during the First World War when, for a time, shopkeepers would perhaps sell tea or flour but only if the customer also bought another product that they might not actually require at that time. A certain amount of profiteering was also alleged, with one letter writer pointing out that a portion of salmon was now 11*d.* against a pre-war price of 7*d.*, and a small jar of jam was now 4*d.* as opposed to 3*d.*[52] There were several other examples, and the writer implored the food controller to quickly get to work and put a stop to these unfair practices. Clearly, the committee would have its work cut out in keeping on top of food-supply matters.

As September 1939 drew to a close, Swansea Council advertised in the local press inviting those who held land that was not currently being used for food production to hand it over (temporarily) to the council so that it could be used for allotment gardening. At the same time, it asked anyone who wished to work an allotment to contact the Borough Estate Agent at the Guildhall. The council's parks department offered 100 vegetable plants (typically a mix of Savoy cabbage, Brussels sprouts and broccoli) to unemployed people in return for a modest payment of 6*d*. Once cultivated, the plants would provide a welcome supply of green food during the autumn and winter.[53]

At the national level, the combined effect of the encouragement of a 'grow your own' mentality (though figures were only collated by the Ministry of Food where the plot of land involved exceeded an acre in size) and the issuing of directions to farmers to bring hitherto-neglected areas of land into production, did make a significant difference in the annual crop yield. This can be shown in the following table[54] (figures are in thousand tons):

	Wheat	Barley	Oats	Potatoes	Sugar Beet	Vegetables
1936–38 average	1,651	765	1,940	4,873	2,741	2,371
1939	1,645	892	2,003	5,218	3,529	2,403
1940	1,641	1,104	2,892	6,405	3,176	2,617
1941	2,018	1,144	3,247	8,004	3,226	2,884
1942	2,567	1,446	3,553	9,393	3,923	3,693
1943	3,447	1,645	3,064	9,822	3,760	3,144
1944	3,138	1,752	2,953	9,096	3,267	3,423

The welcome increase in crop production brought with it problems. A conference held in London on the subject of volunteer labour in agriculture was told that, in 1944 another 500,000 acres had been turned over to food production, but without the necessary labour to efficiently harvest the resulting crops. It was noted that another 120,000 volunteers would be needed, and efforts were being made via the county war agricultural committees, in conjunction with the Women's Institute and the Women's Voluntary Service, to plug the gap. Members of youth clubs, as well as schoolchildren of a suitable age, would all be encouraged to volunteer for work in getting the crops in, and they would receive a modest payment in return for their efforts.[55]

As regards crime and the food production situation in Swansea, it was not all plain sailing, as efforts made to produce more home- or allotment-grown produce were hampered by vandalism. It was reported that 22 men had been working on an allotment in Townhill but the number had dwindled down to only two since local children were 'tearing the hearts out of cabbage, cauliflower, etc., digging out their potatoes as soon as they are through the ground, chopping off broad beans with sticks, pulling up carrots, etc…' Seemingly unable to identify the culprits, the council took no action.[56]

In the early days of the war, the government struggled to make up its mind over the question of food rationing, a measure that was obviously going to be unpopular with the public even if it was essential in order to make the best use of the available food supplies. Rationing soon became unavoidable and it proved necessary to produce some 45 million ration books (based on the entries in a register that was compiled in 1939 – see below), and members of the public, after receiving their ration book, would need to register with a local supplier (typically their corner shop, plus perhaps a butcher and baker) with the supplier(s) then applying to the local food office in order to obtain the appropriate weekly quantities of rationed foodstuffs for their registered customers. Thereafter, the ration book holder would present the book to their supplier who would cut out or cancel the coupons that related to the items supplied for that particular week. Much delay was encountered during the ration book issuing process (both political and practical), the not least of which was the failure of officials at the Ministry of Food to anticipate just how long it would take the poor old Post Office to speedily sort and deliver millions of ration books in accordance with a tight timescale.[57] Despite the detailed planning having been started in September 1939, it was early January in 1940 before bacon, butter and sugar came under rationing control, to be followed over time by meat, tea and preserves. From early January 1940, the weekly ration for an individual would be 12oz of sugar, 4oz of bacon and 4oz of butter. The anticipated personal meat ration (to be set initially at 1s. 10d. worth of meat a week) was expected to meet the usual needs of customers, while edible offal such as tripe, liver, hearts, kidneys and tongues would remain unrationed. Happily, bread and potatoes did not come under the rationing regime during the war and they remained the main sources of calories for the British population.

The Medical Officer of Health noted that, despite food rationing, there appeared to have been no ill effect on the nutritional health of the children of Swansea, and he ascribed this to the diminished availability of sweets and sugar due to the rationing regime. Indeed, he stated that in the pre-war days, although many children were ill-nourished, a 'hungry child' was almost unknown due to the fact that sweets had been used by parents to, in his words, 'dope' the children and dampen their appetites. Another factor had been the expansion of the school meals service during the war so that more children than had hitherto been the case were taking a filling meal at school. Milk was also being provided, and the strictures of the food rationing system across all social classes had unavoidably led to a levelling up in nutritional standards between the poor and the better off. Indeed, the higher wages available to some men for skilled and important war work and the increased use of female labour in well-paid jobs in industry had seen numerous families lifted out of poverty into situations of, at least for the moment, modest affluence.[58]

During the war the number of certain types of farm animals being reared in Britain decreased substantially. It had become evident to the government's planners that animal feed would soon be in short supply in a war situation and, while a steady supply of both beef and milk cattle was deemed essential, it was recognised that there were simply too many sheep, pigs and poultry in the country relative to the likely levels of animal feed available for them. In light of this, while cattle numbers remained fairly constant throughout the war (in 1943 standing at 9.6 million animals), by 1943 the number of sheep had fallen from the 1939 figure of 26.9 million to 20.4 million, while the figure for pigs showed a drop from 4.4 million to 1.8 million, and that of poultry from 74.4 million to 50.7 million. It was a veritable animal holocaust, though, over time, the continuing shortfall in animal feed still meant that by 1941 the meat ration was being reduced down from its heady days of comparative plenty (when it was over 2s. a week per person as excess animals were slaughtered) to just 1s. 2d. per week, per person.[59]

In February 1941 a proposal to establish a piggery in specially adapted premises at Sketty Hall ran into opposition at a meeting of the council. Certain council members were keen to encourage anything that improved the food supply, but thought that the anticipated profit accruing to the council from the scheme was set at too low a level. The plan would see 30 pigs kept at the site at a cost of around £233 over a six-month period. The resulting sales of the animals were expected to produce a modest profit of only £7. There was a fear among some council members that if things did not turn out quite as expected, it would be the council ratepayer who would have to pick up the tab. There was also criticism of the idea that households could contribute waste bread as pig food in support of the scheme. Councillor J Oliver Watkins felt that anyone who had such a precious commodity as 'waste bread' should instead have their ration allowance cut to the point where there was no such waste.[60]

Kindertransport arrival Henry Foner remembered the impact of food rationing on his new family. The Foner's house on Vivian Road had a large back garden where the family kept a small menagerie of animals. Indeed, though Morris Foner was a skilled watchmaker who could make a watch out of the most unpromising pieces of metal, he had originally wanted to become a farmer, and kept in the garden were geese, ducks, chickens and bees. As food rationing later imposed an increasing strain on the family diet, Mrs Foner eventually told her husband that the Aylesbury ducks that strutted around the garden would need to be prepared for the dining table. On the day when the Sunday lunch was enhanced by one of the much-loved and now expertly cooked birds, Morris Foner suddenly discovered that he had lost his appetite, as had the others who were seated around the table. The unlucky bird was donated to some grateful neighbours.

Vegetables were also grown by the Foners, fertilised by the horse manure that Henry was sent to collect off Vivian Road after the horse-drawn carts of several local traders had passed by. He did this task with a bucket and spade, dragging the 'crop' back up to the house on a wooden platform to which were affixed old pram wheels. He was also sent to the nearby Co-operative shop each Saturday to collect food for the chickens, a foodstuff that was also subject to rationing. If food was particularly scarce, it was the practice for Morris and Henry to go down to the docks in Swansea and fish for whiting, a useful supplement to the often sparse wartime rations.[61]

In Swansea during February 1941 it was noted that jams and marmalade were in short supply for no obvious reason.

H F Hood, of the Swansea and District Grocers and Provisions Association, bemoaned the fact that it was the grocer who bore the brunt of the customer's anger at such shortages which had, in fact, been caused by the Ministry of Food setting a control price for the products at such a low level that manufacturers were compelled to retain the items in stock rather than have to sell them at a loss which resulted in empty shelves in the shops. Negotiations were underway, though it seemed that plain, buttered toast would be the breakfast fare for many in Swansea (and elsewhere) until the issue was resolved.[62]

The president of the Swansea Meat Traders' Association told the local newspaper, in addressing reports of disgruntled customers, that, 'If you refuse what your butcher has to offer you… he is not in the pre-war position of ordering what would have been your normal requirements, and consequently you will be the person to suffer for such action on your part.' He added, 'If you have always had home-killed meat and your butcher offers you imported, please do not scorn it, but try to think of the tremendous risks and great sacrifices that our noble seamen have made to bring you meat.'[63]

Food rationing also led to attempts to avoid the regulations or obtain personal gain from the sale of hard-to-obtain foodstuffs on the black market. In April 1943 an Ynystawe greengrocer was jailed for three months after encouraging a farm worker to steal six pullets from his place of work. He had paid the lad six shillings each for the birds, no doubt planning to sell them on at a good profit.[64] A Carmarthen Road fruiterer was found to have charged more than double the allowed price of 4½ d. for a pound of apples and had failed to display the appropriate price list. He was fined £1 and over £2 in costs. A Treboeth scrap metal collector was alleged to have visited Llandeilo in May 1944, returning from the trip with a side of bacon and a quantity of ham that he concealed under some sacking in his car. His defence was that he had simply met a farmer who he did not know and had bought the provisions off him. Llandeilo Magistrates' Bench was unimpressed. The bench was even more unimpressed when the arresting officer stated that the defendant had pressed two £1 notes into his hand with a plea that he be excused from any legal action on this occasion. He was fined over £37 for the food offences and the attempted bribery.[65]

The defence regulations set maximum prices for certain items in an attempt to prevent possible profiteering by businesses. As an example, blackcurrants were assigned a maximum price at which they could be bought by a business for resale to the public. Taylor Brothers of Northampton Lane fell foul of that regulation when the company offered to buy the fruit from a Norfolk business at a price that exceeded the maximum allowed. On receipt of the letter, Norfolk Fruit Growers Ltd forwarded it to the Ministry of Food where officials suspected that Taylor Brothers would attempt to sell the fruit on to the Swansea public at an inflated price in order to more than recover their costs. The company denied that was the case, stating that it planned to sell the fruit to local doctors at the controlled price for the benefit of their patients. The company and its secretary were each fined a hefty £50.[66]

Rationing was also extended to other products that under wartime conditions either became scarce or, when they were available, were earmarked for use in some important area of the war economy. Petrol had actually been the first item to be rationed, with restrictions on its use being introduced in the first few weeks of the war. This was an inevitable consequence of all petrol supplies having to be imported into Britain at a time when shipping capacity was under pressure due to the need to bring in food and other essentials from overseas under wartime conditions.

The need to conserve petrol supplies only for essential purposes seems to have led to an increase in journeys made by rail. While some people might have had to travel by rail if petrol for their motor car was in short supply (remembering that motoring in 1939 was predominantly the domain of the middle- and upper-classes), others did so possibly due to reduced bus frequencies or the need to travel to distant locations for war-related work. Large numbers of service personnel were also being shunted around the country to take up new postings. The Great Western Railway company provided train services that extended from London Paddington to the stations of the South-West, the Midlands and much of Wales. In 1939, even excluding season tickets, it carried almost 85 million passengers (compared to 88 million in 1938), while by 1943 the figure had risen to a remarkable 146 million, very welcome news no doubt for the company's shareholders.[67]

The rationing of petrol naturally caused inconvenience to those lucky enough to own a car and some were faced with temptations that they were unable to resist. George Folland had worked at the docks for some years and was held in high esteem by his employers. In March 1940 he was found guilty of 'tapping' a petrol pipe-line at the docks and thus stealing six gallons of petrol. He had drawn the fuel from a sampling valve on a 12-inch pipe and had subsequently used the petrol in his car, travelling back and forth to his place of work. The magistrates' bench took a serious view of any interference in the petrol supply but, given Folland's previous good character, they imposed a fine of only £3.[68] A similar case involved Griffith Simpson of Frogmore Avenue who was found guilty of siphoning petrol from the tank of his employer's lorry. He admitted seven similar offences and was fined £3.[69] Another case involved a Swansea haulage contractor who had claimed a petrol ration for a vehicle that was off the road while undergoing repair. He was fined £5.[70]

Having decided early on to conscript men by age group, it was important that the government should have an idea of just how many men would be forthcoming in future years for military or other essential service in a time of war. Although the National Service Act gave the government information on the availability of men of 20 years old and over, it provided no data about those who were younger in years, yet still capable of working in a role that supported the war effort, perhaps on the land or in industry. It was also likely that with men being required to join the military, there would be a need for women to step forward and fill at least some of the civilian jobs so vacated, and there was little reliable data available about those numbers. While the census of 1931 contained basic information on the general population, it was eight years out of date for the purposes of wartime recruitment since it was a static snapshot of the population at a single point in time. There was no obvious way of knowing whether an 11-year-old child or an adult male who had appeared in the 1931 census would still actually be available for war-related service in 1939. For example, some of them might have died in the interim or could be currently suffering from industrial injury or general ill health. Others might be serving prison sentences or have moved overseas. Some would, in all probability, be performing work that would be vital in a wartime economy, thus precluding their availability for military service. The same issues applied to women who might need to be deployed in support of the war effort.

To clarify the situation, Parliament urgently enacted the National Registration Act[71] which passed into law on 5 September 1939. The Act provided for the creation of an up-to-date register of the civilian population of the United Kingdom and the Isle of Man and, despite it being a colossal task in the time available, on 29 September 1939 a team of 65,000 enumerators quickly distributed forms that were to be completed by all householders. Shortly afterwards, the enumerators revisited every householder, checked the details on the completed forms and issued an identity card for each resident. Over 40 million identity cards were issued and, as well as forming the basis of a system to possibly assist in introducing food rationing in the future (as did happen), the card could also be requested to be produced for scrutiny as proof of identity by a police officer and certain other authorised people. This would be important where, for example, a town or city suffered an influx of people who had fled or been evacuated from other areas. The other key element was that the register recorded personal details, including sex, age, address, marital status, and occupation. This information would give the authorities a good idea of the number of individuals who might be available for service in wartime across the entire population. Unlike the census, the register created in 1939 was a 'living document' that was updated at the local level (even after the war's end for a time) as people changed address, entered into the armed forces or the Mercantile Marine or died etc.

In the early part of the war the Government hoped that enough women would voluntarily come forward to meet the labour demands of the war effort, thus avoiding the need to introduce any power of compulsion. However, as the scale of the task confronting the nation came into sharper focus, it became apparent that only a large-scale mobilisation of the women of the country for war service would actually suffice. An organised and compulsory approach, although unpopular, would help ensure that tranches of women were moved into the armed forces or industry in the right place, at the right time, and in the right numbers.[72]

In December 1940, a governmental manpower requirements committee had concluded that around two million female workers would be required for munitions work, in the main, and the replacement of men by women in certain jobs. Conscription was not thought appropriate at that time and it was hoped that the ranks of the women's services – the Auxiliary Territorial Service, the Women's Auxiliary Air Force and the Women's Royal Naval Service – would quickly be swelled by eager volunteers. If women could take over non-combatant roles within the military that were currently performed by men, then the men so released could take on other duties of a more martial nature. However, to the great frustration of the authorities, it soon became clear that the number of women volunteering their service was hopelessly inadequate to meet the growing demands of the military and the war economy.

In March 1941, a registration for employment order was made which required women to register by age group at their local employment exchange, and soon afterwards women who had been born in 1920 were contacted regarding possible employment in support of the war effort. Local interviews were held with certain groups of women – those who were not in an occupation, had only household duties or were in unpaid or part-time employment – with a view to encouraging their voluntary enlistment for the nation's cause. Once again, the results proved to be disappointing and an even more direct approach was clearly going to be needed. To that end, an examination of the national register of 1939 gradually enabled the identification of over 500,000 women who had failed to comply with the registration of employment order (as well as over 100,000 men who had also failed to meet their obligations under the National Service Acts). Bringing over half a million somewhat hesitant women into the welcoming arms of the authorities was seen as having made 'a substantial contribution to the war effort'.[73]

Despite the initial misgivings of the Prime Minister and many of his ministers, the National Service (No. 2) Act was enacted in December 1941,[74] allowing for the first time the conscription of women into national service of some sort, subject to a number of safeguards. Only unmarried women and childless widows aged between 20 and 30 were liable for conscription in the first instance, though they could not be forced to perform combatant roles. They were allowed to opt for deployment into one of the three women's services or to industry or civil defence. In the first months of 1942, further restrictions on personal preferences were imposed that meant that women aged between 20 and 30 could only be hired for employment through employment exchanges or via certain, other approved channels. This removed their freedom of choice in employment matters and ensured that they were channelled by the labour exchanges to where they were most needed.[75]

Another issue that taxed the minds of the authorities was the fact that a great many women who were deemed eligible for direction towards war work were, in fact, unsurprisingly hampered by family responsibilities and were therefore tied to a particular location. This lack of mobility meant that they were restricted to working only in their immediate locality and not in areas that actually needed their labour. In April 1942, to partly address this problem, young women aged 19 were required to register for service. It was hoped that the anticipated lack of onerous family responsibilities in that age group would mean that those young women would be more suitable for direction into employment roles away from their home towns. This was an unpopular option for those affected, though steps were taken to ensure that suitable lodgings would be provided in the receiving areas.

Given the pressure imposed on families due to fathers being absent on war duty and mothers being required to work on at least a part-time basis wherever possible, it seemed sensible for the council to open in Swansea a small number of nurseries based at existing schools to look after the children when absent parents led to child-minding issues. During 1942 nurseries were established at the Pentrepoeth (for 27 children), Hafod (24), St Joseph's (27), Llansamlet (19) and Birchgrove (31) schools. Various medical examinations of the children were made over time and numerous problems were identified and dealt with. For example, across the five schools there were 11 children who were treated or kept under observation for tonsillitis. The figure for malnutrition cases was a revealing 34, while six children were found to have posture deformities. During 1942 the nursery school children were each examined several times by a nurse and there were 31 cases of children being seen in an unclean condition.

In June 1942, a nursery school for children between the ages of two and five was opened in a building that had originally been designed as a community centre for the communities of Townhill and Mayhill. It provided care for children while their mothers were engaged on war work and, soon after opening, was playing host to 130 youngsters a day with a waiting list of 156. Care was given between the hours of 9am and 5pm and two meals were provided, as well as a milk break and an afternoon nap – and all for only 1*s*. 8*d*. per child per week.[76] It did not come without risk. Within ten days of its opening there was an outbreak of diarrhoea which affected both children and members of staff over a period of five weeks, while in August an outbreak of mumps occurred which lasted until October 1942, affecting some 18 children. Additionally, at the nursery, during November and December seven children came down with chicken pox, though the incident was soon over due to strict isolation procedures being followed.[77]

Over time women were transferred out of their existing but non-essential work and into employment that supported the war effort, while many others were conscripted and then placed in appropriate roles within the war economy. The overall effect of this for a sample of affected employments in shown in the table below.[78]

Nature of Employment	Women employed in June 1939	Women employed in June 1944
WRNS, ATS, WAAF, nursing services	43,000 (December 1939 figure; June N/A)	466,000
Agriculture	93,000	216,000
Engineering, metals, explosives, chemicals and ship building	488,000	1,764,000
Textiles	600,000	412,000
Tailoring	168,000	124,000

The obligations placed upon women in an effort to boost the ranks of female workers for the military or the war economy naturally affected the women of Swansea in a number of ways. In February 1941, the question of a female member of staff at Swansea Council being allowed to leave in order to join the Auxiliary Transport Service was discussed. Council officers who left its employ to work in the various services usually received an allowance, though this was only payable in cases where the head of the department concerned had agreed to the request for permission to leave. In the present case, it seemed that losing the services of the woman concerned would have a detrimental effect on the work of a department that was already suffering from the loss of male employees to national service causes. It was noted that, to date, only one female employee had obtained the approval of her manager in such a case, and it was suggested that such requests should generally be resisted.[79]

Teenager Elaine Kidwell had already served in the Swansea civil defence service as a very young air raid warden, but as she advanced in age she eventually came to the attention of the employment services, and during 1943 was invited for interview at the old Guildhall in Swansea. She had hoped to join the Women's Royal Naval Service (Wrens), from where she might be able to obtain a posting to HMS Lucifer, the Royal Navy's base depot in Swansea which was conveniently close to her home. However, in an uneven contest, the needs of the war effort triumphed over the personal preferences of the individual and she was given the option of working on the land or in munitions, as that was where the need was currently greatest. Opting for the land she was directed to report to a farm that was not especially close to her home – it was near Haverfordwest. At Glanafon Farm she helped with the cattle, milking and mucking out, as well as delivering the milk to local homes. She also worked in the fields and was regularly chased around the farmyard by some aggressive geese. It involved long hours and a seven-day week with little time allowed for home visits. She remained at the farm until the early part of 1945.[80]

One post-war oral history interviewee (referred to only as 'Margaret' in the archival records) stated that she had been born at Baptist Well Place, Swansea, in 1922 and, in 1936, she commenced work at the Swansea Baths and Laundry, near the Guildhall, working as a presser. She subsequently moved (possibly being directed by the employment exchange) to the Royal Ordnance Factory in Bridgend where she earned over £4 a week, a considerable increase on her pay at the laundry. She travelled to the factory by train and her work involved the checking of fuses for bombs, not the most dangerous of roles performed there but certainly not risk-free. It was not uncommon for fingers to be split or even lost during some of the more dangerous procedures and, over time, there were over 20 deaths at the factory as a result of accidents.

Another Swansea woman referred to simply as 'Joan' was aged 24 in 1940 and had been working as the secretary to a manager at Hancock's Brewery in Swansea before enlisting in the Air Training Service (ATS). She was posted to far-off Chester where she assisted in arranging educational courses for Army soldiers, although during 1943 she contracted a virus and was hospitalised. Spending several months in hospital, she was disappointed to find that – as she saw it – the casualties of combat seemed to receive priority treatment over that of patients like herself. She was eventually invalided out of the ATS and, after completing her recovery, found a role in social work in Liverpool.

'Sarah' was in a reserved occupation, working as a canteen supervisor at Weaver's Flour Mill on the North Dock. She had obtained the job after the previous incumbent retired and there were simply no men available to replace him. The rate of pay for the role was reduced to reflect the fact that she was a woman, while female employees who replaced men who had left for the services also received less than the male rate, despite being expected to lift and carry the heavy sacks of flour. The canteen served hundreds of meals each day, both to the Weaver's employees and also dock workers. When she got married in 1947 she was asked to leave her employment, as men who had been recently demobbed had returned to Swansea and were looking for work.[81]

The impact of the employment of females in roles that had previously been almost exclusively the preserve of men was neatly illustrated by the light-hearted bemusement evidenced in Swansea's General Post Office social newsletters which were written in the masculine style of the times. After the loss of several men to the armed forces and their replacement by women, the newsletter noted:

> Such a number of familiar faces are missing, and the rooms and corridors echo to the chatter of female voices and the clatter of female feet…
>
> Engineering female assistants now blossom on the lower branches [of the organisation chart] and are, in addition to providing local colour, improving the symmetry of the tree… the majority of them are pleasing to the eye…
>
> By the way, one more pair of trousers to our 'bag' in the office. These, a useful-looking pair of grey flannels, adorn the nether members of one of the ladies in 'Fees'…
>
> Not content with slacks they go the whole hog, and a 'Zippy' siren suit now conceals the charms of one of our typists…[82]

One Swansea woman failed to comply with a direction given by a National Service officer that required her to take up employment in Birmingham. It was stated on her behalf in the magistrates' court that the work she was undertaking in Swansea was itself of some importance to the war effort, while she also had a widowed mother who depended on her for support. The court did not accept these mitigating factors but nevertheless gave her 14 days to reconsider her position. In another case, a 23-year-old single woman from Bonymaen had left her employment in Coventry (where she had been directed to work) without the permission of a National Service officer. She told the magistrates in Swansea that:

> I cannot sleep at night because my mind is on my home all the time... The hours in the factory are too long, and I cannot eat the food in the hostel. After working 12 hours on the night shift, I had only a fried egg on toast or a kipper. I cannot eat the food for dinner in the works canteen. I don't like the way it was served.

It was claimed that she was suffering from dyspepsia and the case was adjourned for an independent medical examination.[83]

Another Swansea case concerned a woman who had been directed to work as a domestic at a Young Women's Christian Association hostel in distant Haverfordwest which was being used to house members of the Women's Land Army. Her earlier request to be registered as a conscientious objector had failed and she had not attended Haverfordwest as requested. She was fined £5 plus costs. Two women from Phillips Parade in Swansea, who were Jehovah's Witnesses, had wilfully failed to comply with a direction to work at a hospital in Penycae. They had failed to attend for an interview despite being told that there were vacancies for maids who would work on the wards, a role that was fully compatible with their conditional registrations as conscientious objectors. Given the defiant nature of their stand, they were each fined, with the alternative being three months' imprisonment.[84]

Though enforced conscription was out of the question for them, the issue of utilising young people in some form of 'national service' in support of the war effort was also to the fore in thinking. As early as February 1939, the Swansea Boy Scouts' local association was reminding its Scout leaders of the need for plans to be in place as to how the Scout movement should react if hostilities were to commence. As it said, the motto of the scouting movement was 'Be Prepared' and, despite any personal misgivings among members about getting involved in some way in a major conflict, it made sense to know what was to be done in the event of an emergency such as an air raid. The Chief Scout was of the view that a scout's duty to God, the King and his neighbours compelled him to render his service, were his country to be attacked. That could take the form of working in first aid or air raid precautions for example, though if even that was a step too far for particular scouts then, regrettably, there was no place for them in the scouting brotherhood.

It was also noted that a number of scouting badges required skills that would be useful in a time of war. These included the ambulance, cook, cyclist, fireman and pathfinder badges and scouts should be encouraged to achieve these qualifications as a priority over others. It was also envisaged that scouts between the ages of 14 and 18 could be deployed as messengers to assist the police and air raid precaution services, though any scout volunteering for such service would need the written permission of his parents or guardians. There was also likely to be a requirement for suitably qualified scouts to act as coast watchmen in conjunction with the coastguard service, and holders of the scouting coast watchman's badge would be eminently suitable for this role which would also require a good knowledge of signalling by semaphore flags and morse lamps.

The Swansea Boy Scouts certainly rose to the challenge and it was soon noted that around 75 had volunteered from the Wesley, YMCA and 2nd and 3rd Mumbles troops, and almost every lad had a bicycle that greatly improved their mobility. Other Scout troops in the town were also playing their part. Scout messengers were soon embedded in the auxiliary fire stations at Mumbles, the Guildhall, Sketty, the central police station, St Thomas, Llansamlet, Morriston, Manselton and Mayhill. Working on a rota system, scouts were on duty at the various stations between the hours of 9am to 10pm and, when required, all night. They were equipped with steel helmets and respirators, while suits of anti-gas clothing were available at each station for use in the event of a gas attack. The higher echelons of the scouting movement expressed themselves well satisfied with Swansea's efforts, praising the discipline, courtesy, intelligence and willingness to help of the Scout volunteers.

Additionally, good work was performed by Scout units in aiding the authorities in the distribution of gas masks in areas of the town and in the filling of sandbags, while assistance was also provided by one pack in regularly helping elderly members of the Walters Road church get home during the blackout. The scouts in Swansea were also active in collecting waste paper in the form of newspapers and magazines from Swansea homes and businesses. The paper could be processed and used as a substitute for wood pulp, a vital component in the manufacture of new paper which was in short supply due to the incessant demands of wartime industry for timber, and the hazards of importation having made paper a scarce commodity.[85]

The Girl Guide movement also played its part and, as early as October 1939, it was noted that first aid training was being undertaken, books were being collected for the Mission to Seamen, and wool had been purchased to enable the knitting of items for use in local hospitals.[86]

Emergency legislation that had been passed in the run-up to war or at its declaration gave various government ministries or civil defence authorities extensive powers over the private assets of businesses and individuals, and almost any property that might be of use to the war effort was at risk of being requisitioned for the duration of the conflict. Several plots of land owned by Swansea Council were temporarily handed over for civil defence purposes, though formal requisition was not necessary in those instances. For example, land at Danygraig Cemetery, Delhi Street, land near Mumbles Yacht Club, Norfolk Street and several other locations was taken over for the placement of static water tanks. These tanks could be used for fire-fighting purposes by augmenting the local mains supply or to temporarily replace it where it had been damaged by enemy action. The Danygraig tank had a capacity of 5,000 gallons, while at sites in the Strand and at Vernon Street, the tanks were of 10,000-gallon capacity. A simple register drawn up by officials of the council's estates department eventually listed no less than 210 static water tank locations that had been subject to temporary acquisition (often by requisition) within the borough, usually being 'waste' patches of land, the owners of which sometimes received modest payments (between £1 to £10 per annum) for their assistance.[87]

Some owners appear to have accepted no payment for the use of their land, perhaps keen to be seen to be 'doing their bit' for the war effort. Patriotism had its limits, however, and the operator of the Maxime Cinema in Sketty adamantly refused to hand over a portion of the customer car park that was located at the side of his property so that a static water tank could be positioned there. A compromise was reached and the water tank was erected at the rear of the building during 1942. The site remained under the control of the civil defence body until 1949, at which time the new owner of the cinema (the Odeon chain) was paid £50 in previously unclaimed compensation. Not all additional water supply arrangements were quite so bureaucratic. Swansea schoolboy Alan Osborn remembered some civilians obtaining empty, 40-gallon petrol drums and then placing them close to the home while filled with water. In an emergency, the extra water might come in handy for tackling small fires should the mains supply be damaged. There were at least four of these drums on Robert Street in Manselton.

As well as being an important aspect of the civil defence arrangements, the large tanks also attracted the attention of local youngsters. They provided tempting play and swimming opportunities (though in cold and murky water) in areas where perhaps swimming baths were not available or were financially out of the reach of bored children. It was common for children to splash around or play boats on the water contained within these tanks, which were often above ground and round in shape, while some were of a subterranean design. These juvenile frolics did not come without risk: in Britain around 130 children were drowned in accidents involving the water tanks during 1941 to 1945.[88]

In a similar move, a petrol pump at a garage on Neath Road – one of many that were requisitioned – was taken over in 1941 (at a rental of ten shillings a week) for use in connection with the supply of fuel for civil defence purposes. This arrangement continued until September 1945 when the final bill was paid, as well as a sum of £30 in compensation for damage caused to the pump while in service.[89]

It was also common for the owners of uncultivated agricultural land to be directed to get it into productive use to bolster the country's food supply. In March 1940 the Glamorgan War Agricultural Executive Committee, a body based in Cardiff to exercise powers locally on behalf of the Minister of Agriculture and Fisheries, issued orders in respect of pasture at the Ty'n y Fron (almost five acres) and Garth Fach (around six acres) farms, both of which were located at Glais near Swansea. The orders required the owners of the farms to, 'Plough before March 31st 1940, and carry out other necessary cultivations and acts of husbandry to raise and secure an adequate approved arable crop for the harvest of 1940.'[90] It was not only the farmers who were expected to strain every muscle in the production of food; in September 1941 the men of the 960th Battery, Royal Artillery, based in Swansea, were loaned to a local farmer to assist in getting in the much-needed harvest.[91]

If every possible effort was being made to ensure that man and woman power was efficiently utilised in support of the war effort, steps were also taken to make sure that materials or equipment that were in short supply, due to the wartime disruption, were reused wherever possible. Many forms of transport had been diverted to the transporting of materials for the wartime economy, whether by road, rail or sea. The fact that these modes of transport were now often fully employed on war work meant that there was less cargo space available for the movement of other non-war-related items. Additionally, many commodities that had hitherto been imported from Europe or further afield ceased to be so readily available after the Germans overran the supplying countries, or U-boats sank the ships that were conveying cargoes to Britain. It soon became clear that the best possible use and reuse of what the country already had was necessary in support of the war effort, and the importance of salvaging and reusing existing materials came to prominence.

In July and August 1940, the people of Swansea salvaged 173 tons of paper, around five tons of rags, as well as 110 tons of various metals.[92] The best remembered salvage effort of the Second World War in Britain was probably the scrapping of the ornamental iron or steel railings that topped the walls of parks, schools, churches, gardens and a host of other structures. Swansea played a full part in this salvage enterprise, and by October 1940 it had removed a total of 56 tons of railings. The effort did not stop there, as wartime constraints produced shortages across a wide range of items. In February 1941, the council appealed to householders via a press advertisement to, 'save PAPER, METALS AND BONES, which are urgently required for the Prosecution of the War'. It also requested that bread crusts, unused scraps of vegetable or salad items, potato and apple peelings and scraps of meat also be set aside. If packaged up and left at the side of the normal refuse bin, these items would be collected by a specially appointed refuse operative and used to feed pigs, an important source of meat during wartime.[93] The Ministry of Supply suggested that women should accompany the refuse crews on their rounds, handing out publicity material about issues of salvage (especially that of paper which was used in the making of shells, bullets and other items of military hardware), as well as encouraging every housewife to play an active role in the salvage crusade.[94] Even unwanted personal papers of a confidential nature could be entrusted to the council workers; householders could take such documents to a premises in the High Street where they could be shredded in front of them before being assigned to a new use. Such was the enthusiasm for the scheme that council lorry drivers were working double shifts while, on a designated week, gangs of volunteers were helping the regular crews cope with the workload until dusk each day.[95]

The Ministry of Information (in an advertisement patriotically paid for by the Brewers' Society) appealed for any old shirts or even rags to be passed to the refuse collector. Such seemingly worthless materials could, it was said, be used to make a soldier's uniform, a sailor's blanket or even the padding for a seat in a tank. Even oily rags were apparently items that would fill a refuse collector's eyes with joy.[96] In the year ending 31 March 1944, it was reported that salvage efforts in the town had rescued 853 tons of paper and cardboard, 257 tons of tin and other metals, 534 tons of kitchen waste, 13 tons of rags and string, six tons of bones, 13 tons of rubber as well as over 26,000 bottles and jars.[97] In October 1944, a two-week period was set aside for the donation of old books for salvage purposes, the second time such a campaign had been mounted.[98]

Not all of the salvage news was of a positive nature; during the war it was noted by Swansea Council that some traders in Swansea were proving to be somewhat lackadaisical in dealing with their bombed-out premises. Those properties, though damaged and not in use, usually contained a range of items that could easily be collected for salvage purposes. It seemed that the traders were content to merely sit back and await settlement of a compensation claim while not taking steps to clear their properties of reusable items, an attitude that the council decried.[99]

As well as encouraging the collection of salvaged materials, the government also took steps to restrict the use of materials that would be better employed in the war effort. The manufacture of new furniture (often required by bombed-out families) was restricted to a limited range of designs – referred to as utility furniture – and clothing was treated in a similar way, with function taking precedence over style and little in the way of wasteful embellishment. Even the thickness of coffin wood was reduced, resulting in a surprising saving in wood, while the maximum height of ladies' shoe heels was also reduced, resulting in another saving in leather or similar materials. It really was a case of 'every little helps' as Britain strained to keep up with the demands of the war economy.[100]

CHAPTER 5

Defending the People

AT THE OUTBREAK of war in September 1939, the first thing that could be done to protect the people of Swansea was to examine the papers and activities of every 'enemy alien' (German or Austrian) who was actually in the town. This was a part of a process that had also been undertaken during the First World War, by which adult enemy aliens of military age who resided in Britain were at risk of being interned lest they commit acts of sabotage in support of their home country.

To start that process, the Chief Constable in Swansea, F J May, placed an advertisement in the *South Wales Evening Post* on 5 September 1939, requiring all Germans residing in the town to report to the aliens registration office at the central police station, bringing their identity papers with them. At the national level, on 3 September 1939, there were around 70,000 resident Germans and Austrians living in Britain, and the personal circumstances of all those aged over 16 were soon being examined by a network of internment tribunals. A surprisingly high number of around 66,000 of those examined were exempted from internment and any other restrictions relating to their nationality. As an example, in Swansea it seems that one woman who had been born there in 1902 had later married a Charles Heinson, a man who told the authorities that he had been born in Liege or Antwerp in 1890, but nevertheless identified himself as German. He was living at Field Street in Landore and was employed locally as a tube worker at the Newport and South Wales Tube Company in a role that was probably quite important to the wartime economy. Charles and his wife, Annie Elizabeth, satisfied a tribunal that they were not a risk to the people of Swansea and both were exempted from any restriction. A small number of Swansea women seemed to be the widows of German men, though they were nevertheless interviewed before being released from the prospect of any restrictions being imposed on their lives due to the status of their nationality.[1]

A similar rush of activity linked to the presence of enemy aliens in the town occurred during June 1940 following the Italian declaration of war on Britain and France, and Swansea witnessed some outbursts of violence against Italians in the town in response to what was seen as Italy's treachery. At Cascarini's shop on High Street, a hostile crowd had gathered and windows were broken, while a shop run by the Segedelli family on Carmarthen Road saw the police draw their truncheons in the process of making an arrest from within a crowd of protestors. The breaking of windows allowed access to the shop premises, and in both cases some of the crowd took the opportunity for some quick pilfering of sweets and cigarettes. Several people were subsequently arrested, fined and bound over.[2]

An unusual case was played out at the Recreation Ground in Swansea where the Bertram Mills Circus had recently pitched its big top. Within the circus ensemble of international performers were two Italian brothers, Reni and Burri Manetti, who were employed as clowns and had been working in Britain for around 15 years while never seeking naturalisation. Swansea detectives arrived as the pair were putting on their make-up in readiness for the evening's performance, and it was made clear that they would be taken to the police station for questioning without further ado. If there was any justice in the world then the contemporary press reports would state that the duo made a spirited dash for freedom – pursued by truncheon-wielding policemen – only to come unstuck when the wheels fell off their car before they had exited the big top.

Regrettably, that did not transpire and the arrests appear to have been concluded without comic incident. As regards the wider picture in Wales, it was noted in the press that 33 Italians had been detained in Swansea, with Cardiff rounding up over 60 men. The total for Glamorgan was in the region of 160.[3]

Even before war had been declared, Swansea Council had been preparing estimates of the expenditure that was likely to be required to protect the local population from air attacks. The military thinking at the time anticipated an immediate attempt by an enemy to deliver a knock-out blow from the air in the early days of a new conflict. In May 1939 the council predicted that it would need to dig trenches for around 13,000 people across a number of locations, while the strengthening of cellars and basements in business premises would provide shelter for a further 8,000 citizens. Some test trenches were dug, before the idea was largely abandoned due to the tendency for the excavations to rapidly fill with water. Some trenches were completed where ground conditions proved to be suitable, one example being an excavation on the forecourt of the Plaza cinema. That was completed in April 1940 at a cost of £551 and provided rudimentary shelter for 150 persons.[4] It was also thought likely that money would need to be spent on strengthening domestic property basements where it was impractical to provide a shelter within the rooms or garden of the house, while in many areas effort and money would need to be put into the construction of public surface air raid shelters in suitable locations.

Some elderly or infirm residents would probably require assistance from the council to erect air raid shelters of a government-provided self-assembly type, typically the Anderson shelter, named after the then Lord Keeper of the Privy Seal, Sir John Anderson. These shelters consisted of a number of curved or straight galvanised and corrugated steel panels that could be bolted together forming a shelter of about six feet long and four feet wide, with a height of six feet. They could accommodate six people and were often part-buried in a garden before being topped with earth (and often flowers in a decorative flourish). Though they provided good protection against bomb blast and shrapnel, they could not withstand a direct hit. They could also be set up within a home and surrounded by sandbags, a relevant fact once it became obvious that, while they provided a degree of protection, when placed in a garden they were also frequently cold and dank. The later Morrison shelter recognised that issue and was designed for indoor use. All in all, the council expected to spend a sum of around £106,000 on air raid shelter works.[5]

Just after the outbreak of war, the council took the first steps towards providing public air raid shelters in busy areas, designed to offer a safe place for members of the public who might be away from their home shelter when an attack took place. It initially identified locations at Madoc Place, Wellington Street and St Mary's Square as being suitable for such shelters and each was to be almost 60 feet long, eight feet wide and eight feet high, with the construction being in brick and concrete. The capacity of each would be 50 people and the necessary public notices were placed in the press under the provisions of the Civil Defence Act of 1939.[6] Free-standing public air raid shelters were quickly under construction, and by July 1940 it was reported that there would soon be 46 such shelters in the town and a further 14 in the suburban areas, with yet more being planned. These shelters were intended for the use of people who were literally out and about in the streets; those who were at home during an attack should use their domestic shelters and not cause congestion in what might appear to them to be a more substantial nearby public shelter. It was hoped that, where customers were actually in a shop or other commercial premises when a raid commenced, they would be allowed to shelter within the building, though at their own risk. The public shelters provided a degree of safety but came with their own problems. The Town Clerk lamented that, 'Locks were broken, doors damaged, light batteries exhausted and lamps broken and stolen, fittings were damaged, key cases damaged and keys were missing. Timber seats were stolen or broken. A tremendous amount of cleaning work had to be done.'[7] Even first aid equipment had been stolen, and some thought was given by councillors to the possibility of appointing unpaid shelter supervisors or, following the London lead, actually paying such people. For the moment it was decided to approach local church authorities to see if volunteers could be encouraged to step forward to help maintain order.[8]

In the commercial parts of the town centre it was necessary for the council to requisition the basements of a number of privately owned business premises for use as public shelters. Many of these premises were of solid construction with roomy subterranean basements eminently suitable for shelter purposes. In due course, there were public basement shelters at premises in Castle Street, St Helen's Road, Pleasant Street, the Elysium, the Alexandra Arcade and the Grand Hotel among others. The council was responsible for providing any strengthening works that were required, usually in the form of additional timber supports, while electric lighting was often already available within the premises, but emergency lighting in the form of hurricane or candle lamps was also provided. Protection against the much-feared gas attack, in the form of screens or special curtains, was initially only notable by its absence, while the sanitary arrangements simply utilised any existing basement provision supplemented by a number of chemical closets.

Each basement had at least one emergency exit, often in the simple form of a manhole cover giving access to the street above. The capacity of some basement shelters was surprisingly high, with the combined basements of 32–34 St Helen's Road being able to accommodate 153 people (in more recent times this block included the Wilks Music Store),[9] while the Red Triangle (YMCA) Club basement shelter on Pleasant Street could hold 200 people. The basements of 8–10 Northampton Place provided shelter for 118 persons and had two emergency exits by way of manhole covers to the street above. Works of adaptation at that site were completed in December 1940 at a cost of £263.[10]

At the start of the war some people simply felt unable to wait for the authorities to get around to issuing them with a domestic air raid shelter of an approved type when the risk of attack from the air seemed to be imminent. One such case arose in respect of shelter-building activity at properties in the Hamilton Terrace and Washington Terrace areas of Swansea. After the receipt of information, a council inspector visited the streets concerned and found that one unofficial air raid shelter had been constructed, while several other excavations had been made in preparation for the erection of further shelters. The work completed did not meet the required safety standards as formulated by the Borough Engineer, and an agreement was reached with the people involved so that the necessary safety improvements would be carried out. Beyond that, the police were requested to prohibit the erection of other unofficial and potentially unsafe shelters in the town.[11]

The council had estimated that it would need around 30,000 standard steel shelters (of the Anderson type), and address lists comprising over 22,000 eligible properties had been completed by the end of March 1940. Of the 14,000 shelters that had been received by that time, over 1,000 were found to be missing the required nuts and bolts, causing a serious delay in their assembly. Given the then current rate of delivery of steel shelters to Swansea, it was estimated that the requirement of 30,000 would not be met until August 1940, a worrying prospect given that attacks from the air had been expected from the outset of war and could commence at any time. It was noted that in cases where, for some reason, a domestic property was not suitable for a standard shelter, it was usually the fact that it also did not have a suitable basement. Indeed, less than 20 domestic properties with suitable basements had been identified at that time. The council was also resisting requests from members of the public for the erection of brick and concrete surface shelters at domestic properties, and was instead insisting on providing the less expensive standard steel shelters. Surface shelters would, however, be considered at locations where domestic gardens were too small for even a domestic shelter or where an area was prone to flooding.[12]

When complaints were raised about the lack of shelters in certain areas of the town or the apparently random manner in which they were being distributed, the council was quick to point out that it was a government department that was arranging shelter deliveries from lists provided to it by the council. Deliveries had been subcontracted to the Great Western Railway company which had, in many instances, delivered a shelter but not all of the parts that went with it. Residents who were still waiting for a shelter were advised to try and share a neighbour's shelter in the interim or, for the time being, even to merely retreat to what seemed to be the safest part of their home in the event of an air raid.

Matters were not helped when steel, a vital component of the wartime economy, became scarce in the latter part of 1940. As early as June 1940, the council had been advised that, due to steel supply difficulties, no further steel shelters would be forthcoming from the government in the short term. At that time, some 19,426 shelters had been delivered to Swansea, leaving it short by an estimated figure of 10,574 shelters. The government suggested that the shortfall might be bridged by the construction of brick and concrete shelters, but even that proposal was bedevilled by a lack of the necessary building materials. By December 1940, the number of steel shelters supplied to Swansea had managed to limp up to 22,376, while communal surface shelters provided for another 2,808 families.

A further 95 families had benefitted from an individual brick shelter, while 120 families had been found to have suitable basements in their home for use as shelters.[13]

One householder complained that a large number of Anderson shelters had indeed been delivered to properties in Swansea but had not been assembled by their recipients for unknown reasons. Additionally, even where a shelter had been erected, such were its disadvantages (especially flooding) that many families had simply ceased using them during air raid alerts. The Borough Engineer defended the situation by pointing out that alterations were being made to the shelters to improve their weatherproofing, while he was unaware of the many shelters that were no longer being used by their recipients. He noted, probably with some satisfaction, that even if the complainant (a Mr Bevan of Terrace Road) was unhappy about the situation, someone at his home address had, in any event, applied to the council for a free shelter, defective or not.[14]

The work required for new or replacement air raid shelter provision was large in scale. Some assistance was even provided by local boy scouts in assembling indoor air raid shelters.[15] By December 1941, the council was employing 303 of its workforce on the construction of air raid shelters, while contractors engaged by it on the overall project numbered a further 156. Additionally, the council had 54 men working on the construction of static water tanks for fire-fighting purposes. This robust effort and its extensive use of manpower caught the attention of the Ministry of Labour, and commendable an effort as it was, raised its ire somewhat. The ministry had seemingly previously assessed the scale of the task and, in Swansea, it had determined that there were some 74 men in excess of what it thought was actually needed. If it was a case of 'jobs for the boys' at the local level, then, given the pressing need for labour in all parts of the war economy and the armed forces, it was minded to have those excess employments terminated so that the men so released could be directed to 'jobs for the boys' of its own choosing, in areas where the need was greatest. Every man was an asset that needed to be effectively deployed and the ministry would not hesitate to intervene where deemed necessary.[16]

Air raid shelters were also provided within the confines of schools in Swansea so that pupils and teachers had a place of refuge during a day-time attack though, in the event, such attacks proved to be remarkably rare. By October 1942, almost 50 such shelters had been erected or were under construction. Most of them consisted of reinforced brickwork, but eight were of a lower standard and thus were not quite so capable as the sturdier shelters of withstanding the effects of a nearby explosion. It became apparent that using the school shelters for the use of the public, as well as pupils and teachers, had some advantages when building materials and manpower for the construction of shelters were in short supply. Allowing the public access to the shelters after school hours would go a long way in defusing the occasional clamour for safe places in areas that had none, except those that were often out of reach behind the gates of the local school. The school shelters had initially been quite rudimentary in design, lacking even the most basic of facilities such as electricity and water, which were essential services in the event of a prolonged attack, and it was agreed that in the 40-plus school shelters of stronger construction, works of improvement would be undertaken to increase the comfort offered. This would see the provision of electricity and water, more robust seating (that was suitable for adults as well as children), chemical closets for sanitary purposes, light-tight ventilators to maintain an external blackout, strengthening where required, improved signposting, and painted white guide lines to help aid access in the dark. Across the borough it was estimated that allowing the public to use the school shelters after hours would provide relatively safe places for over 2,000 people. As was often the case, the plan became mired in arguments over funding, with the Board of Education insisting that any works carried out to benefit the general public must be funded by the local civil defence budget, and it is unclear how far the plan actually progressed.[17]

Beyond the passive sort of defence of the people of the town that was provided by the shelter-building programme, there was also the matter of the more active defence measures that were put in place to destroy or frustrate an enemy. By June 1940, with France defeated and its airfields under enemy control, the defence of Swansea by friendly fighter aircraft was provided by the Spitfires of 92 Squadron, RAF, a unit that was to remain at Pembrey airfield until September. It was replaced in September 1940 by 79 Squadron which flew Hawker Hurricanes, and it was those aircraft that would be required to provide air protection over Swansea for almost a year, a task it would perform with some controversy in the coming months.[18] The fighter station under construction at Fairwood Common was on Swansea's doorstep, but it was destined not to open until June 1941 at which time 79 Squadron moved there from Pembrey. By that time Swansea had already undergone its sternest tests that resulted from heavy attacks by enemy bombers.[19]

Another component of the developing air defence system in Swansea was that of the large balloon. Groups of these formed what was known as a 'balloon barrage' and, while being essentially a passive defensive system, it usually resulted in enemy aircraft, keen to avoid hitting the heavy metal cable to which a balloon was tethered, flying at a higher altitude than was desirable for accurate bombing. The balloons were of a significant size, consisting of a rubber-proofed cotton fabric with a gas capacity of just over 19,000 cubic feet, while being around 63 feet long and 31 feet high. They weighed about 550 pounds each and were filled with hydrogen gas, meaning that they were able to rise freely into the air. In the early days of the war it would take around 40 minutes for a balloon to be deployed at the required height. Later in the conflict, with improved methods and training, that time was reduced to around 20 minutes, an important improvement when balloons that had been grounded temporarily due to bad weather or other circumstances had to be speedily hoisted to meet a new attack.

Though they undoubtedly had a nuisance value, the Germans regarded the balloon barrages that hovered above the target areas with little respect, considering the gun and searchlight defences to be much more worrying. It was obvious to the Germans that the balloons could only operate at a limited altitude and they were known to be prone to deflation under certain weather conditions. Indeed, even lightning was a serious issue as, once it was struck, a balloon's hydrogen gas was likely to ignite and quickly bring it down. In one afternoon during the autumn of 1939, no less than 80 balloons caught fire during a lightning storm over London, while in Swansea eight balloons were struck by lightning and destroyed by fire in June 1941, before anti-lightning measures were eventually developed to minimise this problem.[20]

In this early part of the war there was the usual problem of there being too many defensive 'priorities' and not enough men or equipment to cover them all, and balloons were no exception. London and south-east England were clearly the key areas to which the initial balloon defences would be assigned, meaning that other areas, including Swansea, would have to wait until the necessary resources could be made available. On 27 March 1940 an order was issued by the balloon command headquarters to the effect that Swansea was to be provided with only four balloons, while Port Talbot would receive the same number. The anticipated key enemy targets around Swansea were the docks, the oil refinery at Llandarcy and the Mond Nickel Works in Clydach, while at Port Talbot it was the docks that were the main cause of concern. The order requested that a survey of potential sites be carried out and reported back on. For Swansea the sites initially identified as suitable were open ground near to the South Dock, land at Maesteg Park, Port Tennant, reclaimed ground between the south-west corner of the King's Dock and the eastern breakwater, as well as land beyond the eastern end of the King's Dock. There were 16 balloons available for south Wales as a whole and they were to be spread between Cardiff (eight balloons), Swansea (four) and Port Talbot (four) though, unexpectedly, all 16 were initially sited in Cardiff, apparently due to increasing air ministry concerns about its vulnerability.

This aberration was soon rectified by relocating eight of the 16 balloons in Cardiff to be shared equally between Swansea and Port Talbot, thus conforming with the original plan. Though completion of the plan would finally see Swansea and Port Talbot receiving some consideration, it was still likely that four balloons in each area would be hopelessly inadequate when weighed against the likely scale of attack.

The balloon command headquarters placed the overall command of the Swansea balloons under the control of the Cardiff balloon barrage commanding officer. It was noted that, given the need to ground the balloons if adverse weather was anticipated, the distance between Swansea and its control point in Cardiff meant that speedy communication at short notice might be problematic, especially when communication systems might have been damaged during a raid. It was planned that, 'the Barrage Commander will therefore avoid taking undue risks, even if this involves keeping part of the barrage situated in Swansea and Port Talbot close-hauled or bedded down more frequently than would normally be required.' By 5 June 1940, balloon command was able to report that the Swansea and Port Talbot barrages would be flying from noon on 7 June, though it is unclear if that actually succeeded as planned. At the end of the first week of July, it seems that the

Swansea balloons were indeed ready for deploying and, subject to weather conditions, they were to be raised at 7.30pm on the following day and that does seem to have been achieved.[21]

If that was good news regarding the defence of Swansea from aerial attack then, after the fall of France and German control of French airfields within easy reach of Britain, the situation regarding anti-aircraft guns was totally unsatisfactory. With London and the south-east once again being the top priorities for the allocation of what were then the scarce anti-aircraft guns, the shortage of such guns meant that Swansea would face the likelihood of attack early in the war without a single anti-aircraft gun in position. Indeed, by 11 July 1940 (the day after 12 people had been killed during a lone-aircraft raid on Swansea), the town still had no heavy anti-aircraft guns in position for its defence. The guns were in great demand, of course, and there were almost 1,200 heavy anti-aircraft guns dotted around the areas of Britain that were most at risk of attack from the air. The protection, such as it was, had to cover locations as diverse as London, Belfast, the Clyde, Scapa Flow, the Tyne, the Shetlands, and a couple of dozen other important towns and cities. In July 1940, London had 92 guns, Birmingham 64 and Bristol 36. There were just 12 guns in Cardiff and four in Newport and those 16 guns represented the total air-defence strength for Wales as the Battle of Britain began.[22]

Somewhat ironically, although Swansea was currently bereft of such guns, the town was involved in gun barrel refurbishment. Early in the war the Woolwich Arsenal made use of Swansea's metal-working skills and set up a workshop at the premises of Messrs Richard Thomas and Co., Cwmfelin Tinplate Works, Cwmbwrla. Gun barrels that had suffered wear and tear while in use were sent to Cwmbwrla where a specialised team re-plated them and made them fit for further use, a small contribution in the grand scheme of things but nevertheless a much welcome one when every gun counted.

John Gronow worked there as a laboratory assistant, and he recalled the gun barrels – sometimes as many as six a day – being brought by train to the High Street station before being taken to the works on low-loading vehicles. It was an around-the-clock operation with an operative typically working a 12-hour shift, five days a week. A shift would consist of perhaps 15 to 20 individuals, with men performing the heavier work of moving the gun barrels around, while women mixed the necessary cleaning acids and other chemicals and recorded the progress made.[23] This important work was of no immediate use to Swansea, and the town would have to rely on luck in the interim during any enemy air raids. That was a situation that would only improve with the passage of time and, at the end of July 1940, the town finally welcomed the arrival of its first anti-aircraft guns.

CHAPTER 6

Under Attack: The Early Raids

SAPPER J A Lacey of the Royal Engineers arrived in Swansea in June 1940 in the wake of his evacuation from Dunkirk having been, much to his surprise, transferred to the 103 Bomb Disposal Section. Soon after that unexpected news had been assimilated, and before he had even found his bearings in the town, an air raid began and one loud bang was heard, though no damage occurred to the YMCA building on St Helen's Road where he was billeted. The threat from the air had long been recognised, though at the time of this first raid on Swansea – which took place on 27 June 1940 – the town possessed no anti-aircraft guns. Indeed, by the last week of July 1940, Swansea was only defended by eight anti-aircraft guns, a hopelessly inadequate number for an important industrial town that the Germans would undoubtedly target.[1]

During the raid of 27 June a small number of bombs were dropped on the east side of the town, including several on Kilvey Hill which failed to explode. The bomb disposal team's commanding officer soon announced that there were several unexploded bombs in the area, and that the section would have to start defusing them. However, he would first need to borrow some picks and shovels from Swansea Council to help with the task, due to the current dearth of equipment within the new and hastily assembled bomb disposal team. As far as the men were concerned, any training in their dangerous role would be given on the job, with all the risks that entailed. As Sapper Lacey recalled: 'After breakfast we were taken to the site, split into pairs, several holes were pointed out, and we were told, "We think there is a bomb down there, be careful when you get to it." On the first bomb we were careful!'

After the picks and shovels had been nervously wielded for a while, the next step in the process required feeling through the soil with fingers only, until contact was made with the metal of the bomb casing. At that point the officer took over and gingerly deactivated and removed the fuse. The bomb was of the German SC50 type, weighing around 50kg and, happily, it contained no anti-handling devices and was therefore relatively straightforward to deal with. It had proven necessary to dig down almost seven feet to locate the bombs, of which there were seven. All were exposed and destroyed in situ, except for one which was rendered harmless before being taken back to the section's headquarters for examination.

At first, the facilities available in Swansea for such a technically advanced unit existed only in the most rudimentary manner. A room over an empty garage on Wind Street had been requisitioned as its base, and in the early days the 'beds' were merely blankets on a cold floor while the 'office' was comprised of a trestle table and two folding chairs. Official stationery was notable only by its absence, so that any official writing regarding military matters was done on stationery that had been bought off the shelf from F W Woolworths, the Woolies chain of shops which, before its demise in more recent times, was much beloved by those of a certain age. Bathing was achieved by using the showers in Swansea Docks while, according to Sapper Lacey:

> Transport was literally requisitioned from the streets by the OC [Officer Commanding]. Tools had to be borrowed, and there was no special equipment such as a remote-controlled listening device… Slowly equipment began to arrive… Explosives to detonate bombs were obtained, and War Department vehicles replaced the unreliable requisitioned vehicles.

As was usual, the military often found work for idle hands and, when there were no bombs to defuse, much effort was put into using the men to fill sandbags which, when piled around buildings in the town, would reduce the damage from bomb explosions. Sandbags were also filled in order to provide a bomb shelter of sorts inside the unit's own headquarters, especially important as it was located in the heart of the town's commercial district which was already a tempting target for the enemy. It also soon became apparent that many Swansea citizens had obtained all sorts of explosive devices from the 1914–18 war, and had then kept them within their homes as doorstops, ornaments or conversation pieces. Perhaps the worrying thought of what such a device might do in a property that was hit by a 1940 vintage bomb meant that a large number of these almost antique items were hastily handed in to the police who, in turn, requested their urgent collection by the bomb disposal section. A large number of undetonated incendiary bombs from the early air raids were also a common occurrence, representing more collection and disposal duties for the team.[2]

On 10 July 1940, the day that is regarded as the beginning of the Battle of Britain, a lone raider carried out an attack during the morning on the King's Dock in Swansea. No advanced warning of an incoming enemy aircraft (which was apparently displaying French symbols) was issued and, as a result, the surprise attack led to 11 people being killed and almost 30 wounded. Two customs officers, David Evans and Richard Nichols, were among the dead, their official duties sadly placing them in the wrong place at the wrong time. A further fatality due to the raid occurred at the National Oil Refinery in Llandarcy, where Charles Fryer was injured and died of his wounds two days later.

In the future, the town would be regularly attacked by a variety of enemy aircraft, including the Heinkel He 111 type, a medium bomber that could reach a top speed of 273 miles per hour with a bomb load of 2,000kg, as well as the Dornier 17 medium bomber. The original design of the Dornier had been intended for the civilian air transport market but it had failed to impress the commercial airlines and was switched instead to military use. It had a top speed of 260 miles per hour and a bomb load of around 1,000kg. A small number of aircraft of the Junkers Ju 88 high-speed bomber type also took part in the attacks, having a top speed of 269 miles per hour and a bomb load of around 1,500kg.

Given the available technology of the time, future bombing raids on Swansea would, to a degree, be on a 'hit and miss' basis. The Germans were hampered by having to fly at relatively high altitudes in order to avoid the anti-aircraft fire as well as the balloon barrage around the town. This naturally affected the accuracy of their bombing runs even before the difficulty of night-time attacks, bad weather and reduced visibility were taken into account. Two German systems were in operation that depended on radio beams guiding aircraft to the target area and, in certain instances, automatically releasing the aircraft's bomb load regardless of any visibility problems. The first of these was code-named *Knickbein* (bent leg) and the second *X-Gerät*. British counter-measures against these devices soon made the enemies bomb-aiming task more difficult and, in the case of Swansea, most of the Luftwaffe after-action reports indicate that bombs were released 'by sight of ground'.[3] Later experience showed that, whether by accident or design, a lot of enemy bombs fell onto areas that could not be regarded as military targets.

Further consideration of the inadequate number of balloons available for the air defence of Swansea had led to an allocation of another eight balloons in early July 1940, and new sites were identified at Tir John Power Station, Jersey Park, High Street Station, a spot near the tidal basin, the boys' grammar school playground, the civic centre (Guildhall), Elba Works, and a site near the Jersey Marine Hotel. That was not the end of the matter; in early August 1940 it was proposed that the Swansea balloon barrage be increased to 32 balloons, this number allowing for the fuller protection of the town and the oil refinery at Llandarcy. The RAF's 958 Squadron was moved to Swansea on 12 August 1940 and it would be responsible for four flights of eight balloons each, plus three waterborne balloons, making 35 in all, a far cry from the initial four balloons that had originally been allocated to the town. In addition to the locations mentioned earlier, balloons would be located at the east and west piers, various locations within the docks, a site near the Patti Pavilion, the Vetch Field and over a dozen in the Llansamlet-Skewen-Jersey Marine-Coedffranc area.

Sixteen of the balloons were specifically positioned to defend the oil refinery, a clear indication of its importance to the war effort, and it proved necessary for balloon command officers to meet the refinery managers as well as the site chemist in order to identify the best potential balloon sites. It was not a straightforward affair; the surrounding terrain included bog, marsh, poor accessibility and parts of the refinery area were simply not suitable for balloon deployment. It was noted, '... from local information, it is invariably the practice of enemy aircraft to approach the area by way of the River Neath, either from the south or the north. It was, therefore, partially through unavoidability and partially by design that the Barrage has been thickened up on the eastern side.' Permission to inflate and fly the 16 balloons was given by balloon command headquarters by telegram on 24 August.

The issue remained one of concern and a certain amount of repositioning of some of the Swansea balloons soon followed, while in early September it was thought necessary to improve the balloon defence of the lock gate at the King's Dock. It was an urgent request that could be met by either flying the required four balloons from vessels at sea or by way of anchoring them to buoys (the option that was eventually adopted) near to the east and west piers. By February 1941, Swansea's balloon barrage consisted of 38 balloons, while permission for another two balloons had been given, though they had not yet been deployed. The increasing availability of balloons over time had gradually improved the situation in Swansea, though how effective they would be in the face of a massed attack remained to be seen.[4]

There were four further raids on the town during July 1940 but they were all small in size and caused no significant harm since, on those occasions, it had been possible for some advance warning to be given to the population. Within the first four weeks of its deployment, 103 Bomb Disposal Section in Swansea had dealt with 21 unexploded bombs, while many others were defused by other teams temporarily sent to Swansea to assist. The 103 Bomb Disposal Section had been deployed to Swansea in late June 1940 and, between that time and the 31 August, no fewer than 15 air attacks on the town took place. Bombs fell – and many failed to explode – at locations that included Port Tennant, Morriston, the Mumbles, Swansea Docks, Cockett, Manselton, Uplands, Treboeth, Hafod and West Cross, resulting in a heavy workload for the team. The work of the section was not confined to Swansea. Over a week in early July 1940, six bombs were removed from the National Oil Refinery site at Llandarcy near Skewen for detonation in a safe place. Some of these bombs were found at a depth of almost 20 feet underground, thus requiring a lot of hard digging before they could be defused. Visits were also made for bomb disposal purposes to Neath, Llandeilo and Brynamman.[5]

As regards attacks from the air, if the balloon defences had gradually been improved over the summer of 1940, so too had the number of anti-aircraft guns that were available for the protection of the town. At the end of July 1940, orders had been issued that resulted in the 79th Heavy Anti-aircraft Regiment (Royal Artillery) relocating to the Swansea area.

The regiment had been formed in November 1938, with a regimental headquarters in Watford. In October 1939 the unit fired its first rounds against enemy aircraft near to Harwich, where it was tasked with the defence of the port area. It also saw service in France with the British Expeditionary Force between February and June 1940, before being hastily evacuated back to Britain as the Germans advanced towards the French coast. By the end of September 1940, the regiment's 247th and 248th Batteries (with four guns each), as well as elements of the 246th Battery, were in Swansea, with a total strength of around 700 men. The regimental headquarters was established at a property named Ashleigh at Ffynone, which had formerly been used as the Parc Wern School for young children. Guns were soon in position at Mumbles, Sketty and Llansamlet.[6]

Six air raids took place during August 1940, with the most serious one occurring on Saturday, 10 August. This was later recorded as being a 'fairly heavy raid' which saw 30 high-explosive bombs dropped on the Landore, Brynhyfryd, Singleton Park, Clyne and Ravenhill areas. There were 15 deaths and another 15 wounded, some seriously, with the streets affected including Bryn Street, Siloh Road, Penfilia Road and Neath Road. Air raid wardens William Jones and Jack Jones were killed in Brynhyfryd, while Reginald Galvin, an 18-year-old air raid precautions messenger, was killed in Neath Road, Landore, though he lived in Llansamlet. One man had dallied in his home in order to collect some important papers before making his way to the garden shelter. As he made his way down the hall, a bomb exploded in the road outside and the blast blew him part-way up the stairs. In other properties both external and internal doors were blown off by bomb blasts.[7]

A diarist at the time noted that, on 10 August, 'Shelter from 10.30pm to 2.30am, bombs dropped at Ravenhill by Welfare Hall, some at Brynhyfryd causing a lot of damage to about a dozen houses + water pipe (main) + cable which were very quickly repaired, about 17 [*sic*] people were killed.' The diary entries reveal the disruption and stress caused by raids or merely the threat of raids at that time. It notes that bombs were dropped on 2, 3, 6, 9, 10, 15, 16, 24, 27 and 29 August 1940, though it must be noted that not all of these dates tally with the official records of the time. On Wednesday 7 August, the diarist was in the air raid shelter between 11pm and midnight before returning to the house, only to have to re-enter the shelter a little later and then remaining there until 1.30am. In the event, no bombs were dropped during that time, so while caution was the sensible approach it certainly did not help the nerves or sleep patterns of people who might be performing important war work the following day. Though destroying an attacking aircraft by way of anti-aircraft fire was notoriously difficult, it was noted that the Swansea gunners claimed to have seen one such target blow up in mid-air on 24 August. The remainder of August 1940 saw several more minor raids which resulted in only one death, at Gors Avenue, and 15 wounded.[8]

On the morning of 25 August 1940, an official of the Great Western Railway company reported the presence of an unexploded bomb on the railway track at Loughor. Second Lieutenant Ellis Edward Talbot, a 20-year-old native of Newport, had been educated at Harrow and had commenced further studies at Cambridge University before the advent of war, and his consequent entry into the Royal Engineers had resulted in the cessation of his academic pursuits, at least for the time being. In Loughor he was able to confirm the presence of an unexploded bomb and he summoned the assistance of seven men from the unit. Digging commenced at 5.15am on the morning of 25 August and continued until 3pm in the afternoon, with breakfast and lunch for the team being kindly provided by local residents. As the bomb was gradually exposed, it became apparent that its fuse was of a new type, and Second Lieutenant Talbot decided that it would be best to move the bomb a short distance away from the railway lines to a location where it would do less damage if it detonated while being inspected. He ordered his men to take cover before lifting the bomb onto his shoulder and carrying it a distance of some 200 yards to a place of relative safety. For his bravery and devotion to duty, with complete disregard for his own safety, he was subsequently awarded the Empire Gallantry Medal, a decoration that he was soon able to exchange for the newly-created George Cross.[9]

On the night of 1–2 September 1940 a more concentrated raid than had hitherto been the case occurred over Swansea. Given its scale, this raid qualified as being the first 'Blitz'-style attack on the town (there would be six such attacks on Swansea over the course of the war). It is not clear how the designation of 'Blitz attack' was arrived at locally, but it does appear from the records that only raids where it was thought that over 50 high-explosive bombs had hit the town were given the dubious honour. The government's view on the severity of enemy attacks saw raids where more than 100 tons of high-explosive bombs being dropped being classified as 'heavy'. In Swansea, on the night of 1–2 September, just over 100 high-explosive bombs were dropped as well as over 1,000 incendiary devices over a large part of the town, resulting in 33 people killed and over 100 injured, 37 of whom were adjudged to be seriously wounded.

An alarming incident occurred during the raid at the police station on Alexandra Road – external bomb damage caused the station lighting system to fail. An emergency generator was switched on, though the lighting circuits it powered were not fitted with independent switches so that all the station's internal lights came on. That was problematic as the windows and blinds on the east side of the building had been blown out, with the result that the police station was illuminated even as enemy bombers were still overhead. During the raid, Police

Constable Jack Jenks became the first Swansea policemen to be killed during the war, being hit by a bomb splinter on Union Street. He had married only a month earlier.[10]

During the attack, parts of the Eastside of Swansea were hit, with properties in Tymawr Street and Grafog Street damaged. Two deaths occurred at Tymawr Street where an Anderson shelter was hit by a bomb, while at 3 Grafog Street, Thomas Henry Hurford, his wife Ivy and their children Mary (four years old) and Brian (two years old) were killed along with Phyllis Harvey and her three-year-old son, Keith. A property in Russell Street, in the Sandfields part of the town, was also struck, resulting in the deaths of Reginald John Jones, his wife Mary Kate and their three children whose ages ranged from 12 to 26. The Pembroke Hotel on St Helen's Road was a popular haunt of foreign seamen, and four visiting sailors and three civilians were killed when the hotel was hit by a bomb and subsequently burnt-out during the raid.[11]

William Joseph Jenkins was employed by day as a fitter and turner but, in is his off-duty hours, he served as motorcycle messenger for the civil defence services. He was on duty at a suburban post on the night of the attack and was given a message to take to the Guildhall control room, some three miles away. He set off, having to avoid fallen debris and the fires from broken gas mains, occasionally having to dismount and wheel his motor bike over or around difficult terrain. Entering the town, he was knocked unconscious after being hit by falling bricks. Recovering his senses, he continued his journey but was again knocked out by the explosion of a bomb. He was taken into a nearby air raid shelter but, on coming round, insisted on completing his task only to be knocked off his bike for a third time. He covered the last half-mile to the control room on flat tyres before finally delivering his message. He was later awarded a George Medal for his bravery, the first Swansea air raid precautions worker to be so honoured.[12]

The Auxiliary Fire Service was busy both during and after the raid of 1–2 September 1940. The number of firemen involved in dealing with any incident naturally varied on a daily basis, given that the part-time men often had other work to perform and might not be available at short notice. That said, by way of illustration, during the early September raid, the St Thomas fire station was able to muster 23 full-time and 24 part-time auxiliary firemen, while at Fisher Street the numbers were 23 full-time and 17 part-time. The Morriston station produced another 20 full-timers and 28 part-timers. Given that the Fisher Street contingent was described as being 'Section 1 and 2', while that of St Thomas was referred to as 'Section 10', it becomes clear that the Chief Constable's original thought that perhaps an extra 500 Auxiliary Fire Service volunteers would be required had been well judged, given the scale of the task that faced the force during and after a raid.[13]

Even while the raid was still in progress, 103 Bomb Disposal Section's members were involved in fire-fighting and dealing with incendiary devices that had fallen close to their own headquarters. As the situation grew more dangerous, some thought was given to evacuating the explosives which were held on site and were normally used to safely detonate unexploded bombs in controlled explosions. Disaster might ensue were the headquarters to catch fire. In the midst of all this frenetic activity, Second Lieutenant Talbot still had to keep himself appraised of incoming reports about the locations of unexploded ordnance to which the rest of the section could be sent at a moment's notice. Over the next few days, unexploded bombs were dealt with in several parts of the town, including Carmarthen Road, Plymouth Street, Cwmfelin Tinplate Works and St Mary's churchyard. Assistance in this work was also received from a Cardiff-based bomb disposal section. One officer from the Cardiff team, Lieutenant Bertram S T Archer, was later awarded the George Cross for defusing a 250kg bomb that had been dropped on the Llandarcy oil refinery, while also removing its anti-handling device for expert examination.[14]

The raid certainly unnerved some of the towns inhabitants, even if only temporarily. Margaret Kay wrote from Langdon Place to her eldest son a few days after the raid, saying that:

> We are too unsettled even to sit down in the evenings now. Late tea early supper then warning about 9. All the hours in the shelter, home 3 or 4 o'clock & as soon as we're in bed the plane is back again... The people simply pour out of their homes to go out to sleep, it is terrible to see it. The shelters are crowded, they were sleeping under the hedges at Singleton Monday... the next door people close business at 9pm & go to Mumbles for sleeping & everybody that has anywhere to go out of town are off every evening... It's wonderful how quickly they are clearing the debris off the streets & even putting new shop windows in.[15]

The 79th Anti-Aircraft Regiment was based in the town in order to engage enemy aircraft with its heavy guns, and it became mired in controversy due to its inexplicable inactivity during the raid of 1–2 September. The *Regimental War Diary* recorded the attack as commencing at 8.55pm and ending at 3am. The diary noted that there was, 'Very bitter feeling against personnel of the Regt and indignation shown by civil populace who could not understand why all guns were silent.' The answer lay in a restrictive order that had been previously issued by an air vice-marshal at Fighter Command. There were often occasions when a raid took place in weather conditions that prevented or made difficult a definitive visual identification of aircraft that were passing overhead. To fire on a 'target unidentified' basis in such circumstances risked the shooting down of a friendly aircraft when perhaps RAF fighters were flying overhead and attempting to attack the incoming enemy aircraft. The air vice-marshal's order therefore prohibited firing on unidentified targets when friendly forces were also believed to be present in the air. On the night in question, the higher command had indicated that friendly fighters were indeed operating over Swansea (though none seem to have been seen or heard by those on the ground), so that the order became effective and the guns were forbidden to fire before midnight, by which time the unhindered enemy aircraft had inflicted considerable damage on the town and had killed or injured numerous people. The regiment's commanding officer, Lieutenant Colonel R C Raikes, believing that his hands had been unnecessarily tied with adverse consequences for Swansea, made his displeasure known to his superior officers and his indignation soon produced a reaction.

The commander of the 45th Anti-Aircraft Brigade, to whom Raikes reported, told him on 27 September 1940 that, 'In view of the recent unfortunate incidents in Swansea and other places, I have today talked to the General and we have agreed that we are in future going to risk our arm and give you authority to open fire in the event of any town being bombarded.' This was not a *carte blanche* authority; a suspected enemy aircraft merely passing over the town should not be fired upon until it had committed a hostile act, namely by attacking the town by bomb or machine gun. Once that hostile act had occurred, the Swansea guns were free to respond within agreed arcs of fire designed to minimise the risk of hitting a friendly aircraft.

Lieutenant Colonel Raikes had also developed what he thought was an improvement on the normal defensive measure of an anti-aircraft barrage fired over Swansea on predetermined lines. He dubbed the new procedure, rather splendidly, as 'The Ball of Fire', and it was a movable barrage which was fired ahead of enemy raiders in the hope that they would fly headlong into an explosive storm of fire and steel. The procedure allowed control of all the regiment's gun sites to be temporarily passed to the gun site that was best placed to deal with an incoming attack. Based on calculations of the distance to an enemy aircraft and its height, the controlling gun site would plot the target area and coordinate the fire of all guns so as to saturate the selected spot – an invisible square in the sky – with high-explosive or shrapnel shells. The technique certainly seemed to have some merit; the *War Diary* entry for the 24 September 1940 noted that '[Enemy] Aircraft found to jink suddenly when greeted with BALL OF FIRE. This simple form of concentration proving very popular and apparently effective.' Not all gunfire was so effective. By way of comparison, on 22 December 1940, the officer commanding a nearby balloon squadron complained that the regiment's gunfire on the previous night had 'caused great damage to his balloons'. New orders were issued to try and prevent a reoccurrence of that regrettable episode.

Over time, the locations of the 79th Anti-Aircraft Regiment's gun sites in Swansea were subject to change, and there were also regular movements of guns into and out of the area. In December 1940, a perceived gap in the anti-aircraft protection of Swansea was to be filled by an additional four-gun battery. This was to be situated on a hilltop at Ravenhill, closing the gap between the gun sites in Sketty and Llansamlet. It would be a rough affair – the guns would be partly concealed in a hedge, while the gun crews would have the less-than-happy experience of sleeping in subterranean dormitories that were situated between the guns.[16]

After a while, the regular soldiers who manned the new guns in Ravenhill were relieved by newly-trained (and very proud) members of the local Home Guard. Indeed, as early as 1941, Home Guard members across Britain had been manning rocket batteries, while from 1942 onwards some Home Guard men were detailed to operate perhaps one gun in an anti-aircraft battery, the others still being worked by experienced regulars who could pass on their knowledge. As the demand grew for more regular Army gunners who could take part in mobile operations on the mainland of Europe and elsewhere, so the Home Guard increasingly stepped up to fill the gaps thus created in home defence.[17] The training given in Swansea had attempted to ensure that the men were interchangeable as regards anti-aircraft gun roles, so that injuries or other absences could be covered without loss of effectiveness. Almost 90 men served the four guns in Ravenhill, each gun having an 11-man team and the same number of reserves. Arthur Anderson had advanced to the rank of acting captain in the unit and was present when the 'first team' of 11 gunners put on a show for some regular Army observers in Mumbles. The 'target' was towed around 80 yards behind an aircraft, and the first team proved adept in managing to hit it. The reserve team was not quite so proficient and caused some alarm by almost shooting down the towing aircraft, much to Anderson's embarrassment.[18]

As regards the Swansea balloon barrage, in September 1940 the oil refinery in Llandarcy had been attacked by enemy aircraft and had suffered significant damage, and this concentrated the attention of the military authorities in Swansea once again on the strength of its defences. Therefore, in April 1941, when a further four balloons were made available for deployment in Swansea, it was suggested locally that the Llandarcy site would benefit from strengthening in the shape of more balloons. This was questioned higher up the chain of command, since its understanding of the situation was that the importance of the Llandarcy site had actually been lessened as a result of the raid, given that a number of oil storage tanks had been burned out. It suggested that the matter be looked at afresh, with consideration being given to using the additional balloons for the defence of the docks rather than Llandarcy. This was deemed impracticable by the local command, which pointed out that the solid mass of Kilvey Hill and building congestion on the east side of the town limited the potential sites for new balloons, and that those sites might be unsuitable for the easy movement of the hydrogen needed to inflate the balloons. Llandarcy duly received the balloons.[19]

If increasing the number of balloons and anti-aircraft guns around Swansea could only help in its defence, some of the work undertaken on bomb disposal around the town during 1940 proved to be abortive or unnecessary. Nervous local officials or members of the public frequently reported suspicious holes that they had found following air raids, fearing that they might contain unexploded bombs. On one occasion the hole proved to be the entrance to a rabbit burrow, while on another it was simply a hole dug in preparation for the erection of a fence post.[20]

Between the Blitz raid of 1–2 September 1940 and a raid that took place on 5 January 1941, a further nine minor attacks took place, though casualties were surprisingly light with no deaths and only 25 wounded, a light toll but one that nevertheless had painful consequences for those directly affected. That period of relative tranquillity came to an abrupt end when Swansea suffered its second Blitz-type attack and sustained its heaviest casualties to date. The raid took place on the night of 17–18 January 1941 and, based on a post-war examination of captured German records, it was shown that 88 enemy aircraft had raided Swansea, dropping 178 high-explosive bombs and a large number of incendiary devices. While the raid was in progress a sudden and heavy fall of snow covered the town, adding to the difficulties of the emergency services in tackling the situation and recovering the dead and helping the injured. The dead numbered 55 while the seriously injured amounted to 38. A further 59 suffered light injuries.[21]

During the raid, the headquarters of the 79th Anti-Aircraft Regiment was still located in the property named Ashleigh in Ffynone and, while that would have been unknown to the enemy, it nevertheless had more than its fair share of unwelcome excitement. A shower of incendiary bombs landed within 50 yards of the property, though the devices were quickly extinguished by the regimental headquarters team. That matter having been dealt with, a large high-explosive bomb detonated about 100 yards from Ashleigh, breaking a window and no doubt causing a few nerves to flutter. The regiment believed that at least two attacking aircraft had been damaged by its gunfire and large sections of an enemy aircraft's engine cowling – torn and perforated by explosions – did fall in the garden of the property.[22]

The local press reported that, following the attack of 17–18 January 1941 which it described as a 'murder raid', the Auxiliary Fire Service had dealt with ten serious fires and a further 120 smaller ones. Most of the bombs had hit what it termed 'working-class' streets where deaths had occurred, though damage had also been caused to other residential areas. The Oxford Street Methodist Church had been destroyed by fire, a fate that had also befallen the Eddershaws furniture store. Other businesses, the names of some of which will still be familiar to Swansea people today, suffered varying degrees of damage, and included the Rialto Cinema, J T Morgan's, Mundays wine merchants, Currys (wireless and bicycle dealers), British Home Stores and Hancock's Brewery. Also damaged were three warehouses in the docks area, each of which were burnt-out, while electrical and hydraulic equipment, railway sidings and wagons were also damaged or destroyed.

The whole of the regular police force together with the First Police Reserve, the Police War Reserve and the Special Constabulary had been turned out during the raid, and the majority of them were continuously on duty for over 12 hours, with some men even working for 24 hours.[23] Even the Chief Fire Officer, F J May, played an active role in hosing down the flames at one incident.[24] It was indeed a case of 'all hands to the pump'. It was noted that the filled sandbags which had been placed around lamp posts and in doorways throughout the town provided civilians, as planned, with a ready means of quickly extinguishing incendiary devices.[25] Some 38 fire appliances and crews were sent to assist Swansea under reciprocal support arrangements from the nearby districts of Port Talbot, Pontardawe, Llanelli, Neath and Ystradgynlais, while the Newport, Milford Haven and Cardiff districts also sent equipment and personnel. In all, 180 additional personnel were made available for work in Swansea, being a welcome addition to the 414 local men that the town itself was able to muster on the night. Four members of the Swansea police contingent were injured, as well as 19 men from the fire service. Happily, the injuries were of a minor nature, with only three of the fire service men needing brief treatment at the Swansea General and Eye Hospital.[26]

There were numerous incidents during the raid, some of which included undoubted acts of bravery, even if the outcomes were not always successful. Ten incidents had required the attendance of the specialised rescue squads (identifiable by their white helmets adorned with a red 'R'), and they managed to extract six trapped people from the rubble of the damaged buildings, though one of those recovered subsequently died from their injuries. The Goat Street Arcade was saved by the prompt actions of two fire-watchers who, seeing that a confectioner's shop was ablaze within the arcade, fought and extinguished the fire by using a hose pipe and a stirrup pump. An incendiary bomb penetrated the ceiling of one of the town's cinemas, starting a blaze within the premises where some members of the audience had simply decided to take a chance and stoically sit out the raid after ignoring the siren. They were able to help put out the fire.[27]

Among those killed was the wife of Alderman Percy Morris, one of Swansea's most prominent councillors who also served as the deputy Regional Commissioner for Civil Defence (Wales) between 1941 and 1945. Morris was away on business when the raid took place and his wife, Elizabeth, had gone to stay with her husband's relatives in Robert Street, and it was there that a bomb struck the property, fatally injuring her and killing her husband's sister and brother-in-law.[28]

A house on Windmill Terrace in the St Thomas part of the town was demolished by an explosion before parts of the ruins were consumed by fire, leading to the deaths of four members of the Nicholls family. The body of 21-year-old Iris Nicholls was recovered from the rubble, still wearing the engagement ring she had been given by the man she loved and planned to marry. Four domestic properties on St Leger Crescent were also gutted by fire. Some of the casualties were dealt with at the St Thomas fixed first aid post in Welwyn Lodge on Balaclava Street, and a 1940 image shows that the post had a team of two male doctors, two state registered nurses and ten nursing auxiliaries. The fixed first aid post (one of a number set up in the town) only dealt with war casualties – typically the walking wounded – with more serious cases being transferred to a hospital as soon as practicable.

One family of five had taken shelter under the staircase of their home and subsequently found themselves trapped when a bomb badly damaged the property. Their cries for help produced no immediate response and, during a lull, the family heard the voice of a rescue worker saying that anyone inside the house must be dead and there was no point searching the property. Their immediate cries were heard, and after three hours of determined digging by a Mr Kevin Wellington, with bombs and incendiaries still falling, they were freed. While trapped, the young daughter of the family had asked her mother, 'Mam, am I dead?' The brave actions of the rescue party happily answered her question.[29]

Claude Boyd had been visiting Cwm Road in Bonymaen when a number of incendiary bombs fell on the street. After tackling those, he was seen to enter a house just before a high-explosive bomb demolished it. He did not survive. A particularly tragic fate struck the Bird family. They had moved to Bonymaen from their home in Waun Wen following an earlier raid, so as to stay with relatives, in a precautionary move to a supposedly safer area that was sadly to be their undoing. During the January raid, a bomb hit their temporary home at 159 Cefn Road resulting in the deaths of Wilfred and

Gwendoline together with their children Wilfred (junior) who was six, and his sister Mary Ann, two. Also killed were the relatives who had kindly taken them in – five members of the Thomas family. It was reported that a bomb had struck the house and an adjacent property, leaving a crater some 30 feet deep.[30]

At 10pm on 17 January, Police Constable Francis Dart was on duty in the Port Tennant area of the town when a bomb devastated two small houses and a chemist's shop, trapping 77-year-old Martha Shaddick in the ruins of 92 Port Tennant Road. Dart, stripped down to his trousers and shirt, forced his way into a narrow gap in the rubble and debris. A saw was passed to him and he attempted to cut through some woodwork that was hampering his rescue attempt, though to no avail as, sadly, the woman died of her injuries before he could complete the rescue. He rapidly transferred his attention to the bombed-out chemist's shop where he discovered that Gwyn Jones and his wife Annie were trapped. Once again he tackled the situation with vigour, with the assistance of Police War Reserve Constable Ivor Duffy and several air raid wardens. Dart used an axe to smash his way to where the couple lay and succeeded in bringing them to safety. Gwyn Jones later said of Constable Dart, '[He] gave us confidence and kept up our spirits. His act in extricating us was not only a physical achievement, but his cheerfulness under terrific bombing and anti-aircraft fire was a moral inspiration and I cannot speak too highly of his bravery throughout the whole rescue.' Police Constable Dart was subsequently awarded the British Empire Medal (Civil Division) for his bravery.[31]

Another Police War Reserve Constable, Haydn Powell, tackled one incendiary bomb with a sandbag and, while he was extinguishing the device, his uniform caught fire. The flames were quickly brushed down by a soldier, and with his uniform no longer ablaze Powell then put out a fire in a nearby house before attending at another property where he dislodged an incendiary bomb from the rafters with the help of a garden rake. That job completed, he was persuaded to pause while he received medical attention for his burns. ARP wardens William Morgan Ayres and John Pillar managed to rescue several people who were trapped in a bomb-damaged house and they both later received the British Empire Medal for their efforts.[32]

A rest centre, one of dozens in the town, had been established by the council in a chapel at Mount Pleasant, with the aim being that it could receive people who had been rendered homeless in the aftermath of an attack. A number of families who had been bombed out in Shelley Crescent and Byron Crescent during the raid arrived there in need of temporary assistance. Though the council provided food, clothing and other necessities, the centre was actually run by members of the Women's Voluntary Service (WVS). One who worked there, a Miss Walters, remembered (in an oral recording made in 1979) that the driving forces behind the organisation of the WVS effort at the chapel were two women from the Jewish community in Swansea, Mrs Foner and Mrs Hyman. As already mentioned, it was Mrs Foner and her husband Morris who had taken into their care the young Heinz Lichtwitz (later Anglicised to Henry Foner) after he had arrived in Swansea on a Kindertransport rescue mission from Berlin in 1939.[33]

This searing raid of 17–18 January 1941 undoubtedly left a mark on both the fabric of the town and the morale of its population. It was, however, merely a prelude to a far greater trial that would almost overwhelm the town in a little more than a month's time.

CHAPTER 7

Catastrophe:
The Three Nights' Blitz

SWANSEA UNDERWENT ITS greatest trial of the war during the period 19–21 February 1941, when German air raids on three consecutive nights resulted in heavy casualties with severe damage inflicted on the town centre and several residential areas. High-explosive bombs of varying weights (some of which were fitted with delayed-action fuses) of both the blast and fragmentation types, as well as thousands of incendiary devices, were dropped on the town each night. Given their severity, these three raids were each regarded as 'Blitz attacks' by the Swansea authorities. Given the variety and numbers of bombs dropped on the town during the raids, it can best be shown in tabular form (below). The prefix 'SC' indicated that a bomb was of the *Spreng Cylindrisch* type, a high-explosive bomb that was contained within a thin casing so as to allow for maximum blast effect. The number following an SC designation was the weight of the bomb in kilograms, so that an SC 1000 was a bomb with a weight of 1,000kg. In one respect Swansea was 'lucky' in that the enemy did not deploy bombs of up to 2,500kg that were available within his armoury.

Bombs of the 'SD' (*Spreng Dickenwand*) class consisted of a thick walled casing that produced a lot of fragmentation on detonation. The suffix 'LZZ' meant that the bomb was of a delayed-action type, designed to explode many hours after hitting the ground and thus posing an ongoing threat to bomb disposal teams and passers-by. Bombs of the B1 E1 type were incendiary devices weighing 1kg that ignited on contact. Those with the suffix 'ZA' contained a small explosive charge that detonated while the device was aflame, sending burning material over a radius of about 50 feet.[1]

Bomb Type (High-explosive unless otherwise indicated)	Number dropped: 19–20 Feb 1941	Number dropped: 20–21 Feb 1941	Number dropped: 21–22 Feb 1941
SC 1000kg	4	2	0
SC 500kg	10	26	19
SC 250kg	80	93	79
SC 250 LZZ kg	14	30	9
SC 50kg	334	183	322
SD 50kg	0	70	0
B1 E1 incendiary	14,184	17,832	17,671
B1 E1 ZA incendiary	1,536	2,112	2,765
Number of high-explosive bombs/ tonnage dropped	442/49.2	404/58.4	429/47.6
Enemy aircraft over Swansea	61	64	59
Enemy aircraft destroyed – crashed after leaving Swansea	0	2	2

German records state that a total of 1,275 high-explosive bombs were dropped on Swansea during the raids. Local Swansea records report a total of 896 high-explosive bombs being dropped over the three nights. It is possible that, in the frenzy of an attack, some bombs were quickly jettisoned outside of the Swansea target area or into the sea.[2]

It would have astonished and probably incensed those in Swansea who lived through the three nights of attacks to be told that the raids had not been 'major attacks'. This was because the authorities defined a 'major attack' as being one in which over 100 tons of high-explosive bombs were dropped, and that was not the case for any of the February attacks on Swansea. In the first quarter of 1941, a number of raids did take place on towns or cities where over 100 tons of high-explosives were dropped, including Portsmouth (193 tons), Liverpool-Birkenhead (303 tons), Hull (316 tons), and London (467 tons).[3]

Swansea's three-night ordeal began on the evening of 19 February 1941, when a preliminary warning of a possible air raid was issued at 7.23pm before, just 14 minutes later, the alert status was elevated to that of a raid being imminent. The first enemy aircraft approached the town from the north-east at an altitude of between 8,000 and 17,000 feet, while later attacks arrived from the south-east. Anti-aircraft gun batteries had been established in Morriston, Jersey Marine, Mumbles, Sketty, Ravenhill (the guns not yet emplaced at the time of the raids) and Neath. Each battery had four 3.7-inch guns (though Mumbles had only two at first), capable of firing a 13kg (28lbs) shell to a height of between 23,000 and 45,000 feet, depending on the fuse chosen and other settings. Even the four guns that were sited at Pembrey attempted to engage the enemy at long range in a desperate attempt to at least disrupt, if not destroy, the enemy aircraft attacking Swansea. The guns fired 857 rounds of high-explosive shells during the raid, while other guns that were placed at 'vulnerable points' (such as the oil refinery in Llandarcy) added a further 109 high-explosive shells, as well as 13 rounds of shrapnel, to the maelstrom.[4]

German records state that on the night of 19–20 February, 61 Luftwaffe aircraft attacked the town and began dropping parachute flares in an attempt to illuminate the target areas. That was quickly followed by a shower of incendiary bombs which proceeded the dropping of high-explosive bombs onto the town by enemy aircraft. Fires soon began blazing at numerous locations, providing useful aiming points for the following waves of attackers. In the opinion of F J May, Chief Constable and Chief Fire Officer of the Swansea Fire Brigade, the incendiary devices, though apparently of a similar design and size to those seen on earlier attacks, nevertheless seemed 'of a much higher standard, and combustion was rapid and violent'. May noted that the areas of the town affected by the raids of 19 and 20 February were mainly located outside of the town centre and included Manselton, Cwmbwrla and Mount Pleasant.[5]

A bomb exploded near to Corrymore Mansions on Sketty Road, blowing out the windows and demolishing a house on the other side of the road. The explosion killed three men who were working as members of an ARP rescue squad. Nestor Morgan (of Kilvey Terrace), George Thorne (Llangyfelach Road) and Exel Jones (Station Road, Landore) had all left their home streets to assist those in need elsewhere in the town, with tragic consequences. The local press, while not revealing information that would assist the enemy, was able to report that a Methodist chapel, two hotels, a chemist's shop and a public house were all damaged by explosions, some to the point of total demolition, with rescue squads assisting in the recovery of several people from the resulting ruins. Also damaged was a cinema, still running the film for the benefit of those patrons who had decided to sit out the air raid, presumably with their fingers tightly crossed. Incendiary bombs had crashed through its roof and landed in a backstage area, disrupting the operation of the projection equipment and bringing the film to a sudden halt, while producing a shower of sparks that was visible to the startled audience. The cinema manager appeared and attempted to head off any panic by announcing that it was only an incendiary device, implying that it could soon be made safe. His words were followed by a loud bang and he swiftly added 'of an explosive type!' to his comment.[6] One family had a lucky escape when a bomb struck its Anderson shelter in the garden, though, happily, they had chosen to take refuge under the stairs of the house.

As the thousands of incendiary bombs fell to earth, their arrival on the ground was usually met by a scramble of local people (often including children) who rapidly threw sand over the flaming devices. Fires were extinguished before they had a chance to develop and it was noted that many of the streets and open spaces of the town were soon dotted with small piles of sand, each one marking the final resting place of an enemy device.[7]

During the raids of 19 and 20 February it proved necessary to relay water for the fire-fighting appliances from ponds in Cwmbwrla to the Manselton area (a distance of around a mile), while a 5,000-gallon supply stored in a tank was passed via hose pipes from the community centre in Townhill over a distance of about half a mile to St Teilo's Crescent in Mayhill. This latter supply was further augmented by water that was relayed from the ponds, some 300 yards away, at the Tawe Lodge Infirmary in Mount Pleasant. At around 8.44pm on 19 February, the trunk water main was ruptured at Plasmarl, meaning that the water hydrants in the central part of the town remained dry for several days until repairs were effected. It also resulted in a temporarily restricted water supply in the St Thomas, Morriston and Landore areas.[8]

If the civilian authorities were struggling to cope with the rapidly deteriorating situation, the military were experiencing problems of their own. As noted, the gun operation room of the 79th Anti-Aircraft Regiment was situated in the property named Ashleigh in Ffynone, and it had already experienced a couple of 'near-misses' during previous enemy attacks. Sadly, on the night of 19 February, its luck finally ran out. The gun operation room suffered a direct hit by a high-explosive bomb at 8.13pm, and the adjutant of the 79th Anti-Aircraft Regiment was killed, as was the gun control officer and two signallers. All communication from the wrecked gun operation room to its subordinate anti-aircraft guns was cut until a telephone line to the Cardiff control room was patched up – though, even this proved problematic, as bomb damage elsewhere subsequently cut the GPO (General Post Office) cables between Cardiff and Swansea. Frantic repairs to the telephone cables were carried out to help retrieve the situation.[9]

During a flurry of activity in response to the attack of 19 February, the Auxiliary Fire Service in Swansea began recording requests it was receiving for attendance by the central control room at the Guildhall or by other official or even unofficial means. Though not a comprehensive list of incidents in Swansea during that period, it does convey the urgency and extent of the growing crisis. The first report reached the Auxiliary Fire Service at 8.05pm on 19 February 1941, and concerned an incendiary bomb that had hit a house in Rhondda Street. A light trailer fire pump was sent to the location, though the fire, which slightly damaged the first landing of the house, was actually extinguished by the simple use of sand. Within minutes further reports had come in regarding incendiary devices at Tawe Lodge (the former workhouse), Oliver Watkins' yard, the Blind Institution and a domestic property on Manor Road, Manselton. Within an hour of the first report, no less than 42 further reports had been recorded involving additional domestic properties, public halls, garages, cinemas, the Cwmfelin Tinplate Works and the George Hotel on Henrietta Street, among others. By the end of the first night's attacks the tally of incidents stood at 71, with the last incident – a house being demolished by a high-explosive bomb – being logged at 3.15am on 20 February. The range of damage sustained by particular properties varied, but the contemporary records include descriptions such as 'house completely demolished'; 'building partly destroyed'; 'building gutted' and 'complete destruction'.[10]

Swansea was again the target for German bombers over the night of 20–21 February 1941, and on that occasion 64 enemy aircraft arrived. The attacking force approached shortly after 7.30pm from the south, north, south-east and north-west and at heights of between 10,000 and 20,000 feet. The first wave to reach the town from the south released flares and incendiaries before breaking off to the north. The second wave also came in from the south, dropping high-explosive bombs before the first wave returned from the north to do likewise. Subsequent attacks arrived from the south to simply drop more flares before returning from the north to drop high-explosive bombs. The final raiders approached from the south-east before returning to drive home their attack from the north-west. While the town's population and its defenders were being hard-pressed on land, enemy aircraft were also observed conducting mine-laying operations in Swansea Bay, travelling from west to east at a height of only 1,000 to 2,000 feet. The results of that enterprise would threaten shipping as it entered or left the port in the days and weeks ahead.

Particularly badly hit was Teilo Crescent in the Mayhill area of the town. It appears that on the night of 20 February, initial bomb damage and fires were in the process of being furiously tackled by civil defence personnel and civilians when further bombs hit the area with devastating effect. No less than 38 people were killed in what was Swansea's worst single incident of the war. Among those killed was Charlie Rees of Eigen Crescent, a butcher's van driver with a wife and daughter. As an air raid precautions warden he attended at Teilo Crescent to assist with the fire-fighting on the night of 20 February. With the situation seemingly coming under control, Charlie told an ARP comrade, George Ham, to escort a female friend to the relative safety of his home shelter. George and his companion set off shortly before another explosion in the area of Teilo Crescent was heard, causing George to hurriedly retrace his steps. He arrived to witness a scene of devastation, with numerous casualties being visible, though of Charlie there was no sign. Indeed, Charlie's body was never found and it seems that he must have been very close to the epicentre of the explosion, with catastrophic consequences. The fact that Charlie's body could not be found or positively identified meant that he was not listed as a civilian casualty by council officials (his body never having reached a mortuary), though his name did find commemoration in the records of the Commonwealth War Graves Commission.[11]

The Williams family of 27 Teilo Crescent were all killed during the attack. William Morgan Williams was a 57-year-old master mason who had seen active service during the Great War with the Royal Garrison Artillery. It appears that he was killed on the night of 20 February along with his wife, Emma Catherine, and their daughter Betty who was 20 years old. Their bodies were recovered from the ruins of their home in the days following the attack.[12] Barbara Griffiths lived at 31 Teilo Crescent, a short distance from the Williams family home. On 20 February, Barbara came home from school and later that evening entered the family air raid shelter as the warning sirens sounded yet again. Her father, James, a 58-year-old railway wagon examiner, soon left the shelter – despite the protests of his family – being anxious to assist others in dealing with the incendiary bombs. During a lull in the bombing, a soldier appeared and led the family away from the shelter to a place that was deemed to be less dangerous. Along with numerous other properties on Teilo Crescent, the Griffiths' home suffered a direct hit and fires blazed at several locations on Teilo Crescent, while the family pedal organ was blown into the street and lay amid a pile of rubble. As Barbara remembered, 'Teilo Crescent was like a battlefield. There were bodies everywhere – in hedges and gutters. I'd never seen anything like it. There didn't seem to be many people moving in the street as we made our way along. There was no shouting, no screaming. It was weird...' As dawn broke, Mrs Griffiths went in search of her missing husband, but it was a search that would end in sorrow; the rescue and recovery services had found and removed James's body to the St Faith's mortuary at 3.30am on the morning of 21 February.[13]

As the raid had developed, the anti-aircraft guns around Swansea were in almost continuous action for approximately four hours, with target plots being provided from Cardiff given that the bombed-out gun operation room in Ffynone was still non-operational. As enemy flares intended to illuminate the target area descended, they were fired at with shrapnel shells with limited success, extinguishing some before they could land. Beyond that preventive measure, 932 shells of the 3.7-inch variety were hurled at the enemy aircraft, along with almost 200 of a three-inch calibre. Nine rounds of shrapnel added to the desperate efforts of the defenders to protect the town. Although searchlights were busily scanning the skies during the raid, it only proved possible to illuminate two aircraft, though even then it was impossible to judge whether they were friend or foe.[14]

Following the second raid the people of Swansea and its civil defence units struggled to cope with and understand the scale of what had befallen their town over the two preceding nights, while German attention was firmly focused on delivering one final and heavy blow that would hopefully shatter morale and seriously hamper wartime production in Swansea. So it was that, at 7.30pm on the night of 21–22 February, the air raid warning was sounded once again, for the third night in succession, to the horror of an already exhausted population. German reports indicate that on the night of 21–22 February, 59 aircraft attacked Swansea.

The anti-aircraft gun teams again worked tirelessly in attempting to disrupt the incoming aircraft, while the searchlight batteries scoured the sky – though largely without success – in trying to pick out the enemy machines. The guns fired 851 high-explosive shells at the enemy aircraft as well as 15 rounds of shrapnel. Within the cacophony of sound produced by the explosion of bombs, the rumble of falling masonry and the tinkling of breaking glass, the roar of the anti-aircraft guns at least gave the people of Swansea, mostly huddled in their garden shelters or under the stairs of their homes, the consoling thought that at least the enemy was not having it all its own way.

That idea was shattered when, between 8.20pm and 8.56pm, the guns fell silent. Though it was not obvious at the time to the population of the town, the reason for this unexpected and most unwelcome occurrence was the fact that friendly fighters (16 Hurricanes) had been sent from the RAF base at Pembrey (RAF Fairwood not yet being operational) to try and intercept the attackers. It was the headquarters of the 10th Fighter Group that had therefore ordered the guns to cease firing in case they should hit incoming friendly aircraft. With the guns inactive and the Hurricanes failing to locate and engage any attacking aircraft the enemy was, for a short period, free to bomb the centre of Swansea without distraction and with devastating success.[15]

The third consecutive night of attack proved to be the most destructive in terms of physical damage to the town. The raids of 19 and 20 February had already caused numerous deaths and serious damage and the early efforts at recovery and repairs to vital infrastructure were hampered by a number of unexploded bombs that lay within the town centre and its suburbs. Chief Fire Officer May felt that the raid on the third night was the most concentrated attack of all, and once again the German aerial onslaught had included a blizzard of incendiary bombs, many of which fell on the already damaged town centre. This caused immediate problems, since the presence of unexploded bombs in the central area of the town, from the earlier attack had led to its virtual evacuation prior to the hard-pressed bomb disposal teams being sent in. This had unavoidably left the town centre short of fire-watchers and other personnel who would have normally been on hand to report and tackle blazes as they arose and before they could gain a solid foothold. In the absence of such vital first responders, many fires soon began to burn out of control with devastating effects.

Strenuous efforts were made by May (who was out on the streets himself) and his ash-covered colleagues to try and regain control of the situation. Damage to the water supply meant that it had proved necessary to join together fire hoses and run them for lengthy distances from currently undamaged water sources to the scene of the fires. Given the obvious and daunting scale of the conflagration that was engulfing the town, a nearby source of much-needed water lay in the dark depths of the North and South Docks. As May later reported, on the night of 21 February:

> A relay from the North Dock was made to the 5,000-gallon steel dams on the Central Hotel site, High Street, and the Great Western Railway, High Street Station site, and from there further relays were put into operation to the vicinity of (1) the Central Police and Fire Station, (2) De-la-beche Street, (3) Page Street, (4) Welcome Lane, (5) High Street, (6) Orchard Street, (7) Dynevor Place, (8) Rutland Street, and (9) Castle Street.

The central part of the town had been used for water relay training exercises in the recent past, and May thought that the experience previously gained had helped during the present emergency, even if new and painful lessons had been learned as well. Though the water relay system was vital, it was nevertheless prone to leaks – usually from where one hose joined another – while the hoses themselves were often damaged by shrapnel or by being draped over rough debris. Even the rapid movement (where possible in the debris-strewn streets) of emergency reaction vehicles often damaged any hoses that they might unavoidably run over.

In addition to the North Dock, water was also relayed from the South Dock to Wassail Square, Oxford Street, and adjacent areas. The St Helen's Road area was served by a well that was situated in the premises of the William Hancock's brewery on Western Street, while even the water in the Swansea Baths was made use of for fire-fighting purposes. It was a monumental effort, even if it sadly failed to save much of the town centre from destruction. The North Dock alone covered an area of around ten acres and water taken from it for emergency fire-fighting saw its level drop by an astonishing seven feet. May estimated that the North Dock had provided around 16 million gallons of water, most of which had been rapidly deposited onto the blazing streets of Swansea with regrettably little effect. Additionally, on the night of 21 February, water containers with a total capacity of 20,000 gallons had been brought into the town from south and west Wales, Bristol and Birmingham. Though no doubt a much appreciated gesture, it does seem that 20,000 gallons of water was a mere pinprick in the full context of Swansea's gruelling and fiery ordeal.[16]

Swansea's civil defence teams had responded to the three consecutive nights of crisis with commendable vigour, desperately attempting to help and recover the wounded or trapped. George Long was able to fire-watch over a part of the town despite some fire-watchers being unable to use their normal posts due to earlier damage or danger from unexploded bombs. On the night in question, he occasionally heard:

> ... the sound of women's and children's voices... as wardens directed them from shelters which were threatened by the flames. I saw one such party being brought from a back street in the region of the parish church. It was like daylight in the glare of the flames as they were hurried through debris to another shelter. Less than half an hour later, they were hurried out of this basement to another spot as the building above them had caught fire... The fire thus spread and increased with immense speed, and the heat became intense. It was impossible to approach some streets which had both sides ablaze. When a store directly opposite my post was a great

flame of fire, it was obvious that fire-watching had passed beyond the practical stage.[17]

Chief Fire Officer May, in reviewing the events of the three nights, stated that on the night of 19 February, in addition to his small force of dedicated firemen, he was able to deploy 183 full-time and 175 part-time Auxiliary Fire Service fire-fighters to deal with the blazes that affected various suburbs of the town. Probably due to the strain of the task, the numbers decreased slightly on the following two nights, with 160 full-time and 121 part-time men attending the raid on 21 February. He also made use of the reciprocal aid scheme that existed between neighbouring local authorities and, indeed, of authorities from far further afield, and on the night of 19–20 February assistance had been forthcoming from Port Talbot, Neath, Llanelli, and Pontardawe. This had produced four large trailer pumps and their crews, while the Newport district had provided ten crewed trailers and Cardiff twenty, with even Milford Haven and Carmarthen dispatching a trailer pump each to assist their stricken neighbour.

The external support effort had grown in size over the following nights. On the night of 20–21 February, there were 35 'foreign' trailer pumps and crews in Swansea, while on the night of 21–22 February no less than 71 such appliances and crews were present in support as the town faced its greatest challenge. In addition to all of that, firemen who had no fire-fighting appliance to work with were nevertheless sent to Swansea from other districts to simply provide extra pairs of hands to tackle the numerous tasks required to help try to restore the situation in the town. Bristol sent 77 such men, while Birmingham (35), Bath (26) and Wolverhampton (25) all provided much welcome manpower for whatever work was required. A further 40 men came from Kidderminster, Smethwick and several other locations. A woman who served in the wartime fire services in Swansea recalled that 'the old school' (presumably the grammar school at Mount Pleasant) had large rooms which could accommodate around 60 visiting fire-fighters on simple beds and mattresses in rooms which had, so far, escaped any serious bomb damage. No doubt other men were billeted wherever space could be found.[18]

Numerous examples of unstinting heroism during the three-night ordeal were later reported and often recognised by an award for civil gallantry. The actions of auxiliary fireman Samuel Williams compelled F J May, the head of the Swansea Fire Brigade, to bring them to the attention of no less a personage than that of the Minister of Home Security, Herbert Morrison. Williams had been fire-fighting at Teilo Crescent in the Mayhill area of the town. Houses on this street were already ablaze and a number of residents and civil defence members were attempting to quell the flames when several more bombs exploded in the area, killing over 30 and injuring numerous other people. Samuel Williams and his section officer, George Hughes, a schoolmaster from Cockett Road, surveyed the damage to prioritise the response required before entering a house that seemed on the brink of collapse. They struggled to reach a male casualty inside the dwelling and, despite the pressing danger, they succeeded in bringing that man to safety though, regrettably, he died during the rescue. An official at the Ministry of Home Security subsequently told Samuel Williams that he would be awarded the King's Commendation for his bravery.[19]

There were similar heart-breaking attempts at rescue that also sadly failed. William Thomas and Albert Hinder attempted to rescue a male and female from a damaged house in Elfed Road. They entered the property with Walter Davies, a fire brigade officer. Davies later told the *South Wales Evening Post*:

> I located the part of the wreckage from where cries were coming. The top part of the building had collapsed. We

removed some of the wreckage and had to crawl in one by one.
We had to pass back the masonry and debris... We had to keep
propping the overhead pieces of debris with pieces of timber,
to stop it collapsing on ourselves...

It soon became apparent that a man and woman were
trapped, and while the man was shouting the woman remained
silent. Fire officer Davies could see the man's hand through a
gap in the rubble and later recalled:

Just as we were getting into closer touch with them, an
explosion took place, quite near to us, and brought down more
debris, and the man's hand could not be seen. On calling him,
he was begging us to be quick as he could not hold out much
longer. He was calling to the woman but receiving no reply.
We continued to clear the debris, and eventually we got his
head uncovered and his shoulders, and also the head of the
woman.

Tragedy then intervened. It was apparent that the female
casualty was already dead and, as efforts to free the man
continued, the smell of escaping gas became apparent. The
gas supply to the house had been damaged and matters were
soon made worse when hot coals that had been scattered from
a fireplace following the explosions started a fire. Efforts were
frantically made to put that fire out but the gas meter then
burst into flames bringing with it the risk of explosion and
forcing the hurried retreat of the rescue party. There was no
alternative other than to leave the man to his fate and the
entire house was soon engulfed in flames.[20]

Detective Constable Victor Rees and Constable Percy Cork
attended at a damaged property in Plymouth Street and found
that two men were trapped inside. The ceiling had collapsed
and the clearance between that and the floor of the building
was only about two feet high, though, after crawling in, a
man, Thomas Copp, a sprightly 76 year old, was soon located.

With Constable Frederick Morgan supporting the dropped ceiling with his back, a chain of men removed rubble from the vicinity of the trapped man who kept up a spirited conversation throughout the rescue attempt. He was duly freed and initially taken to an air raid shelter as bombs were still occasionally falling. The body of another man was also discovered at the property.[21]

Mrs Marion Roberts of Sketty Road was an air raid warden who did not hesitate to assist when efforts were made to free a man who was trapped in the rubble of his bomb-damaged home. As Sergeant Frederick Price and Constable Sidney Baker attempted to reach the man, she helped remove the debris and shone a torch to light up the scene, a useful aid in the darkness as it was feared that using a Hurricane lamp might ignite escaping gas. Even when further men arrived to help in the rescue, Mrs Roberts refused to leave her position, insisting that she fully intended to 'do her bit'. Sadly, the victim died before the rescue could be completed.[22]

Even when not attempting to rescue trapped members of the public, the police were running risks as they went about their work. During the attack of 21–22 February, Police Sergeant William Bolton Flitter was near the police station in Orchard Street when a high-explosive bomb exploded nearby with fatal consequences. In the same incident, Constable Stephen Jones sustained severe injuries which led to his leg being amputated.[23]

Joseph Martin Burke and William Arthur Miles were both aged 16 and working in the air raid precautions messenger service. They had taken refuge in the Ragged School air raid shelter but later emerged to see what they could do to help the civil defence services. Both were killed by explosions in the High Street area on 21 February, with their bodies being discovered several days later in the rubble of the burnt-out Picture House.[24]

Peter Williams had moved from Newport to Swansea in

1940 at the age of 15 and, as a member of the Boy Scout movement, began working as a messenger for the air raid precaution service. Working from the Central Hall on Orchard Street, he took messages to local doctors, probably checking on their availability during a crisis situation. Travelling by bicycle or on foot in the blacked-out streets, care had to be taken due to the amount of debris that frequently littered the roads. On the second night of the three nights of attacks, he was released from duty as the bombing intensified and tried to make his way home along the blazing streets. Compelled to enter a surface air raid shelter, he found it tightly packed with a mass of humanity and edged his way along its length without finding a place where he could rest. He simply exited from the other end of the shelter before finding refuge in the basement of the Ragged School. As the bombing gradually reduced in intensity, he ventured out and was surprised to find a No. 23 bus, complete with driver, parked outside the school. When the driver decided shortly after midnight that it was safe enough to take a chance and commence a journey with his bus, the young Williams made sure he was on it. He arrived home safely.[25]

The Wesleyan chapel on Goat Street (close to modern-day Princess Way) had adapted its basement for use as an air raid shelter that could accommodate 195 people. Constructed of concrete and timber, it had also received additional strengthening and had two emergency escape exits, but no protection against gas.[26] During the Three Nights' Blitz attacks, the chapel was burnt-out and rumours later abounded in the town that hundreds had perished in its shelter, with the site later flattened so as to act as a mass grave. In fact, a sharp-eyed member of the civil defence services had spotted the growing danger and led those sheltering there to safety before disaster struck. That sort of alarmist rumour was not uncommon at that time. Eileen Chilcott remembered that during that period she might be told that somewhere in the town had been hit by a large bomb and perhaps 90 people had been killed, only to find out that, in fact, the death toll from the incident, tragic as it was, amounted to only two or three people. Indeed, the *South Wales Evening Post* of 28 February 1941 referred to rumours of 'imaginary holocausts' in the town, where many people were supposedly trapped in ruined air raid shelters after the three nights of raids. Miss Chilcott later recalled that the intensity of living at that time of great danger led to some people displaying signs of almost 'hysterical gaiety' during a crisis, being keen to show that, despite all the risks, they were determined to conquer their fears.[27]

As well as the Wesleyan chapel, another chapel on Pell Street (near Dynevor School) was also burnt-out during the February 1941 attacks, with only its walls left starkly standing, even though above its main door a sign still proclaimed:

> The Lord is our refuge and strength,
> A very present help in trouble,
> Therefore will we not fear,
> Though the Earth do change.
> Psalm XLVI, 2:3.[28]

And in the Swansea of February 1941, the Earth was indeed changing as the enemy did its worst. At De La Beche School it was noted in the school journal:

> Feb 20th. After a very heavy night raid, it is necessary to close the school; a bomb has fallen in the playground and burst a water main; there is a deep crater + much debris in the playground, and no heating, as the boiler-room is flooded. There are broken windows in the Dining Room + Annexes, and a damaged door in the Physics Laboratory. Incendiary bomb on flat roof.

The journal records that, as a result of the next raid on 21 February, most of the school was destroyed by fires caused by incendiary bombs, resulting in the loss of all the equipment used by the music, art, science and geography departments. Arrangements were soon put in place for some tuition to be provided for De La Beche pupils at the Llwyn y Bryn school.[29]

The men of the 103 Bomb Disposal Section received numerous reports of unexploded bombs during the attacks, two of which needed urgent attention: one at Castle Street, the presence of which meant that traffic could not safely use that key road for travel to and from the docks, and the other close to the prison where it threatened trains on the nearby high-level railway line. Lance Sergeant Thomas Henderson led a team of men to the Castle Street site, while another group made its way towards the prison. Digging down to the bomb at Castle Street was a lengthy process, but on 21 February it was finally revealed. Sapper J A Lacey noted that it was in the range of 1,000kg and was fitted with a delayed-action fuse that was controlled by a clock device. There was also an anti-handling mechanism designed to prevent the fuse being tampered with. Normally, bombs of that type would be left alone for 96 hours, assuming they had landed in a location where it was safe to do so. Clearly, the Castle Street and prison site bombs needed speedy attention so that, once disarmed, normal road and rail traffic could resume and any delay to the movement of materials for the war effort minimised. Consequently, team members soon began working on the bombs despite the risk involved.

Since any rough handling of the Castle Street bomb might trigger the anti-handling device with deadly consequences, it was decided to remove the explosive material from within the bomb rather than try to defuse it. Somewhat alarmingly, this required the removal of the bomb's filling plate and the drilling of another hole in its body. This allowed the insertion of a steam steriliser into the bomb casing so that pressurised steam entering through one hole could eject the explosive matter from the other. Usually, when defusing a bomb, it was normal practice to have just one man in its immediate vicinity but, where the steaming method was used, it was necessary to have several men clustered close to the device with each performing an important role.

At 1.30pm on 21 February 1941, Staff Sergeant Munford commenced what was often referred to as the steam sterilising process and, by 4.25pm, the explosive matter still remaining inside the bomb casing rested below the level of the fuse and was thus incapable of detonation in the normal way. Lieutenant W D Rees was still uncertain that the device was in fact totally safe, though Munford reassured him that the use of a stethoscope had not picked up any ticking noises and all seemed well. It was therefore decided that the bomb could be removed from the hole and taken to a safe place where the rest of the explosive matter could be steamed out at leisure. To that end, a rope was attached to the bomb and then anchored onto a lorry, while the other members of the team were told to take cover as a precaution.

The first attempt to get the bomb out of the hole was aborted when Sergeant Finney noticed that the rope was slipping along the bomb casing. While he quickly re-secured the rope, the men had in the meantime emerged from their hiding places to observe what the problem was. Regrettably, they had not taken cover again when the lorry recommenced its work of pulling the bomb out of the hole. It exploded, immediately killing seven of those who were attempting to render it safe. Lieutenant Rees and Sergeant Finney were both affected by shock and punctured ear drums that later required a lengthy stay in hospital. On hearing the loud explosion, the team working on the bomb near to the prison immediately made their way to Castle Street to see what assistance they could give. That there had been a serious incident was beyond doubt, and on arrival it was clear that there was little they could do to help as they surveyed a scene of utter devastation.

As they tried to make sense of what had happened, they were jolted out of their bewilderment by an explosion from where they had come – the bomb near the prison had also exploded but, luckily for them, while they were re-gathering their senses at Castle Street.

After departing from Castle Street, the sombre surviving members of the section made themselves busy in filling their lorries with essential equipment, while their cook prepared an evening meal. Hardly had the meal been eaten than the third raid commenced. Before Lieutenant Rees was taken to hospital for treatment after the explosion at Castle Street, he had instructed Sapper Lacey to get the men away from the likely target area of Swansea town centre if another attack was made that night. It was pointless for the men to remain at risk in the danger zone when their services would be sorely needed at numerous locations once the raid had ceased. With their lorries loaded with the equipment and materials that they would need in the aftermath of another raid, the group quickly set off for the relative safety of the Gower peninsula. They regretted leaving the town in such circumstances but knew that they would soon be returning to recommence their dangerous work after the latest raid had ended. In the Blackpill area of the town they were challenged by a sentry who told them that they needed to keep moving – the location they were now in was about to be used to set fires in the darkness that would hopefully confuse the Germans as to the precise location of the town centre. They resumed their journey into the fringes of a blackout darkened Gower and a place of temporary safety.

On 22 February 1941, Sapper Lacey had the unpleasant task of touring a number of temporary mortuaries in order to identify his fallen comrades. In due course, the bodies were placed in coffins and kept overnight in the section's new billet at Langland before they were taken to the railway station for return to their families.[30]

W Rhys Nicholas was a mature undergraduate student at the University College, Swansea, between 1938 and 1942. He had been at home in west Wales on the night of 19 February 1941 when the first attack took place. He recalled watching the searchlights piercing the darkness over Swansea before an 'ominous glow' appeared, an indication that somewhere was ablaze. He was present in the town when the third raid commenced:

> Flares were dropped in many parts, mainly outside the town. As we watched them float in threes and fours down to earth, we heard the swish and clap of hundreds of incendiaries as they dropped in every direction. People were soon rushing and scurrying to smother and trample the incendiaries. There came cries for water and sand and standing pumps. Doors were hacked down – bedrooms and garrets were broken into without the least ceremony…[31]

As regards the heavier bombs that fell in the wake of the myriad incendiary devices, Nicholas stated:

> Some fell unpleasantly near, their shrill whine increasing in intensity as they neared us and reaching a climax with an ending crash and a thousand different noises as glass and rubble and stone fell on the roofs and on the streets… I could see the town itself. The sight of it was almost staggering. It seemed that the shopping centre was a huge wall of fiercely burning flame. Dark clouds billowed upwards into the night sky and seemed like a heavy curtain over the moon and stars. To my nostrils came a sharp acrid smell – the smell of burning wood as if a great forest was burning and sending forth its smoky offerings.[32]

Glyndwr (Glyn) Lewis of Pentretreharne Road had the misfortune that his 16th birthday fell on 21 February 1941, the climactic third night of the Blitz attacks. After finishing his shift at the Baldwins steel plant at Landore (he had started work there at 14), he ventured into the already battered and smouldering centre of the town intent on seeing a film in one of the cinemas that had so far escaped damage. However, before the film had finished the cinema was evacuated as the air raid sirens sounded once again, and he had to make his way back to Landore on foot, occasionally dodging from door to door as the bombs rained down around him. Though it might have seemed impossible to him at the time, in a remarkable transformation of the fortunes of war, within four years he would find himself fighting his way into Nazi Germany as a private in the 2nd Monmouthshire Battalion.[33]

A diary entry for 21 February portrayed the shock experienced on seeing Swansea after two nights of raids, and indicated that there were still dangers within the smouldering ruins of many much-loved buildings and their associated businesses:

> Ben's [the Ben Evans department store], David Evans, Woolworths, Strides [Jewellers], Castle Street... St Mary's Church, only walls standing. Trinity Chapel in Park Street damaged, ruined also Trinity Church. High Street Arcade + hotel + tailors shop opposite H[igh] St station down, market all down, only walls and framework left... Oxford Street, Castle Street + High Street closed for traffic, waiting for delayed bombs to explode, many unexploded bombs around town, police + soldiers guarding. Large fires in several parts and firemen did wonderful work, hundreds of houses saved by fire-watchers who worked hard in putting out incendiary fires...[34]

W Rhys Nicholas walked through Swansea on 22 February, the Saturday morning after the final raid. It was a sight that was bound to sadden anyone who had known the town before the vicious aerial attacks had devastated it. He recorded:

The sight of the market was heartbreaking. That homely spacious building which one used to think of as a miniature Swansea in itself. The glass roof has disappeared, and the tangled, twisted girders stood out harshly against the cloudy sky. The floor was a mass of devastation – even like a wilderness that had been devoured by cruel, gnawing flames. The streets presented a sad picture. They were covered with stones and bricks and slates, and glass and dozens of trailing hose pipes. Water was everywhere and here and there a crater gaped with ruins right around it. Churches and schools and shops had suffered alike, and it really seemed that morning that Swansea – that old, friendly, familiar town – was gone forever.[35]

In the aftermath of each of the raids people had fled the town to what they hoped would be safer areas. Mr Birt, a highways engineer, recalled a stream of people passing his home in Pennard as they made their way to the relative safety of the local golf links or even further into Gower, laden with sleeping bags and a plethora of other items that would help them endure a few days in the wild, well away from the dangers of the town. An anonymous female had her memories recorded (in 1979) and remembered 'droves and droves of people' leaving the town, some for the open countryside where perhaps they could camp in their holiday-type tents, while others were heading for the relative safety of the suburban home of a relative or friend. In her own case it had become customary at the sounding of the air raid warning siren to dress in good clothes before entering the air raid shelter, since one never knew just where one would end up or for how long home might be just a memory in such circumstances. Appearances did matter even among the death and destruction. A leather attaché case was also always brought out of the home, containing important family papers and even the deeds to the house. Again, in a dangerous and uncertain world, it was best to be prepared for all eventualities.[36]

If many of the buildings within the central part of the town had been devastated by the three nights of attack then the human cost was of tragically high proportions. The Council was required to compile a list of civilian casualties; and that was done though, for reasons that are unclear, there are some minor anomalies between the local records and those of the Commonwealth War Graves Commission. An attempt has been made to clarify the position though, even after that effort, there remain a few inexplicable differences or gaps in the detail. Using the Commonwealth War Graves Commission data (which covers civilian casualties only), it seems that at least 39 civilians died in Swansea on the 19 February 1941 or succumbed sometime later due to the injuries received on that night. Working on the same basis, the 20 February figure was 105 killed or later died of wounds and on 21 February it was 60 such cases, making a total of 204 civilian deaths being attributable to the Three Nights' Blitz. That said, a council file listing the names of the dead runs to 220 names with the difference of 16 fatalities consisting mainly of Army sappers and other military personnel who were killed during the attacks; while a separate file baldly states that the death total resulting from the Three Nights' Blitz was 230. Further detailed work would be required to arrive at a more accurate figure though it seems likely that the higher figure of 230 includes several unidentified bodies which are not included in the list of names of those killed. It might also include a small number of grim cases that involved only unidentified body parts. There were also 260 seriously and 137 lightly wounded due to the attacks.[37]

During the 1930s the authorities in Britain had been concerned that, in a future conflict, the trauma associated with the mass bombing of civilian targets would produce something akin to mass hysteria within the population, adding to the problems of those bodies tasked with trying to restore some sort of normality to a heavily bombed town or city. The morale of a bombed populace was a constant worry for those in authority. Though it is possible that the local press might have put a 'gloss' on the story, a prominent local doctor was reported as saying, regarding civilian behaviour during Swansea's fiery ordeal:

> In the days before the war, we imagined that under conditions of great strain there would be groups of frightened people trying to get to hospital having nothing much the matter with them except fright and nervousness. Exactly the opposite has been the case. I saw only two cases whom I really thought were nervousness. One had quite sufficient cause for his nerves and the other was drunk. Even with severe injuries the patients simply lay in bed, smiled, spoke quite patiently, and were content to wait until their turn came for attention. These were men, women and children and there was hardly a whimper even from the youngest child.[38]

No doubt many calmed their nerves after a raid by busying themselves with domestic chores or assisting in the multitude of tasks that needed completion in clearing up the bomb-created debris in or around their homes. Some may have found solace in drink. One youth of 17 was brought before the magistrates to answer a charge that he had been found 'helplessly drunk' on Mumbles Road in the wake of the final raid. In evidence, it was stated by the lad's father that his son had been out on each night of the attacks, putting out incendiary bombs and assisting the police in whatever way he could. Indeed, his father noted that at one point his son didn't even know what day it was, such was his exhaustion and mindset. The youth told the bench that he had left the town after the final raid for the comparative calm of the Mumbles and, being somehow unable to obtain a cup of tea, had unwisely drunk a cupful of port, an ill-judged action that led to his drunken state. The case was dismissed.[39]

On 23 February 1941 a party of 150 Royal Engineers

arrived in the town to assist with making safe or demolishing the numerous damaged buildings. This was clearly a much-welcome if something of a knee-jerk reaction, since they arrived without any of the equipment or other stores that would be required to help them in their work. The already harassed staff of the Swansea garrison commander spent a lot of time making the necessary enquiries and telephone calls in order to rapidly obtain the required items.[40] Many buildings in the centre of the town had been totally burnt-out, leaving only the walls standing, often in a precarious manner. There was no safe alternative other than to dynamite what was still standing in such cases.[41]

Not all the rescue and recovery work following a raid concerned human lives. The Swansea branch of the People's Dispensary for Sick Animals reported in February 1941 that the traumatic effect of noisy bombing raids on family pet animals and birds was often considerable, more so when the family home had been damaged. A local branch of the organisation's national Air Raid Precautions Committee was active in the town, and had previously registered the contact details of over 13,000 animal owners, covering a correspondingly large number of pets. Within Swansea there were 32 people acting as chief guards and another 192 people working as animal guards at the behest of the committee. In the aftermath of a raid, many animals that had become temporarily separated from their owners had subsequently been reunited with their families due to the efforts of the committee's volunteer workers.[42]

As the Three Nights' Blitz devastated the town centre and damaged other areas, the resultant casualties had been removed to medical facilities as soon as was practicable. Since the Swansea General and Eye Hospital could not cope with the numbers involved, use was also made of the Cefn Coed Hospital, and the former infirmary and other wards of what used to be the Swansea Workhouse, since renamed

'Tawe Lodge' in an effort to remove the stigma of pauperism that had long been attached to it. Following the attack of 19 February, Cefn Coed Hospital had admitted just over 40 casualties, including eight French seamen who had arrived in the harbour on board the SS *Fort Médine* before being caught up in the bombing attacks. The oldest person admitted to the hospital was 76, while the youngest was only nine. The injuries sustained by those admitted included burns to the face and body, concussion, abrasions, scalp wounds, as well as a small number of cases that required the subsequent amputation of limbs.[43]

At what was referred to as the 'Tawe Lodge Hospital', there were listed 21 casualties, with injuries that included the 'usual' burn injuries, two amputated legs, a compound fracture of the arm, shock, and one woman who had gone into labour while being not quite six months pregnant. At Tawe Lodge, it seems that 12 of the admissions had been brought there after being injured in a bomb blast at the Swansea General and Eye Hospital.

The matter of the anti-aircraft guns falling silent for almost 40 minutes on the night of 21 February was investigated in the week after the town's ordeal. As the *War Diary* of the 79th Heavy Anti-Aircraft Regiment noted, 'There was (as in Sept. 1940) great indignation in the town directed against the A.A. defences, since the civil population had not been told that the guns had been silenced in favour of some other weapon.' Enquiries by the commanding officer of the regiment, when he visited the 10th Fighter Group at Pembrey, elicited the information that there was no plan in existence that set out a safe point of entry into the airspace above Swansea for friendly fighters who were trying to engage enemy aircraft. Indeed, when summoned on the night of 21–22 February, the Hurricanes had flown on routes well to the north of the town that were designed to keep them away from friendly fire, a pointless precaution when the guns had already been silenced in anticipation of their arrival. Unsurprisingly, in those circumstances, they had not encountered the enemy. Lieutenant Colonel Raikes, commanding officer of the regiment, returned to Swansea from the RAF base in Pembrey and, after mulling over his options, sent a terse signal to the fighter base stating that, in future, he would not consider himself bound to obey a 'ceasefire' order that he thought would endanger the town.

On 27 February 1941, Raikes and his superior officer attended on the Mayor of Swansea in the presence of Lang-Coath, the Town Clerk, to explain the situation regarding the silence of the guns in what must have been a very uncomfortable meeting for the military men. Lang-Coath was reported as saying that he would raise with the Regional Commissioner for Civil Defence the fact that, '… the destruction of the centre of SWANSEA had happened during this silent period and the town had no knowledge of the reason for this silence, which it bitterly resented.' He was as good as his word, and subsequently told the regional commissioner, Colonel Sir Gerald T Bruce, by letter that:

> It was during the cessation of the Gun Fire that the real 'mischief' was done. It would appear that for 45 minutes the Enemy had things entirely his own way and there was no resistance of any kind offered to him. Of course, I cannot definitely say that the Hurricanes did not go in to the Attack, but I have been able to find no evidence that they did.
>
> My submission is that all our efforts to maintain the Public morale, entailing as they do the greatest effort and energy, to say nothing of the time involved, are worthless if the Public's confidence in the Military Defences here is shaken, as I fear, it is in view of the disastrous destruction on Friday evening, which might apparently have been avoided, or in any event mitigated, if the Enemy had not been given a free hand for three-quarter's of an hour as apparently, from the information available, he had.

He added that another area of concern was the fact that he had been advised that the complement of guns allocated for the air defence of Swansea was 24, though, during the three nights of raiding, only 18 had actually been available for action.[44]

One teenage diarist had left Swansea for the safer area of Burry Port before the attacks of 19–21 February took place. She had cause to return to the town a few weeks later and, after first visiting her home to check on its condition, walked into the town centre. Her reaction would have brought a smile to the face of Prime Minister Winston Churchill, displaying as it did the gritty determination to see things through, whatever the ending might be, something that he had so often encouraged in his broadcasts. She wrote:

> We had to walk part of the way as our road was bombed rather badly and buses could not pass owing to large craters in the road. I cannot describe to you my feelings when we got into town. I think sometimes that what I saw was a dream, something fantastic, unreal, the looks of grief and suffering on people's faces, the smell of burning still in the air, the signs where streets were roped off, 'Danger unexploded bomb'. It was all so tragic and so unjust…
>
> That blitz has done many things to people but above all it has made them bitter and, if anything, more eager than ever to carry on the fight for freedom, for the right to live like human beings and not like frightened rabbits running into their burrows when Goering's Luftwaffe comes to bomb them, to murder women and little children.[45]

Though it would not have been known to the diarist and the people of Swansea, the town's worst trials of the war were now behind it. There would be many more dark days ahead before Churchill's 'sunlit uplands' would come into view but, come into view they would as eventually the united forces of the free world finally destroyed Hitler's malign and much-vaunted 'Thousand-year Reich'.

CHAPTER 8

The Aftermath

No one had a fuller picture of the disaster that had befallen Swansea as a result of the February 1941 raids than Town Clerk and Air Raid Precautions Controller, Howell L Lang-Coath. At a council meeting held on 18 March 1941, he had to fend off criticism from certain councillors regarding his perceived failure to convene a committee meeting the morning after the attack on the third night. He defended his position successfully and his verbal report to the council, carefully noted down in shorthand by an official and later transcribed, provides a vivid description of the frantic efforts made by council officials and many others in their attempts to deal with the numerous emergencies that arose during the attacks. He noted that the raids that had commenced on the evenings of the 19 and 20 February had created havoc in the town, 'and had taxed the energies and resources of those engaged in combating the attacks and dealing with the many difficulties which were left in their wake.' Indeed, many of those in positions of authority who were bearing the heaviest burdens had had limited sleep over the preceding 48 hours before the town was engulfed in crisis yet again, as the third and final attack was launched on the night of 21–22 February 1941. He challenged those present, including his critics:

> Can you just realise the position of affairs here on that Saturday morning? We had had three nights, a most terrible ordeal. You should sit in that control room – hear all those reports coming in – hear all the terrible things that are

happening. I can assure you it is not a sinecure – it is a very responsible position, and one which I would rather not go through again. The other officials can speak for themselves, but I am there in that room, Mr Mayor and Gentlemen, and I know what is going on. I can imagine part of Swansea falling down, I can't go out to see for myself, but there it is, and it is a very apprehensive position to be in, and one in which you feel your position very acutely.

He proceeded to lay out the stark situation the town had found itself in, both during and after the three raids. Over 8,000 messages had been received in the Guildhall control room and 561 incidents had been logged. The food office on Northampton Lane had been completely demolished, resulting in the loss of all rationing records (happily duplicate copies of the records had been securely stored in the Guildhall), while the market and the central shopping area of the town had been 'wiped out', resulting in the loss of over 170 food shops. There had been a remarkable 43 butcher's stalls in the market alone, supplying some 22,000 customers, and it was immediately obvious that feeding the citizens of the town and those who lived on its outskirts was going to be a major problem. Whether food was available or not, in many cases there was simply no easy way to cook it. The gas and water supplies had been badly affected during the raids and many householders had seen their homes damaged and the kitchens rendered unusable. Even where a kitchen had escaped serious damage, it might not be possible to use it due to the instability of the house or the danger posed by an unexploded bomb that had landed nearby.

After an urgent discussion at 2.30am on the morning of Saturday, 22 February, with one of his officials whose role encompassed food supply, Lang-Coath had contacted the food authorities in Cardiff and arranged for the rapid deployment to Swansea of 16 mobile canteens. He also, in a move that must have later raised the eyebrows of his often parsimonious critics on the council, conferred quickly with the mayor and the chairman of the Air Raid Precautions Committee and then authorised the opening of emergency cafés in the nursery school at Nelson Terrace and in the workingmen's club on Alexandra Road. These cafés met the immediate needs of those who, perhaps, even if not bombed-out, had no ready means available to prepare and cook meals. Around 1,000 meals were soon being prepared each day in the cafés, while other options across the town provided another 1,000 or so. Canteen meals were priced at 8*d.* for adults and 4*d.* for children, though, in the event that someone had no money to pay for a meal, one would be provided free of charge. Common humanity in the midst of a crisis dictated that that should be done, as did the fact that many people were performing key roles in support of the war effort and could hardly be expected to work on empty stomachs.[1] Lang-Coath praised the help given to the ARP services by members of the Women's Voluntary Service and the Young Men's Christian Association in dealing with the numerous crises that had arisen due to the attacks.[2] The YMCA operated several mobile canteens within Swansea, bringing sandwiches and hot drinks to members of the military, police, fire and civil defence services wherever they were in action. As the organisation later reported:

> The second Blitz night was a repetition of the first… The mobiles were on the scene in good time and were working in the docks area as well as on Townhill and Mayhill, serving the men of the A.F.S. in Teilo Crescent, who had a very gruelling time, and had had no refreshment except that provided by our canteens. One cannot go out on this service without having a great admiration for the men working on the fires, and it is indeed an honour to be able to serve them.

On Thursday, 20 February, given the extent of disruption to the food supply within the town, Swansea YMCA requested assistance from other areas. Soon, around 15 mobile canteens

The shape of things to come: the Ben Evans department store ablaze during the air raids of February 1941.

(West Glamorgan Archive Service, P/PR 95/4/27)

The Swansea town centre of 1939 included some impressive buildings. The dome of the Ben Evans department store is visible in this image.

Oil storage tanks near the Swansea foreshore, with a glimpse of the docks in the distance (left). Both were tempting targets for Hitler's Luftwaffe.

(www.swansea.docks.co.uk)

Howell L Lang-Coath, the long-serving Town Clerk of Swansea. He was also the Air Raid Precautions Controller.

Henry Foner (formerly Heinz Lichtwitz) in February 1939 at the time of his arrival in Britain on a Kindertransport from Germany. Henry later had no doubt that, in kindly taking him in, the Foner family of Swansea saved his life.

(Henry Foner)

Anti-aircraft guns of the type used in Swansea. There were no such guns in Swansea when the first air raid took place.

Barrage balloons over London. Swansea eventually had more than thirty balloons flying over the town.

Air raid wardens at Bonymaen, Swansea. The sign board mentions posts, divisions, groups and sectors, illustrating how extensive and organised the civil defence structure was.

(Lyn Courtney)

A Home Guard unit from the Brynmill area. Ernest Hayward of Francis Street is on the far right of the front row.

(John Hayward)

Swansea Home Guard soldiers man a barricade during a training exercise.

A modern image of a pill box that defended the railway line near Clyne Valley, Swansea.
(Gareth Lovering)

Anti-tank blocks still in situ (2024) in the Swansea Docks area.
(Ceri Thomas)

Not all defensive works in Swansea were passive in nature. There were a number of flame fougasse sites and the image shows a demonstration of the device somewhere in England.

A Heinkel HE 111 bomber, one of several types of German aircraft that attacked Swansea between 1940 and 1943.
(Bundesarchiv, Bild 101I-343-0694-21/Schödl (e)/CC-BY-SA 3.0)

Swansea's premier shopping destination: the much-loved Ben Evans store which stood opposite the town's castle.

The burnt-out ruins of the Ben Evans store. The council later developed the site as a memorial garden.

(West Glamorgan Archive Service, D 235)

The F W Woolworth shop at Castle / High Street. A sign displaying an 'S' is visible on the lamppost, pointing to the nearest air raid shelter.

(West Glamorgan Archive Service, D 280/2/13)

Looking up Temple Street, with the ruins of the David Evans store to the left. Today, Castle Gardens would be on the right of the image.

A solitary policeman surveys the bomb damage on Castle Street. Castle Buildings (still extant) are burnt out on the right.

(West Glamorgan Archive Service, P/PR 95/4/21)

Men of the Auxiliary Fire Service at a station in St Thomas. Such units provided vital support to the regular fire brigade.
(John Fitzjohn)

The Chief Constable of Swansea in 1939, Mr F J May, whose role also oversaw the work of the town's fire brigade. Invariably close to the danger, during one incident he worked a water pump himself.
(South Wales Police Heritage Centre)

A first-aid-post team at the Welwyn Lodge, St Thomas. These posts provided speedy treatment for the walking wounded, with more serious cases being referred on to a hospital.

(Jeff Stewart)

Strenuous efforts were made to ensure that civil defence workers were able to get a snack and a hot cuppa amid the destruction. A YMCA mobile canteen serves the workers outside the Bush Hotel on High Street.

(West Glamorgan Archive Service, D 280/2/12)

Many civilians were left without homes to cook in and, even where a home had survived, there were often problems with gas and water supplies. Another canteen distributes sandwiches and tea to those who need them.

A bomb-damaged Teilo Crescent in February 1941. The street saw the most concentrated loss of life in the town during the war.

(West Glamorgan Archive Service, P/PR 95/4/19)

Men of the 103 Bomb Disposal Section who served in Swansea. There were seven deaths in a single bomb-defusing incident on Castle Street in February 1941.
(West Glamorgan Archive Service, D 258/1)

The Prime Minister visiting Swansea in April 1941. He is pictured with (L–R): Councillor Thomas James (Mayor), Mrs Churchill, Mrs James and Mr John Winant, the American Ambassador. The tower of St Mary's Church can be seen in the distance.

Mike Lewis (second from the left) was evacuated from Swansea to Ystradgynlais in the wake of the February 1941 air raids.

(Mike Lewis)

Women's Land Army members. Many jobs that were previously largely male domains were successfully performed by women, freeing up men for more martial duties.

The D-Day build up begins: American soldiers in Swansea.
(www.swanseadocks.co.uk)

Equipment for the D-Day invasion begins to arrive at Swansea Docks.
(www.swanseadocks.co.uk)

Happy times return to Fleet Street, Swansea. Victory celebrations in the town were adjudged to be well conducted with no untoward drunkenness.

In 1947, Dylan Thomas wrote about bomb-damaged Swansea in the radio play *Return Journey*, having been in the town during the devastating attacks of February 1941.

(@ CTK Photobank/ Mary Evans)

turned up, keen to help, and their activities were centred on Mumbles (to where many townspeople had temporarily fled), the Guildhall and the YMCA building on St Helen's Road. These depots were soon turning out sandwiches on an almost night-and-day basis, aided by numerous volunteers. This impromptu service continued for around a week after the attack of 21 February 1941, on some days supplying almost 3,000 sandwiches a day.[3]

While the provision of food from a canteen could help meet the craving of hunger, another craving was met by the urgent distribution of ten tons of cigarettes. As a result of the attacks, over 6,500 people had been rendered homeless and the council's billeting officer had worked tirelessly to find alternative accommodation for those affected, sometimes in nearby local authorities. The council had previously established 61 rest centres across the borough, and 19 of those were brought into action in the bombed areas to cope with those people who needed assistance. Upon arrival at a rest centre, each person was given a basic 'iron ration', which included tea, canned milk, sugar and a few biscuits. Once their nerves had been settled they could, if necessary, obtain a hot meal at one of the emergency cafés. The wonderfully named Area Bread Officer had been contacted and was able to quickly arrange a delivery of 10,000 loaves on 22 February, a very welcome development but nowhere near enough to satisfy the hunger of Swansea's 160,000 citizens. As the town's market had been totally destroyed, a temporary market was set up on the roof of the United Welsh bus station on Singleton Street, so that Swansea's shoppers could begin to get back into some sort of domestic routine and start fending for themselves wherever possible.

Damage to the town's gas supply was dealt with by the local gas company, while council employees attended to the problem of broken water pipes. There were 57 public water mains that needed attention, and emergency repairs were carried out with some difficulty, hampered by the problem of some of the urgent work having to be carried out during the hours of blackout. In the interim, regional assistance arrived in the form of 22 water-tank lorries that distributed 1,800 tons of water, covering a distance of over 3,000 miles in a circuit of those Swansea streets that were still passable to vehicular traffic.[4] The council's waterworks department soon placed an advertisement in the press stating that it was currently vital to restrict the use of water for non-essential purposes. Dirty water could be used for toilet flushing purposes and, for the time being, baths should not be taken nor clothes washed in clean water. Drinking water was also required to be boiled before consumption.[5]

Within days of the final raid, the *South Wales Evening Post* published a number of advertisements from local businesses that pronounced that, in the light of their premises being destroyed or made unusable, they would soon commence trading from a new location. The *Post* itself was forced to relocate following damage to its premises that stood in the shadow of Swansea Castle, temporarily moving to George Williams and Co. on Mariner Street.[6] Customers of the Star Supply Stores on the badly-hit College Street were advised to visit an alternative shop on Walter Road, while those of John Moriarty Ltd of Castle Street made their way to Wind Street, not too great a distance, though some allowance would no doubt need to be made for the effect of debris in the streets and any unexploded bombs. Not so lucky were the customers of Hill's Furnishers of Gower Street and C F Walters, opticians, who were told that they would need to travel to Neath to have their needs met. Matthews Nurseries stated proudly that new premises would be found within a week and, in the meantime, 'We Carry On!'[7] Willsons of Oxford Street declared that they were 'BOMBED BUT NOT BEATEN!'[8] On a more sombre note, the Swansea Gas Light Company advised its customers, whose fittings had been damaged, to turn off all taps and bypasses on their gas appliances pending the safe reconnection of their supply by its engineers.

The local press also provided information on where certain services could be accessed in the aftermath of the raids. Allowances for an injury arising from the raid, that resulted in a loss of work for over seven days, were claimable at the Walter Road Congregational Church or the Elysium Building on High Street, while the dependants of those killed during the raids should enquire about pension possibilities, again at the Walter Road Congregational Church. As noted, Swansea Council could assist where billeting was required after damage to a home, as well as providing replacement food rationing books in circumstances where they had been lost or destroyed. Claim forms for damage to property could be obtained from the Guildhall or from the district valuer's office on Wind Street, while people in need of immediate assistance in respect of clothing, furniture or food could apply for payments in advance of compensation at several locations in the town, including the Bethesda Chapel schoolroom and St Jude's Church in Mount Pleasant.[9]

In the aftermath of the raid, several dignitaries visited the town to see the extent of the damage for themselves and to assess the performance of the civil defence service. William Mabane MP arrived on behalf of the Ministry of Home Security while Herbert Morrison, Home Secretary, also visited, accompanied by the Regional Commissioner for Civil Defence, Colonel Sir Gerald T Bruce. Mabane later wrote to the mayor, saying, 'Swansea has real reason to be proud of the manner in which the attack was met, both in the courage of its people and the efficiency of those responsible for its government. I have, in my report, made particular reference to the excellent initiative of the emergency market,' an allusion to the speedy establishment of a temporary open-air market on the roof of the bus station in Plymouth Street.[10] The temporary market could be reached via a concrete ramp that usually allowed the passage of buses. It was a large space with a concrete floor that was 'covered with row upon row of trestles covered with produce of all kinds'. As had been the case with the 'old' market, the outer part of the temporary hall was replete with butcher's stalls, each butcher carefully weighing out a customer's weekly meat ration allowance, while in the inner areas the usual market items could be purchased, including cockles, laverbread and farmhouse cake.[11]

The Ben Evans store was indeed gone, its high walls still standing though the interior of the shop was completely burnt-out. In earlier times it had apparently been the practice for some of the unmarried female staff to live above the shop, though that seems to have stopped some time before the enemy air raids, thus avoiding potential catastrophe. Given the destruction of the store and the level of disruption in the town, the managing director of Ben Evans, George Wheatley, placed an advertisement in the press asking all staff members to attend a meeting at a premises on St Mary Street, in order that a way forward for the business could be discussed. Before the first aircraft had appeared over Swansea on the evening of 19 February, one Swansea man had visited the store to buy his wife a bed-jacket. She had been hospitalized with a minor ailment and, spotting the bed-jacket on display in Ben's window, he thought he would buy it to cheer her up. His daughter was impressed by another window display that featured several expensive fur coats, all destined to be destroyed as fire later engulfed the premises.[12] Sidney Heath Ltd, a well-known Swansea business, stated in a press advertisement that it had taken the precaution of earlier removing a considerable portion of its stock to premises outside of the town centre so that it could recommence trading once a suitable property had been acquired.[13]

In different parts of the town, jewellers were seen looking on anxiously as efforts were made to recover the heavy metal safes from their bombed-out shops. A recovered safe had to be left – under the watchful eyes of its owner – until it had cooled down enough to be opened. Happily, it seems that in most cases the steel sides of the safe had protected the contents within, much to the relief of its owner.[14]

Efforts soon began to clear the worst of the rubble from the thoroughfares of Swansea so that vehicles and people could at least pass through the town in order to go about their business, always assuming that whatever business they had to deal with was still able to be operated in the rubble-strewn town. One woman recalled catching a bus to take her out of town, though it could only convey her as far as the Palace Theatre on High Street, from where she proceeded to her home in Landore on foot. She saw rescue parties furiously digging away at the shattered remains of what had once been homes or shops, while fires still smouldered in numerous locations. It was, she said, like walking down a country lane, except that there were 'hedges of rubble either side' of the narrowed street. There were few sounds – people seemed to be walking in something of a daze, not talking as they tried to grasp what had happened to the town they knew and loved. The shuffling of their feet made a rhythmic sound that was clearly audible in the general silence as they stepped on layers of rubble and broken glass.[15]

As previously noted, Heinz Lichtwitz had arrived in Swansea as a small boy on a Kindertransport rescue mission from Germany in 1939, and been entrusted to the care of the Foner family, adopting the name of Henry Foner. When the very first German air raids had taken place in 1940, the Foners and Henry had taken shelter under the stairs of 99 Vivian Road, though, as time went by, that practice was abandoned and the family sheltered instead in their garage which had been clad with a protective layer of filled sandbags. It is possible that Morris Foner's work as an air raid precautions warden had persuaded him as to the advisability of taking shelter outside of the family home in the event of any further raids. The family dog developed the remarkable ability to recognise the sound of German aircraft – at which he whined – while remaining calm when a British aircraft passed overhead. Presumably, the bangs and crashes which followed the passing overhead of German aircraft provided the dog with a sharp contrast to the silence that usually followed the routine sound of a patrolling British aircraft on a quiet day.

During the Three Nights' Blitz of 19–21 February 1941, the Foner family had gone up to the top of Vivian Road and were able to see the awful vista of a blazing Swansea town centre. Indeed, Henry remembers that the light from the multiple fires meant that it was possible to read a newspaper in the dark, despite the distance to the town centre. During one raid, a bomb landed in a property opposite that of their home on Vivian Road and, in due course, a bomb disposal squad arrived and told nearby residents to remain inside their homes and to open the doors and windows so as to minimise the effect of any unexpected explosion. After a while, two of the disposal team emerged from the crater carrying a bomb. They took it to their lorry and, without much ceremony, threw it into the back of the vehicle causing onlookers to suddenly drop to the floor of their homes in fear. It soon became apparent that the device had been successfully defused and posed no threat other than to the heart rates of the residents of Vivian Road. Mrs Foner was active in the Women's Voluntary Service, and assisted at a canteen that cooked meals for those whose homes had been damaged by the bombing. As noted, she was also involved in fundraising for the Swansea General and Eye Hospital, a body that largely depended on voluntary subscriptions and played an important role in treating the wounded.

Swansea's plight after the raids was recognised far and wide and a steady stream of donations in cash and kind began to be received in the town. Messrs F James of Newport, a company that imported a range of foodstuffs, sent a lorry containing rice, flour, tinned mutton, tea, biscuits, jam and condensed milk, plus several other items to the town. Johnston, Hewson and Company of Golden Square, London, stated that they had received, via 'American friends', a number of food parcels and were anxious to send them on for the benefit of the townspeople. The British Legion branch in Richmond offered to send a mobile canteen vehicle and the Post Office Social Service Association in Worcester sent the mayoress a quantity of knitted garments, while a Mrs Walters of Tonyrefail sent her week's rations for the benefit of a Swansea resident. Several people from Bridgnorth, Radlett, Newcastle Emlyn and Llandudno, among other places, offered to take in one or two homeless children, and their offers were passed to the council's billeting officer – an official who was faced with the onerous task of quickly finding accomodation for almost 7,000 displaced people. Councillor Geary of Neath suggested that his town would be happy to accept 300 people, though Swansea Council, while grateful for the offer, did not think it was as yet necessary to accept it. The residents of Aberdyberthi Street sent support in neither cash nor kind. Instead, they sent a letter to Lang-Coath, Air Raid Precautions Controller, thanking the air raid precautions teams 'for the very able manner and good work which they put into their efforts, during the recent "Blitz".'[16]

Cash donations were also received, and the *Times of Wales* newspaper (which was published at Denbigh) launched an appeal for funds to assist the stricken town. Then, as now, some people believed that money donated locally for good causes should be kept and used at the local level, and some readers of the newspaper queried whether it was the case that Swansea donations would actually be spent in the town rather than elsewhere. Somewhat surprisingly, though with good cause, the mayor of Swansea stated:

> I have to say that all the money which we receive in Swansea is being sent on to the Lord Mayor of London's Air Raid Distress Fund. We are doing this because we have found that we cannot possibly hope to raise sufficient money in Swansea

to cover the needs of those people who have been rendered homeless as a result of raids of the magnitude we have experienced in Swansea, and therefore all we receive we are sending to the Lord Mayor and in return we get grants from that Fund.

I may say that although money has been coming in exceedingly well in Swansea, we have drawn much more from the Fund than we have received.[17]

Amid the outpouring of support for a bomb-battered Swansea, within the town there were numerous troubling events in the wake of the raids. Looting of war-damaged premises was viewed as a serious crime and, in England and Wales, there were 426 cases in 1940, while during 1941, with Britain repeatedly under attack from the air, there were 2,508 cases. In Swansea during 1941 there were 105 instances of looting from premises damaged in enemy bombing raids, and a number of cases (32) involved juveniles who often tampered with pre-payment gas meters in bomb-damaged properties.[18]

Robert Donovan Murray, aged 39, was 'doing his bit' as a fire-watcher in 1941, but in March that year he was rather grandly charged with the offence that 'in an area which had been subjected to an attack by the enemy by means of aircraft, he feloniously stole two ladies' handbags and two purses, valued in all at £1 0s. 4d., the property of Messrs Salisbury's Ltd., Swansea, which had been left unprotected as a result of war operations.' His defence that he had found them in the gutter and had intended to return them to the shop was not accepted, and he was sentenced to six months' imprisonment for looting. In a statement that seems at odds with the Chief Constable's report for 1941, the presiding magistrate noted that at that time only two cases of looting had, so far, been brought before the court following the February attacks, a record that Swansea could be proud of. It is likely that he was ill-informed on the matter.[19]

In one case, in April 1941, four boys were bound over and

another three fined after being involved in the theft of food as well as money from gas and electric meters in bomb-damaged properties. Three of the group were charged with looting. All pleaded guilty and the suggestion of one parent, that the council should take steps to make damaged properties more secure, fell on deaf ears.[20] In March 1942 it was stated at a meeting of the council's Housing Committee that children as well as adults had been involved in looting war-damaged premises, especially in the Townhill area. Lead piping, flooring (probably linoleum) and other articles were being stolen from empty properties, and it was agreed that the Education Committee should be asked to instruct head teachers to speak to their pupils. The council's Highways Committee expressed its exasperation in early 1943 at what it called the 'wanton damage, pilfering and looting' that took place after bombing raids. Additionally, for some reason, street lamps and fittings seemed to be popular targets for vandalism across the borough, and several thousand pounds would need to be spent when conditions allowed on making good the damage. It was disappointing to see that, despite the supposed camaraderie of the 'Blitz spirit', temptation proved just too hard to resist for some.[21]

After the first two nights of the Three Nights' Blitz in February 1941, Malcolm Smith broadcast over BBC Radio his account of walking through Swansea while the rubble of bombed-out buildings was still hot. Given the terror, casualties and substantial damage experienced and witnessed by the people of Swansea over those two nights, it was a remarkably upbeat broadcast, perhaps in the spirit of 'Britain Can Take It!', but it caused widespread offence, with people feeling that he had underplayed the severity of the suffering within the town. Smith had reported:

But there are the usual smiles even from those who have lost friends and relatives are [sic] not really depressed and their stories are told in a subdued manner but with a sense of pride. I can honestly say that the two nights of heavy raiding here have not had the slightest effect on the morale of the people of Swansea…

Early this morning I saw some elderly men and women running through the streets clutching small cases and parcels in their hands. These were all they had left in the world. Many of them raised their hands and gave us a cheery greeting.

Reports of local complaints about the Swansea broadcast were considered by officials at Home Intelligence, a division of the government's Ministry of Information. That unit aimed to provide the government with timely information about the state of public opinion and morale across the country as the war developed. It was noted that while broadcasts, such as that which had upset the people of Swansea, were subject to censorship on matters of security, there was little else to guide broadcasters as to the suggested tone of their comments. An official at Home Intelligence stated, 'This particular talk was given after the second night of the Blitz, and the comments of the inhabitants after the third night of Blitz I leave to your imagination.'

Swansea was not the only place to feel aggrieved at the BBC's coverage of its trials. An account of the attacks on Coventry upset local people, as it seemed to imply that there were gaps in the civil defence provision, while Portsmouth was incensed as the BBC overlooked completely the efforts of its civil defence services – although, to look more closely would have drawn attention to serious shortcomings in their response to the emergency. It was apparent that it was difficult for the BBC to tread a line that provided useful information to the British public while not upsetting this or that group of people. An attempt to provide guidance for the future was made and forwarded to the regional information officers, many of whom no doubt had the required local contacts for briefing purposes in the various sources of news. The guidance issued referred especially to the aftermath of heavy air raids, noting that many who experienced such events would be left dazed and, to a lesser or greater extent, shocked. Those who had also suffered direct loss, whether human or material, would be feeling sad and depressed. Information might be hard to come by for civilians after an attack, since the supply of newspapers might be temporarily disrupted and radio sets might have been lost or damaged in bombed-out buildings. Rumours were likely to spread quickly and any signs of failings in the civil defence operation would be seized on as a cause for concern by the local population, given the likelihood of repeat attacks.

To try and counteract these morale-sapping conditions, Home Intelligence suggested that when information was communicated to the population, hearsay evidence should be excluded and general comments on the state of morale or any heroics performed should be avoided. While it might be tempting to minimise the extent of any damage sustained during a raid, it was better to be open and frank in the knowledge that the enemy would undoubtedly eventually see the relevant news reports. To minimise, in media reports, the damage caused to a certain town might only encourage the enemy to return again and finish the job, a possibility that was clearly not desirable. References to the work of a local civil defence team should instead be tempered with caution, and glowing reports of particular actions (whether justified or not) were likely to cause upset where the experience of a part of the local population and the support it received was, perhaps, markedly different to that portrayed in a report. There was no harm, however, in describing what happened, for example, in a rest centre after a raid, without casting a judgement on the efficiency of the operation. Though it would be difficult to understand for those who had suffered directly, it was relevant to point out that the experiences of a raid on a particular town or city were very similar to those of other places that had also been attacked. Everyone was in it together, and the suffering undergone and the subsequent rebuilding undertaken by a community would all contribute to an eventual victory.[22]

An investigator from the Mass Observation organisation visited the town shortly after the Three Nights' Blitz and submitted a report on the conditions found. It was stated that, in common with similarly bomb-ravaged towns, Swansea was now seeing more of its people routinely carrying gas masks where that had not been the normal practice before the heavy raids. It was also apparent that, as well as those who had been officially evacuated from the town due to their homes being damaged, a large number of people had decided to simply seek safer quarters further afield, whether by staying with relatives or renting a room or property outside of the town (it was not uncommon for such people to return to a bombed town on the following day in order to fulfil their work commitments). Many people had simply travelled to the seaside village of Mumbles, some six or so miles from the town centre, where it was noted that church and village halls, cinemas and private properties had willingly opened their doors and offered shelter to the new, albeit temporary, arrivals.

Though inaccurate or alarming rumours were not too widespread in Swansea, the raids were nevertheless a key topic of discussion among the townspeople, though not in an obsessive manner. There was a feeling that what had happened had happened and it was sensible to just try and make the best of an undoubtedly difficult situation. The Mass Observation investigator thought that, though people were understandably shaken by the casualties suffered and the damage caused to the town, it was still possible for them to adopt a positive attitude and deal with issues in a matter-of-fact manner. Many of those affected just 'got on with it' by temporarily moving in with friends or relatives, a move that provided them with a familiar and reassuring presence. Even where friends or relatives were unable to help, the Welsh trait of offering hospitality to strangers played its part and saw some people being accommodated or assisted by someone to whom they had no real link. All in all, morale in Swansea was judged to be good despite the trauma so recently undergone. Indeed, it was seen to be better than that exhibited by the citizens of some similarly affected towns in England. The investigator also noted that a frequently expressed opinion by those spoken to was along the lines of 'Oh well, we'll just have to grin and bear it' – a suitably pragmatic outlook on a situation and uncertain future that was simply beyond the control of the people of Swansea.[23]

The Inspector General of Air Raid Precautions passed favourable comment on the performance of Swansea's Town Clerk, Howell L Lang-Coath, in his role as Air Raid Precautions Controller and especially for his work during the attacks of February 1941. The Inspector General noted, in late March 1941, that, 'Probably no town in the country, and certainly no town in south Wales, has been subjected to such severe raiding as Swansea.' He added that it was due to Lang-Coath's '… leadership and to his efforts that the whole civil defence organisation in Swansea was able to stand up to such a severe trial.' He went on to say:

> In regard to the 'after Blitz' arrangements, Lang-Coath's organisation has been quite exemplary, to such an extent that the regional commissioner was entirely content to leave the whole matter is his most capable hands.
>
> Mr Lang-Coath has set a magnificent example of leadership and organising ability under the most trying circumstance. He has never been ruffled and has met every situation, as it arose, with the utmost confidence, success and cheerfulness.[24]

Howell L Lang-Coath was duly made a Commander of the Civil Division of the Most Excellent Order of the British Empire (CBE) for his work during the air raids and the award was announced in a supplement of the *London Gazette* on 25 April 1941.

As was the case with Lang-Coath, the unrelenting efforts of Swansea's Chief Constable and Fire Officer, F J May, during Swansea's three-night ordeal did not go unnoticed. He had been in the police service since 1917, when he had commenced work as a constable in the Tynemouth force, having been a clerk there since 1914. He soon showed an aptitude for policing and was promoted to sergeant in 1920 and then to inspector in 1921. In 1927 he had obtained the post of Chief Constable in Stalybridge before being essentially head-hunted for the role of Chief Superintendent in the much larger Sheffield force during 1929. He was seen as a keen advocate of modern policing methods, including the use of fast cars and other modern systems. He was appointed to the post of Chief Constable in Swansea in March 1931.

In the aftermath of the attacks of 19–21 February 1941, Colonel G H R Holland, one of His Majesty's Inspectors of Constabulary, visited Swansea and spoke to May as well as other prominent people in the town. Holland later told his superiors that he wanted:

> ... to bring to your notice the excellent work done by the police both during and after these attacks, and more particularly the great gallantry and fine leadership displayed by Mr May himself. On each of these three nights Mr May was out and about, constantly in the main target area during the height of the attacks, inspiring members of his force and of the fire and other services by his fine example of courage and leadership. It is only necessary to go to Swansea to appreciate the force of these attacks on the business centre of the borough and to hear on all sides praise of Mr May's personal leadership and example.

Colonel Holland went on to recommend that F J May be awarded an Order of the British Empire (OBE) 'without any hesitation' and that honour was reported in the supplement of the *London Gazette* on 25 April 1941.[25]

The most high-profile visitors to the town in the aftermath of the air raids were the King and Queen. The visit, which was understandably cloaked in secrecy, took place on 19 March 1941. The 'cloak' proved to be not especially 'secret' since, on the eve of the visit, the general secretary of the Swansea YMCA, W B Hilton, wrote to the Town Clerk requesting an invitation to the proceedings, mentioning the work that had so willingly been done by YMCA members after every air raid. The Town Clerk was unable to accede to his request as it was only a 'flying visit', with the royal party arriving at the Great Western Railway station at High Street at 10.50am and leaving the town for Cardiff at 1pm. On the day of the visit, the King and Queen, accompanied by the Regional Commissioner for Civil Defence, Colonel Sir Gerald T Bruce, were met at the railway station by the mayor of Swansea, Thomas James (in civilian life a colliery traffic manager), who introduced them to Percy Morris, chairman of the ARP committee, H L Lang-Coath, Town Clerk and ARP Controller, and F J May, the Chief Constable.

The party set off by car along Alexandra Road and Dyfatty Street, heading to Morriston where they were to inspect rest centres at the Soar Baptist and a Methodist chapel. It had been noted that, in the event of an air raid during the royal visit, the air raid shelters along the route would be prepared for the emergency use of the party, though it had to be borne in mind that they were in no way bomb-proof. It was a risk that would just have to be taken. The five-car convoy (which included one car that was filled with detectives and another that was kept empty as a 'spare') then proceeded to Robert Street where all alighted and inspected the damage sustained there due to the attacks. After being driven to Carig Crescent, they walked via Emlyn Road to the heavily damaged Teilo Crescent, a distance of about 200 yards. The final stop on the journey was Milton Terrace, a location that afforded the party a bird's-eye view of the town and the damage it had suffered.

After being conveyed back to the town centre, the group then observed the damage to Castle Street, Temple Street, Oxford Street, Lower Waterloo Street, St Mary's Square, Lower Union Street and Nelson Terrace. At Nelson Terrace they visited the communal feeding centre in the nursery school (later renamed as a 'British restaurant') before proceeding to the Guildhall, where they met other senior officials of the council as well as representatives of the various civil defence units, including the air raid warden service, the rescue and first aid parties, among others.[26]

Soon after the visit of the King and Queen in March 1941, Swansea saw the arrival of Winston Churchill and his wife Clementine, who visited the town in early April. It was another visit that was intended to show support for the stricken town and to boost the morale of its people, and it certainly had an impact. The Prime Minister walked several miles through the battered town and its suburbs, often at a pace that found some of those accompanying him struggling to keep up. As he walked through the streets to loud cheering, he occasionally placed his hat onto his walking stick and flourished it aloft so that even spectators at the rear of the crowd could see that he appreciated their support. When he enquired of the crowd, 'Are we downhearted?', he received a lusty 'No! Not likely!' in reply. While visiting the docks, one workman mildly chided him for not carrying his gas mask and the Prime Minister acknowledged his error and had the item swiftly retrieved from the back of his car. He continued his tour with the gas mask dangling conspicuously from his shoulder. Even the Prime Minister understood that it was desirable to stay on the right side of a Swansea docker![27]

Though the Prime Minister had been warmly received as he was driven through or walked along the streets of Swansea, in the background the arrangements for his visit caused a few ripples in municipal circles. At its meeting in April 1941, several members of the council questioned the role of Colonel Sir

Gerald T Bruce, the Regional Commissioner for Civil Defence. They thought that Bruce was bypassing the local officials and simply imposing his will on the town in respect of particular issues, including that of the Prime Minister's visit. It was claimed that the arrangements had, in any event, proven to be inefficient as the Prime Minister had been asked to attend on the mayor at 8.30am for breakfast, while the mayor had been told to expect Mr Churchill at 9.30am. The mayor had duly arrived closer to that time only to find the Prime Minister already there and kicking his heels, an embarrassment that had apparently been caused by simple administrative muddle. The criticisms were rejected by the chairman of the Air Raid Precautions Committee, Percy Morris, who stated that the notice given regarding the visit had been short and Bruce had merely asked the Swansea officials to make the appropriate arrangements without imposing any conditions. It was the authorities in London who had decided that, as regards those who were to be presented to the Prime Minister, the focus was to be on ARP personnel, meaning that those serving in Swansea with the Navy or Army (including the Home Guard) were excluded. Morris added that Sir Gerald's only concern was to see that Swansea's travails and suffering were recognised by all in authority.[28]

One support service that had been introduced in Swansea in the light of the February 1941 attacks was that of the communal cafés, which urgently opened on the instruction of the Town Clerk and ARP Controller in order to provide food, mainly for those who had been bombed out of their homes. This was not purely a Swansea innovation; early in the war some thought had been given at governmental level to the possibility of providing focal points in each likely enemy target area where emergency kitchens could be set up. This idea was dropped however after it proved impossible to identify enough suitable premises in the right locations. The idea of travelling field kitchens, which could be dispatched to wherever they were needed, was also found to present innumerable logistical problems, while inter-departmental haggling at government level over who should run and pay for such an expansion of the state's involvement in welfare issues hardly helped matters progress.

Gradually, despite all the difficulties, the idea of communal feeding facilities gained acceptance, offering the possibility of a system that could deal with both urgent and non-urgent needs. Once again, there was some reluctance at governmental level to embrace what was likely to be a major expansion of the state's welfare provision, and there were also concerns that access to non-rationed food in publicly provided café-like settings might undermine the efficiency and fairness of the food rationing system in general, as well as having an adverse effect on the trade of commercial catering establishments. Nevertheless, the need to make provision for all eventualities, as well as concerns that the poorer classes of people were already hard-hit by rising food prices, eventually won the day and tentative plans began to be put into effect for communal feeding services in all parts of the United Kingdom.

It was appreciated that communal feeding outlets would be useful to those who had been bombed-out, those who worked unusual shifts due to the wartime emergency, as well as to a host of civil defence volunteers who would welcome a modestly priced snack or a more substantial meal after a difficult turn of duty at often unsocial hours. The government view was that food could be provided to a town's citizens by the local council at more or less cost price, plus the addition of a small percentage to cover the expense of staffing and equipment. Control would be exercised by having the local food supply undertakings submit regular financial returns to the local authority; there was no question of the Exchequer providing a blank cheque to local councils. The service had to pay its own way or provide full explanations regarding any specific financial problems for the consideration of the higher authorities.

Earlier dithering at all levels meant that in Swansea the council only established a Communal Feeding Committee in 1942 to direct the work of the yet-to-be-established communal feeding facilities (though communal cafés had been opened on the initiative of the Town Clerk at Alexandra Road and Nelson Terrace in the aftermath of the February 1941 raids). No less a person than Prime Minister Winston Churchill had voiced his distaste at the term 'communal feeding', suggesting it smacked of Communism or the much-loathed workhouse system. He suggested that such facilities should be called 'British restaurants' as, in the eyes of most people, a restaurant was a step up from a simple café and far removed from an uninviting workhouse dining room. In the event, though Swansea Council did establish several British restaurants, it resolutely retained the term 'communal feeding' in its committee structure.[29]

A number of sites for British restaurants were examined by the council before it was agreed that, over time, restaurants would be located at the workingmen's club on Alexandra Road, the Scala Cinema at St Thomas, and at the nursery school in Nelson Terrace. Plans for a further restaurant in Castle Street foundered due to the chosen site being judged as unsuitable by the Cardiff-based officials of the Ministry of Food. The service was initially managed by an official who was seconded from the staff of the council, before R Stuart Murray from Norfolk was appointed to the newly-created role of catering manager in September 1942. The menu offered traditional dishes, and most people seemed to opt for a main course of meat and vegetables followed by a pudding, all provided at a competitive price.

The service proved to be undoubtedly popular in helping those who, for whatever reason, might be struggling to provide themselves and their families with meals at particular times of the day. This might be due to damaged homes, shift-working patterns, or the periodic absence from the home of women who were engaged in war work and thus unable to cook for their families, a daily task that was usually left to women at that time. During the four weeks ending on 30 January 1942, the British restaurant based at the Scala Cinema at St Thomas served 378 breakfasts, 1,987 dinners and 869 teas. The figures for the Alexandra Road establishment were 122 breakfasts, 2,730 dinners and 723 teas. Nelson Terrace provided 127 breakfasts, 2,637 dinners and 709 teas. Very welcome hot beverages were also provided, the cuppas dispensed totalling 4,481 at the Scala, 4,420 at Alexandra Road and 4,491 at Nelson Terrace, during the four-week period.

Until the early part of 1943, the food served at the restaurants was actually prepared at cooking depots that were located at Ynystawe and Pontlliw, with the food being transported to the restaurants. By the spring of 1943 it was considered necessary to utilise the two cooking depots solely for the provision of school meals as scholars gradually returned to their usual classrooms as the risk of attack from the air diminished. This meant that if the town's British restaurants were to continue operating, they would need to be equipped with previously unnecessary kitchen equipment. Given the resultant cost implications, it was decided to close the Nelson Terrace restaurant, while fully equipping the other two for the cooking of food on-site.

As was always the case with the finances of Swansea Council, the pennies spent on the British restaurant service were watched closely and it became apparent that takings at the Nelson Terrace and Scala Cinema sites did not cover their estimated expenses. The sums involved were actually quite trivial but, nevertheless, resulted in a jaundiced eye being cast over their operations. Indeed, after the Nelson Terrace site closed in 1943, the Scala Cinema premises came under even closer scrutiny. It was noted that in the financial year ending on 31 March 1944, the Scala had made a loss of £172, to which had to be added a further cost of £408 in respect of capital spending (largely on kitchen equipment) and establishment costs. The council's Communal Feeding Committee was told that the opening of a canteen at the docks had affected trade at the Scala, while some potential customers were put off by the prospect of eating at what they considered to be little better than a soup kitchen.[30]

The decision was then made to also close the Scala site as soon as possible, despite it having provided almost 50,000 dinners in the 12 months to the end of March 1944. It closed in August 1944, and those whose needs it had catered for presumably had to visit the Alexandra Road site or simply cook for themselves. As it happened, a similar fate awaited the Alexandra Road premises after it was reported, in December 1944, that it had lost the grand sum of £14 on running costs alone in a four-week period. It seems that the council had decided that, minor though the losses seemed to have been, it no longer wished to provide a loss-making service that had not existed before the war. Accordingly, the Alexandra Road site went the same way as the Scala and Nelson Terrace restaurants. During the period that the restaurants had operated, a total loss of £2,871 had been borne by council funds and enough, it seems, was enough for the parsimonious guardians of the council's coffers.[31]

CHAPTER 9

Evacuating the Children

RELATIVELY MINOR GERMAN air attacks on Swansea continued into March and April 1941 with two fire-watchers, Kenneth Evans and Henry Price, being killed at 1264 Neath Road on 12 March, while James Williams, an ICI worker from Landore, died in hospital the day after the raid. On 31 March 1941 a lone enemy aeroplane dropped its bombs which hit the electricity power station on the Strand. Hubert Harris, John Nicholls and Percy Williams were all killed as a result of the explosions, while Thomas Atherton lost his life during a raid on 28 November 1941.

After the harrowing raids of February 1941 and amid the ongoing air raid warnings and occasional explosions, the council again turned its attention to the question of the evacuation of the town's school children to safer locations. Since the outbreak of the war in 1939, schools in Swansea had attempted to continue very much as usual, allowing for the fact that plans had been made and discussed with parents regarding what would happen at the school in the event of an air raid. At St Thomas' Infants' School, the rhythm of pre-war school life had been maintained after the declaration of war, although the summer holiday period had been extended until 25 September 1939 in case enemy attacks from the air commenced immediately after war was declared. The local vicar visited the school regularly, as did the 'nit nurse', while teeth were still examined and those children who were in receipt of free milk were regularly measured and weighed to check on their development. A small number of children who had been voluntarily evacuated from the supposedly more dangerous areas of Britain to Swansea were also present for lessons.[1] At Newton School, near Mumbles, the procedure adopted when an air raid warning was sounded (an increasingly frequent occurrence) was for the children to be taken by their teacher to the school gate, from where those who lived nearby would be directed to their homes while those who lived further afield would be temporarily accommodated in nearby houses.[2] Later in the war, the school benefitted from the construction of an air raid shelter. Amid the constant worry, it still proved possible for Father Christmas to visit the school and distribute small gifts to the children prior to the commencement of the festive holidays.[3]

In the wake of the German air raid of 10 July 1940, which had targeted the nearby docks area with fatal consequences, the headteacher of St Thomas' Infants' School was instructed on 12 July by the Director of Education to close the school until further notice, with the teachers transferred to other locations. The thinking seems to have been that since the docks area would be a prime target for the enemy, the school was a little too close for safety to where the focus of attack was likely to be.[4] Schooling was still provided in the town as far as was practicable as the war progressed, even where a school had suffered bomb damage. For example, in 1944, Henry Foner, who had arrived in Swansea on the Kindertransport in 1939, started studying at Dynevor Grammar School. The school had been badly damaged in air raids of February 1941 but it was still possible to use some parts of the buildings for teaching purposes, and every effort was made to continue providing tuition to those children who were still present in the town.[5]

By early 1941, with the aerial attacks intensifying, it was becoming clear that additional action was required regarding the safety of all children in Swansea, but there was nevertheless an understandable reluctance on the part of parents to be separated from their offspring at a time of danger, even though the risks involved in their remaining in the town were all too evident. Indeed, in some homes children played important roles as errand runners and, where appropriate, in looking after their younger siblings while perhaps dad was in the services or mam was at work in a factory. There was also a feeling in some homes that if danger was to come calling from the sky, then it was better for the family to face it together.

In April 1941 the council resolved that it would make an application to the government to declare Swansea an 'evacuation area', while at the same time testing the reaction of parents to the prospect of their children being removed from the town for their own safety. In order that the parents were fully aware of what evacuation might entail, teachers were encouraged to highlight key facts when discussing the issue with them. They were to stress that any evacuation was likely to be for the duration of the war, which was a worryingly imprecise time for a loving parent. Only children were to be evacuated and there was no option, at that time, for a mother to accompany her child or children, provided they were of school age. There was currently no information available on just where children might be sent, though, once they were moved to a place of safety, those parents that could do so would be expected to make a financial contribution towards their billeting costs. The more affluent parents would be required to meet the full billeting cost, while those on lower incomes or on public assistance would pay less or, in some cases, nothing.

It seems that in the minds of some parents the fact that no indication could be given as regards the areas that the children might be taken to probably meant that the authorities were concealing the fact that the destinations were possibly as far away as the north of England or even Scotland. This doubt probably influenced the subsequent decision on the issue of some parents in a negative manner. The result of what was termed a 'census' of parents' opinions on the evacuation of children from Swansea was stark. The parents of 13,312 Swansea children participated in the process, though the names of only 2,802 children (21 per cent of the total) were eventually put forward for evacuation. Shortly after this disappointing result, the council was nevertheless able to announce that Swansea would indeed be imminently declared an evacuation area (in May 1941), an indication that the government considered Swansea to be still at high risk of further attacks. This seems to have produced a reconsideration of the matter among some families, and when those who wished to register their child or children for evacuation were requested to visit a school to do so, a rather more encouraging 4,030 children were actually registered. Of that total, there were only 296 secondary school children, some of whom had siblings in the elementary schools. Nevertheless, that still left over 9,000 children who would remain in the town and at risk, though it was likely that some children – or even entire families – might independently move away from Swansea to stay with relatives or friends in safer parts of the country. At Newton School it was noted that not a single pupil had been registered for evacuation by July 1941, and despite teachers being available to register potential evacuees during the summer holidays, yet again no child was actually registered.[6]

Some families did take steps that allowed them to remove their children from Swansea, while retaining more control than would have been possible had they simply handed them over to the local authority. Bert Little, who was originally from Trowbridge in Wiltshire, and his wife Alma, lived on Danygraig Road in the Port Tennant area of the town at the time of the February 1941 attacks. The family was able to privately arrange the evacuation of their eldest son, George (who had been born in 1927), to the relative safety of his grandmother's home in Trowbridge, before he soon moved again to the home of an aunt in nearby Bratton. George's introduction to the leafy byways of Wiltshire impressed on him the stark contrast between his new, albeit temporary, lodgings and the more familiar territory that surrounded his home in the largely industrialised landscape of the Eastside of Swansea. He began to keep sketchbooks and found enjoyment in painting the farms, woods and fields around Bratton. Before the war was over, George returned to Swansea and promptly enrolled at the Swansea School of Art. In later life he became a noted artist in the town, chronicling in photographs, drawings and paintings the industrial and urban decay that became so prevalent in post-war Swansea.[7]

For those who had decided to entrust their children for evacuation purposes to the care of the council, events soon moved on apace. On 21 May 1941, over 4,000 Swansea child evacuees were medically examined by a hastily assembled team of doctors and nurses, and the record of any child found to be suffering from an infectious disease, such as scabies, was specially marked for the attention of those in the planned receiving area. In such cases a period of quarantine before going into a billet was thought likely to be needed. The initial plan in Swansea was that such children should actually be held back and only sent to their billeting area when they were free of infectious disease, though that idea was ruled out by officials at the Ministry of Health who thought that the greater risk lay in the children remaining in Swansea for longer than was necessary. They were to go to their appointed areas as soon as possible, be they infectious or not.

At the Swansea Guildhall and in the schools themselves, a flurry of activity was undertaken in preparation for the planned moves. Instructions were issued and thousands of forms were completed, checked and analysed. Nominal rolls of those travelling were drawn up, transport was arranged and the locations of numerous reception areas were finalised, with most of them being in not-too-distant locations in south or west Wales, a decision that, given their closeness to Swansea, would cause Education Department officials in the town numerous problems in the future. The children were to typically proceed in school groups and there was a contingent of some 186 teachers that would be split across the parties to accompany them to their temporary homes.

As the Director of Education in Swansea, T J Rees, later noted with some pride:

> In five working days, arrangements had been completed
> for the first group of children and teachers to be evacuated
> from Swansea – arrangements of the kind for which English
> authorities had been given five months to prepare. Those
> hectic five days will never be forgotten by the officials and
> others who had anything to do with it. The mental and
> physical strain was intense, but there was scarcely a hitch in
> carrying out the final organisation.

Within the body of schoolchildren were 588 of the Roman Catholic faith, and the leaders of that group requested that any areas to which their children were evacuated had to be able to provide for the religious needs of the new arrivals. They were duly sent to Llanelli and Ammanford. A similar request from the Jewish leaders in Swansea proved to be impractical due to the simple non-availability of synagogues in the receiving areas. That difficulty was overcome by requiring the Jewish families in Swansea to withhold their children from the official evacuation parties, and instead to make their own arrangements to remove them to locations where there were synagogues. Once that had been done, the Director of Education would issue each child with a billeting certificate entitling them to the same benefits as official evacuees.

Even after the first registrations and evacuations had been completed, pupils continued to be added to a list of those requiring a belated removal from the town as parents, presumably, had second thoughts about the matter. In the first week of June 1941 alone, the names of another 237 elementary pupils and 42 secondary school pupils were added to the list. By the 20 June, five 'late' parties of children had been added to the original list of official evacuees, resulting in a total of 4,477 elementary school and 350 secondary school pupils being evacuated from Swansea, a grand total of 4,827 children. It was, of course, a figure that was still far below the actual number of children in the town at the start of 1941. The children who had not been moved away by their parents outside of the official arrangements simply had to take their chances in a bomb-shattered Swansea that might well be attacked again.

Most of the children who were being taught in elementary schools were relocated to the areas of the Carmarthen or Llandeilo Rural District Councils, though some were sent to Haverfordwest or Ystradgynlais. Billeting certificates were issued for each unaccompanied child that was officially removed from Swansea, and the weekly payments for their support made to the receiving family ranged from between 8s. 6d. for a child aged under ten, to 15s. for a child aged over 16. In the occasional case where, for exceptional reasons, a parent had been allowed to accompany a child, the receiving family was entitled to 5s. for the parent, 5s. for each child aged over 14, and 3s. for each child aged under 14.

Brynhyfryd School children were sent to an area containing Talley, Trapp, Salem and other nearby villages, while Townhill School children were typically sent to the area of Pontyberem and Tumble. As another example, children from the Danygraig boys' and girls' schools were sent to Ystradgynlais.[8]

Naturally, the personal experiences of those evacuated varied depending on the place they were relocated to, the reception they experienced, and the care that they received. Ongoing interest in their education and welfare, plus the abilities of the supervising teachers who had accompanied them, were also important factors. One such evacuee was Michael (Mike) Lewis from Danygraig Road in Swansea. His father had dug out a pit and erected an Anderson shelter in the garden of the family home, though, when used in the winter of 1940, it was found to be waterlogged and cold, while the bunk beds were also damp and uninviting. In February 1941 the family had abandoned the primitive comforts of the shelter after the first night's attack and, for the subsequent two nights, retired to the more hospitable environment of the kitchen – where they huddled under a table – while Lewis senior crouched under the stairs with a bucket of sand at the ready to deal with any incendiary bombs. A high-explosive bomb exploded near to the house and, aged just five, Mike Lewis recalled the terror that later led to his parents thinking it would be better if he was moved away from Swansea:

> The thuds of ceilings falling down, glass being blown in. All I knew was I was safe in my mother's arms as the three of us were huddled under the kitchen table – mother, sister and me… bombs had exploded just outside 96 Danygraig Road, blowing a big gap in the cemetery wall, and had also brought down a large tree on the opposite side of the road. I expect the blast and thunderous vibrations were what caused the front bedroom and parlour ceilings to collapse, one bringing down the other, as well as smashing the windows in both rooms.

Among the crash of the bombs, falling masonry, breaking glass and the sound of the anti-aircraft guns firing furiously, Mike's father had been running around with his bucket of sand desperately trying to extinguish incendiary bombs wherever he could reach them. As the dim light of a February morning arrived, Mike emerged from his shelter under the kitchen table to see the amazing sight of Kilvey Hill looking 'like a gigantic Christmas tree' as incendiary bombs gradually burned themselves out. The ground-floor rooms of the family home were covered with rubble and there was a strong smell of escaping gas, and the area around his home was pock-marked with bomb craters, while his school had also been badly damaged. The gas supply to the house had been interrupted, the pipe that led into the meter having become dislodged by the violent vibration following a nearby explosion. As a temporary measure, Mike's father drove a number of wooden wedges around the pipe, thus resecuring it and stopping the escape of gas until professional help arrived.

If his parents had harboured any misgivings about having their son evacuated out of Swansea, it is likely that the impact of the February 1941 bombings quickly removed their doubts. In May 1941, Mike found himself congregating with about 40 other boys and girls in the shelter of Mount Calvary Baptist Chapel on Ysgol Street, near to his home. It took the children a while to realise that they were about to be evacuated out of the town, but the procession soon set off on foot along the Danygraig and Port Tennant roads towards the Midland Railway Station. Carrying his small suitcase and a child's gas mask, Mike Lewis was unable to spot his mother in the watching crowd as he passed by, since – as she told him years later – she had gone back into the house being unable to control her tears.

The train took Mike and his school chums to Ystradgynlais, and they were assembled in the yard of Ynyscedwyn School where they waited patiently as prospective families viewed them, trying to decide which ones seemed 'right' for them. As he waited, a local youth approached him and, by way of introduction, punched him firmly on the nose before running off. Blood flowed freely over Mike's white shirt, with the result that the blood-stained evacuee was the last one to be chosen by a local family. A woman he came to know fondly as 'Mam Bess' stepped forward and offered her hand, and he soon found himself settling into a terraced house in College Row, Ystradgynlais. He went there with another pupil, Gethin Mitchell, and they found themselves sharing a house with Mam Bess, her three daughters (two of whom were working in a munitions factory), and a grandson.

The arrangements for schooling in Ystradgynlais were

complicated by the fact that the local children were being taught in Welsh while the Swansea children spoke only English. Mike recalled that in the Port Tennant area of Swansea where he lived, two languages were actually spoken but they were the English language and bad language with Welsh being quite uncommon. The issue was resolved by schooling the Welsh-speaking contingent in the morning and the English-speaking evacuees in the afternoon, and doing the opposite in the following week. It was not a great success. A half-day of schooling each day was quite a reduction from the norm and, to Mike, the teachers seemed impatient, so much so that he described his education in Ystradgynlais as being 'terrible'. Indeed, after his later return to Swansea, he and his fellow pupils spent some time in a class with the youngest pupils so that they could quickly get back up to speed, their educational progress having been hampered by their time away. Mike remembered that having to sit comfortably on the smaller chairs of the youngest class was quite difficult and the subject of much laughter.

While in Ystradgynlais, Mike and Gethin, his pal from Port Tennant, made themselves useful by assisting a local woman in delivering milk from a horse and cart, while help was also given in picking up hay and loading it onto another horse and cart. Inevitably, coming into regular contact with Welsh-speaking pupils and villagers meant that he soon picked up various Welsh words and phrases. He also made an unsuccessful bid to run away after the novelty of his new placement wore off and he became homesick.

At some point Mike returned home to Port Tennant as the risk of further serious raids on Swansea decreased and as the fortunes of war changed in the Allies' favour. There was no fuss made around his departure from Ystradgynlais and he simply said goodbye to Mam Bess (who he described as being 'a lovely woman') before proceeding home in a works vehicle that was driven by his father.

After the war Mike went back to Ystradgynlais several times to visit Mam Bess, the woman who had taken him in. He was completing his National Service in the Army in Germany during 1958 and, while on leave, he went again to Ystradgynlais, only to find that Mam Bess had passed away.[9]

Another group of evacuees consisted of 37 pupils from various schools, including Waun Wen, Sketty, Glanmor Boys, Dynevor and the Junior Technical School. The group was billeted in Llanybydder, Pencader, Velindre and several other west Wales villages. It had left Swansea on 30 May 1941 and had initially travelled to Pencader where additional medical inspections were undertaken and a light tea provided. The distribution of evacuees to receiving families took place at Llanybydder Council School, and one of the supervising Swansea teachers, Mrs E Cook Rees of Ynystawe, visited the various billets on the following day to introduce herself and to make sure that the children had settled in to their new homes as well as could be expected. The fact that she was able to speak in Welsh to what she termed as the 'foster parents' undoubtedly helped ease her reception and, happily, all the children appeared to be content with their allotted families.

Most of the children opted to attend some sort of religious service on Sundays, while the supervising teacher assembled the group each weekday for an hour or so in order that she could chat to them, read a story and go for a walk, providing the weather was suitable. Despite the good start and the attempts to keep the children happy and contented, by 3 June one child had already opted to return to Swansea and the relative closeness of the evacuation area to the town soon proved to be an habitual problem. As Mrs Cook Rees noted on 7 June 1941:

Parents have kept on coming up to see the children this week – and have unsettled them. Children who, seemingly at any rate, were contented, cried when they saw their parents who were then sorry that they had come along. Anyway, in most cases the children eventually returned to Swansea with their parents.

Between 2 June and 7 July 1941, no fewer than 17 children were collected by their parents. At least one child was moved to a different home due to problems with the initial placement, while two other youngsters firmly informed the supervising teacher that they intended to take the next train back to Swansea – on their own. It was quickly agreed that their grandmother would come and collect them.

School lessons for those who remained were provided at Aberduar Vestry School, and included reading, writing, arithmetic, scripture, Welsh and nature. Time was also found for art, needlework, music and clay modelling. Government inspectors called at regular intervals to ensure that all was well on the personal and schooling fronts with the children. It was not all hard work for the children since, living in a rural area, they were able to visit a horse mart in Llanybydder, take part in the Teifi Valley School sports day, go winberry picking, and observe the intricacies of sheep shearing at close quarters. In the difficult circumstances of 1941, many evacuees had an enjoyable time spent out in the countryside and away from danger. As it happened, the children had only been evacuated after the worst of the raids on Swansea were over, though that would not have been known back in the spring of 1941.[10]

T J Rees, the Director of Education in Swansea, estimated that 4,827 children had eventually been evacuated from Swansea under the auspices of the council, while another 2,274 were removed privately by their parents or guardians, making a total of 7,101 evacuees. This was still only a little over 50 per cent of the number it was thought might be removed and, even then, over time, 945 of those who did leave Swansea later returned to it, despite the inherent dangers. The Swansea civilian casualty records indicate that, thankfully, no children who were kept in Swansea after May 1941 or returned there soon after the evacuation were killed in the later raids though, sadly, 43 Swansea children aged 13 or younger had already lost their lives.

Rees also noted that once the novelty had worn off, some of the receiving carers were keen to return their temporary charges to their real parents as soon as possible. Some children had been brought up in Swansea in conditions which Rees said were 'a disgrace to our boasted civilization', leaving them largely devoid of any idea of cleanliness, decency or Godliness. Inevitably, those children proved to be ultimately unacceptable to the receiving families once their personal habits became clear. One grubby urchin loudly complained that, at his placement, he was being made to wash four times a day, a totally alien experience to him.

Rees knew of one Swansea child aged under ten who had, within 48 hours of his arrival in Pembrokeshire, picked up a bottle of milk from a doorstep and presented it to his temporary 'mother' as a present he had supposedly bought for her with his pocket money. He visited a slot machine premises and claimed, untruthfully, that he had inserted a shilling into a machine with no effect. The assistant promptly 'refunded' him the shilling. The lad then went to a shop used by the family he was staying with, and claimed that he had been sent to collect some money – the shopkeeper having mistakenly short-changed the family earlier – another claim that was untrue. On attempting the 'I've lost a shilling in the machine' trick again, he was found out and his other transgressions revealed. Clearly, such a boy was unsuitable for a family placement.[11]

CHAPTER 10

Defending the Town

BEYOND THE EVER-PRESENT danger of attacks from the skies on the towns and cities of Great Britain during the war, there was also the worrying threat of a German invasion by sea. The miraculous evacuation of the British Expeditionary Force from Dunkirk and its neighbouring ports in the summer of 1940 could not conceal the harsh fact that, while just over 330,000 men had been safely brought back to Britain, the bulk of the force's heavy equipment lay abandoned in France, Belgium and Holland. The losses included some 600 tanks, over 1,000 artillery pieces of varying calibres, 500 anti-aircraft guns, almost 900 anti-tank guns, large numbers of lorries, cars and motorcycles, as well as huge quantities of ammunition and other military supplies. It was an unmitigated disaster. There were serious concerns about whether British industry could provide the equipment needed for the home defence divisions as rapidly as might be needed, should the Germans launch a speedy invasion. In the spring of 1940, 25-pounder field guns were being turned out at the rate of only 35 a month; the poorly equipped home defence divisions (of which there were 27) needed around 1,900 such guns to simply meet their establishment strength. There were similar difficulties in the production of other weapon types and, while strenuous efforts were soon underway to plug the gaps, it would clearly take time.[1]

General W E Ironside was appointed to the position of Commander in Chief, Home Forces, on 27 May 1940, and he had to devise his plan for the defence of Britain while commanding units that were currently ill-equipped and unsuited for mobile, offensive warfare against an invading force. He concluded that the best option was to arrange static defences, backed up by his scanty mobile forces, at key points in the south of the country. The hope was that these measures would at least help to break up and delay any German advance from the coastal areas until mobile forces from the general headquarters reserve could be deployed in targeted counter-attacks against the invader. Use would also be made of a fortified 'stop line' running from the vicinity of Richmond in Yorkshire, down to the Wash, Cambridge and Aldershot, before terminating on the coast near Bristol. German forces could, hopefully, be contained within this long loop which formed a defensive crust so as to prevent London and the important industrial centres of the Midlands from being overrun. Though initially accepted, Ironside's plan soon came in for criticism, not least due to the fact that a number of Royal Air Force (RAF) bases were located on the 'wrong side' of the defensive crust and would, in all probability, be quickly captured by an advancing enemy. Additionally, many Army units which contained new recruits were actively involved in creating the necessary defensive works to the detriment of their much-needed training. Following these concerns, on 20 July 1940, Ironside was replaced by General (later Field Marshal) Sir Alan Brooke.

Brooke had the advantage of taking over at a time when the position regarding vehicles and weapons had shown some improvement. He changed the anti-invasion plan from that of a simple linear defence to one of a more aggressive and mobile offensive posture. The defensive crust provided by the Richmond-Bristol stop line would no longer be the primary defensive line. Instead, mobile reserves would be positioned closer to the likely landing areas so as to be able to rapidly engage – and hopefully destroy – enemy units before they could establish settled bridgeheads on British soil. To help achieve that aim, in July 1940 he confided to his wartime diary that he fully intended to spray any beaches that the enemy chose to land on with mustard gas. In the event of an invasion, it would be a total war on a no-holds-barred basis. The invading enemy was to be destroyed at all costs and with whatever weaponry was available.[2]

By the time that Brooke assumed command during July 1940, Adolf Hitler had already asked his senior commanders to draw up plans for the invasion of Britain. When these were produced it soon became clear that if a successful invasion were to be launched, mastery of the skies would first have to be gained. The Battle of Britain had begun on 10 July 1940, and would continue until the end of October, with the German Luftwaffe attempting to prise control of the skies from the hard-pressed RAF. In fact, though Brooke was unaware of it, after 15 September 1940 the plan to invade Britain was put on hold by Hitler as it had proved impossible for the German Luftwaffe to obtain the necessary aerial supremacy. Bombing attacks were to continue, however, in an ongoing effort to damage essential infrastructure and undermine the British will to resist.

Meanwhile, on the ground, it had been apparent from the earliest days of the war that many men in Britain who wished to perform some type of work in defence of their country were prevented from doing so by age, fitness or personal circumstances which might include them being involved in roles that were important in the wartime economy. Though a certain amount of pressure about this had been applied to those in charge of Britain's defensive preparations by the time that Germany invaded Belgium and Holland on 10 May 1940, no major meaningful steps had been taken to make use of this largely untapped source of manpower. Following the early German successes on the Western Front, the issue became much more pressing, as it was apparent that the enemy might soon be able to reach the French coast and so be poised for an invasion of Britain. So it was that Anthony Eden, Britain's new Secretary of State for War, addressed the nation in a radio broadcast on the evening of 13 May 1940. He proposed that a new, voluntary and unpaid organisation be formed, to be known as the Local Defence Volunteers, consisting largely of men between the ages of 16 and 65 who had fired a rifle or shotgun and were capable of 'free movement'. The effect on the British population was dramatic, and only a week later around 250,000 volunteers had been enrolled, with the number reaching a third of a million by 31 May.[3] By the end of July, no less a person than Winston Churchill had intervened in the matter, insisting that the rather uninspiring name of 'Local Defence Volunteers' should be abandoned in favour of the more resolute (in the Prime Minister's eyes, at least) name of 'Home Guard'. Numbers enrolled in the new organisation by that time were approaching half a million men.

A modern reader might find their opinion of the Home Guard somewhat coloured by its depiction in the popular and long-running TV programme *Dad's Army*, where old age, pomposity, incompetence and endless muddle were presented to great comedic effect. There is no doubt that among a force of 500,000 men there would be those willing volunteers who, for a range of reasons, were hopelessly unsuited to the tasks allotted to them in a time of war, but that is not to say that the entire force was of little value. After all, a man who had been aged just 20 in 1916 might well have experienced significant military action, whether on land, at sea or in the air, by the end of the Great War in November 1918. By 1940, he would be a not-especially doddery 44 year old who was familiar with military routine, discipline and weaponry, while being keen to defend his homeland from a ruthless invader at almost any cost.

Of particular concern to those who planned the defence of Britain in 1940 was the threat from German paratroopers who might be dropped behind the defensive line held by regular

Army units, thus landing in areas where there might only be a modest Home Guard presence for defence purposes. An early Home Guard training manual noted that, during the attack on the Netherlands, German paratroopers had been dropped onto Dutch airfields to clear and secure the runways so that follow-up formations could be quickly flown in to build up a force in the rear of the Dutch defenders. Indeed, when the Swansea press reported on the speedy enlistment of men into the Local Defence Volunteer force, the forerunner of the Home Guard, it referred to them as 'parashots'.[4] In Swansea, an enthusiastic meeting held at the Central Hall on 4 June 1940 saw 150 men signing up for the new organisation on the spot, while others were compelled to return at a future date as the supply of enlistment forms had simply run out.[5]

Enlistment stations had been set up on a district basis around Swansea and included facilities at the St Helen's Rugby Ground, the church hall on Port Tennant Road, the police station at Llansamlet, the Ravenhill Social Club and the church hall on Castle Avenue, Mumbles, among other locations. By January 1941, volunteers in Swansea had been largely formed into battalions, with the number of men in each varying a little depending on circumstances. The principal local Home Guard units detailed to help protect Swansea from possible invasion were the 12th Battalion (with around 2,500 men) and the 14th Battalion (which contained around 2,700 men), while the 15th Battalion would protect Gower.

The flow of men into a Home Guard unit had to be constantly maintained as, throughout each year, some of its eligible members received their call-up papers for the military and were soon taken away on other duties. Under the Defence (Home Guard) Regulations of 1940, local officials of what had been renamed the Ministry of Labour and National Service were active in contacting the employers of men who had been required to register by age group for additional employment in support of the war effort, and a man would be expected by the ministry to carry on with his normal job while also devoting some of his 'spare' time to Home Guard duty. The Swansea office of the ministry wrote to the employer of a man named Hounsell (a builder's labourer) of Granville Road, St Thomas (in a 'date as postmark' letter), stating that it proposed to:

> ... direct [Hounsell] to enrol in the Home Guard. Normally a member of the Home Guard will not be required to perform training and operational duties for periods exceeding a total of 48 hours in each period of four weeks. He may, however, in the event of his unit being mustered for the purpose of resisting an invasion, be required to serve continuously and, if necessary, to live away from his home.

The letter added that if the employer was of the view that Hounsell could not be released from his normal duties, even in an emergency, then representations should be made to the ministry (which had an office on Northampton Lane) against his enrolment in the Home Guard within seven days.[6]

Even after the disastrous losses of equipment and other material in France and the Low Countries, and despite Britain being short of just about everything in 1940, it was not long before every Home Guard volunteer had a uniform – if not a weapon. The uniform was essential if there was to be any hope of a Nazi invader observing the requirements of the Geneva Convention, and, after an invasion of Britain, treating captured Home Guard personnel as combatants rather than mere armed civilians who could be shot without further ado. Though not part of the regular Army, Home Guard volunteers could help it by easing the pressure on regular Army units in performing tasks such as patrolling beaches, manning roadblocks, checking for evidence of 'fifth column' activity, examining the papers of anyone who was seen to be acting in a suspicious manner and, most importantly, in the event of an invasion, defending a set location or strongpoint so as to defeat or at least delay an invading force.

In Swansea, as elsewhere, many industrial or other organisations had enough manpower available to form their own Home Guard units, which could, as a minimum, provide men for patrolling purposes around their works or other establishments. A case in point is that of the University College of Swansea which, in October 1941, welcomed a former Dynevor schoolboy through its doors in the firm expectation that, as well as studying, he would also join its Home Guard unit. And that is what he soon did, parading on Wednesday afternoons when there were no classes to attend. As he recalled:

> In those early days there were no uniforms and no weapons.
> Can you imagine some 50 or so of us charging around
> Singleton Park in civilian dress carrying broomsticks to
> represent rifles and shrieking wildly – this was supposed to
> represent a bayonet attack! After some weeks of this I decided
> that I would make a better contribution to the war effort
> by helping out on the farm of mother's aged uncle – I could
> plough with a team of horses, milk the dairy herd, clear out
> the cowsheds and the stables and so on. After a few weeks of
> this I was called before my betters!

His 'betters' comprised a three-man panel made up of a representative of each of the principal armed services, who left him in no doubt that his attendance was indeed required for university Home Guard purposes. Suitably chastised, his attention to military matters soon showed a remarkable improvement until he was required to join the regular Army in December 1942.[7]

In a similar vein, the Home Guard unit formed of employees of the National Oil Refinery in Llandarcy could commit almost 350 men to its defence, while the Great Western Railway company at the docks produced no less than 321 Home Guard members. The Weaver's and Co. Home Guard unit had 95 members, the Prince of Wales Dry Dock Company had 75, and the Mond Nickel Works could muster 230. In all, the various major employers in the Swansea area provided around 3,000 men for their dedicated Home Guard units. That said, it was a sobering fact that, by January 1941, rifles were provided for only a third or so of those available for duty – though it was not a critical problem, provided no invasion took place. It was, after all, fairly simple for one man finishing Home Guard duty at his workplace to hand over 'his' rifle to a chap who had just arrived to replace him. The threat remained, however, that in the event of a 1940 invasion, almost two-thirds of Swansea's Home Guard members would not have a personal weapon to hand, even if much useful work could be done in simply carrying supplies or ammunition and delivering messages in an emergency. There might also be a chance to throw hand grenades or improvised 'Molotov cocktails' at enemy troops and tanks, though such close-quarter actions could only be performed at great personal risk.[8]

Involvement with the Home Guard in Swansea was not without its elements of comedy and tragedy. Arthur Anderson had been born in 1913 and had joined what was initially the Local Defence Volunteer force at Fforestfach soon after its creation. As was common within the organisation at that time, at first there were simply no uniforms available for the men (Anderson was given an armband) and certainly no rifles – a broomstick acted as a largely ineffective weapon until the supply of rifles to Swansea units slowly improved. Eventually, uniform trousers arrived, though battle tunics only limped in some time later, thus completing the uniform.

In one training exercise in which Anderson took part, the headquarters of a Home Guard unit in Birchgrove was to be 'attacked'. Those in command of his unit had the bright idea of approaching the objective from an unexpected direction – by crawling through a marsh – in order to gain the advantage of surprise. The attackers emerged covered in mud after crossing the marsh on their stomachs, only to discover that the defenders were indeed surprised – they had no idea that an exercise was taking place. To round things off, one poor chap who had been positioned as a lookout in the upper branches of a tree was still there, cold and forgotten, while his mud-splattered comrades enjoyed their post-exercise refreshments in a local hall. On a more sombre note, the sergeant assigned to familiarise the Fforestfach men with a rifle was a Great War veteran who appeared keen to demonstrate his experience and weapon-handling prowess. In doing so, he accidentally shot one of Anderson's comrades in the leg. The man subsequently died from the complications of pneumonia.[9]

On 17 October 1940, a new unit of the regular Army, the 15 Defence Regiment (Royal Artillery), began forming in Swansea under the command of Lieutenant Colonel J F S Bullen though, by November, following an administrative muddle, the regiment had been re-designated as the 14 Defence Regiment. A number of defence regiments were established in various parts of Great Britain during the autumn of 1940, and they were usually equipped with whatever old artillery guns happened to be to hand. They were tasked with defending areas of beach where it was thought the enemy might attempt an invasion, and their deployment usually resulted in more modern heavy weapons, already at a particular location, being taken away for use by the regular Army mobile counter-attack units.[10]

The daily regimental *War Diary* was diligently completed by the assistant adjutant, Lieutenant H E Gilmour, and his frustration with the innumerable difficulties that he faced in helping organise the new unit is evident from his first entry, in which he bemoaned the fact that paper was in short supply. He noted that, in due course, the function of the regiment would be to guard the '… docks, beaches, vital road junctions and aerodromes from Carew Cheriton Aerodrome [an aerodrome some five miles west of Tenby] to St Athan's Aerodrome [some ten miles west of Cardiff], a coastline of over 100 miles.' To cover that large area, there were initially only 25 guns of varying types, namely 4-inch (ten in number), 4.7-inch (two), 6-pounder (11) and 12-pounder (two). Swansea seems to have been allocated seven guns, with the others being spread around the Cardiff and west Wales coastlines. Swansea had two guns of the 4.7-inch variety, a weapon that had been developed as far back as the 1880s, while the 6-pounder (of which Swansea had two) was of a similar vintage, though that is not to say they could not still be effective when used well. Completing the mix were three guns of the 4-inch type. The guns were sited on the foreshore, at Jersey Marine and Gowerton, among other places.

With the weaponry not being of the highest quality, Lieutenant Gilmour also found cause for complaint in the standard of men assigned to the regiment, one of whom was described as already having 'a lengthy charge sheet and got into further trouble very soon after he arrived'. He was also unhappy at the building chosen for the regimental headquarters, which was a hall adjacent to the rather prominent St Andrew's Church on St Helen's Road. In December 1940 he noted with pleasure that a new headquarters building had been chosen and it was to be 'Enniskerry, an unoccupied house on Sketty Green, which is not only more convenient and more pleasant but seems less obviously a target than buildings of a church in the centre of Swansea surmounted by two conspicuous turrets.'[11] The advantages of not attracting attention to a headquarters building was brought forcibly home to Lieutenant Gilmour during an anti-invasion exercise that was staged in Swansea in August 1941. Though the use of Enniskerry as a headquarters building was not especially obvious to the casual observer, the parking of two staff cars outside its front door during the exercise soon attracted the attention of the invading 'enemy', as did the three uniformed staff officers who were clearly visible through a front-room window. One subsequent 'enemy attack' was repulsed by the headquarters staff, before a second attempt – reinforced by the use of Bren and Tommy guns – was judged to have rather embarrassingly captured the premises and all those in it.[12]

As the Battle of Britain raged over the southern coast during the summer and autumn of 1940 and, indeed, on occasion in the skies above Swansea, efforts were made to better prepare the town for the possibility of invasion, though it seems that the pressure of circumstances, coupled with a shortage of manpower and building materials, prevented the early construction of a comprehensive series of defensive strong-points. However, in January 1941, a plan, the Swansea Defence Scheme, was issued by the officer commanding troops in Swansea after the end of the Battle of Britain, though at a time when the prospect of invasion had still not been totally discounted. Indeed, during 1940 and into 1941 the threat of Britain being invaded by Germany's armed forces still remained high in the thoughts of Britain's political and military leaders.

The plan set out the likely scenarios surrounding a possible invasion of Britain and how the town of Swansea might be affected. It envisaged an attack either by enemy parachute landings, by a seaborne invasion, or possibly by a combination of both, the attack being undertaken to secure a land base from which future operations could be staged by the invader. Alternatively, it was thought that an apparent invasion attempt on Swansea might only be a feint by the enemy in a bid to draw British and Allied reserves away from the location of a more serious and determined attack. The forces available to the garrison commander for the defence of the town (excluding Gower) amounted to almost 6,500 men, around 5,700 of whom were Home Guard soldiers of the 4th, 12th and 14th Battalions, though only 2,800 or so rifles were available to battalion members at that time. Apart from Home Guard volunteers, only 133 regular Army infantrymen (of the 16th Home Defence Battalion of the Welch Regiment) were available, as well as a smattering of men from the Royal Artillery, Movement Control (usually employed in making sure that military use of the port, road and railways functioned efficiently) and any other military units that happened to be based in the town.

The focus of the defence plan in 1941 was largely on the town itself and its port facilities, probably due to the fact that the shortages of manpower, as well as construction materials, prevented the completion of a comprehensive scheme of fortification construction across the wider borough. The Swansea garrison commander spelled out the seriousness of the situation in his plan, stating that the town was to be defended as a fortress preventing the enemy from entering its central area by way of its beaches or from its landward side. Any invasion attempt was to be met with an immediate counter-attack by the nearest friendly forces, and such an attack was to be pressed home 'REGARDLESS OF LOSS' (emphasised in capital letters). Every opportunity was to be taken to 'act offensively and destroy the enemy' before it had time to reorganise after a landing, and there was to be 'no withdrawal from defensive positions'. Instead, such positions were to 'be held to the last man and the last round'.

The land perimeter of the town was to be defended mainly by the 12th Home Guard Battalion, utilising a number of roadblocks or strong-points which would be camouflaged and also protected, as far as possible, against attack by enemy flame throwers. Anti-tank obstacles would be manned by Home Guard members at the southern entrance to Singleton Park, near the St Helen's Ground, at culverts leading from the beach between Blackpill and Brynmill, and at all entrances to the docks area. Prominent in Blackpill and several other areas were lines of 'anti-tank cubes', large blocks of reinforced concrete that could at least delay the advance of enemy armour. The defensive doctrine associated with their use stated that it was essential that, while enemy tanks were delayed by the blocks, they should be engaged with all suitable weaponry. Indeed, the blocks were occasionally sited so as to steer the enemy towards an area that looked easier for tanks to negotiate but was, in fact, well defended. Two heavy guns located in the South Dock area would cover approaches from the sea, as well as firing, if necessary, at beaches to the west of the dock. Similarly, two heavy guns situated in the docks area on the eastern side of the river would engage any enemy craft approaching from the sea, as well as being available to fire at beaches to the east.

To ensure that mobility could be maintained for as long as possible under invasion conditions, all motor transport used by the defending units was to have its fuel tanks topped up every evening. In an emergency, petrol supplies could be obtained while on the move by urgent requisition from local garages. It was, however, recognised that in some circumstances valuable supplies of fuel, oil and lubricants might need to be destroyed to prevent them falling into the possession of the enemy.

The regular Army units in Swansea were required to hold two days worth of reserve rations (typically preserved meat, biscuits, tea, sugar, flour and tinned milk), while depots at Cockett, the Francis Garage in Pontardawe, together with the Miner's Rest in Waunarlwydd, held a combined total of an additional 7,500 reserve rations. Home Guard members, however, were required to eat food in or brought from their home; though how, in an emergency, that was supposed to work is hard to understand. It was suggested that some reserve rations for the use of Home Guard personnel could be held at local police stations, and no doubt a flexible approach would need to be adopted should the enemy arrive at the doorstep.[13]

Work on anti-invasion defences in and around Swansea picked up after just over 200 men of the 194th Tunnelling Company (the 194th Company of the Auxiliary Military Pioneer Corps to give it its proper title) set off from Birmingham on

27 February 1941, joining a party of around 60 men who had arrived from Wrexham the day before. Though designated as a tunnelling company, the unit would actually undertake various works to improve the defences of the town against invasion. By the beginning of March, there were 279 tunnellers in the town, based in Mumbles, though some were working on detachment in Llanelli and, somewhat oddly, on railway work in Birmingham where presumably there was a greater need for their services at that time.

Though the precise nature of the work is not always detailed in the unit *War Diary*, it was carrying out tasks in Singleton Park and was also active in 'planting' poles in the ground at several open locations so as to discourage the potential landing of enemy forces by glider. It is possible that it performed similar anti-invasion pole-planting work on the beaches around Swansea in order to impede the progress of enemy landing craft in the event of an invasion. On 31 March 1941, an officer and 21 men of the unit kindly helped get the Mumbles lifeboat on to the foreshore, while in Llanelli there was a detachment of over 100 men engaged in erecting anti-invasion obstacles on a beach. Work was also carried out at the Fairwood Aerodrome in readiness for its use by the RAF. The inevitable trench-digging was undertaken at Pengwern Common on Gower, while certain minefields in Swansea and Gower were wired off to protect the public and domestic pets from harm. The preparation of ground for new minefields was also undertaken. Naval mines nicknamed 'toadstools' were laid, coal was stacked at a depot in Cockett, and ammunition was moved into a reinforced magazine near to Llansamlet. Some work on pillbox construction was also performed – certainly at Blackpill and Killay – though it is unclear whether the unit also worked on the placement of the large, oblong concrete anti-tank blocks that lined parts of the promenade and elsewhere in Swansea during and after the war. Bomb craters that were restricting movement in areas such as Oxwich were filled in, while hutments were constructed at several locations, including Mumbles Head, Penclawdd and Langland.[14]

Another unit that was active in improving the defences in Swansea and its surrounding area was the 719th General Construction Company of the Royal Engineers. The company had been based in Acton, West London, but a 28-strong advance party arrived at Porthcawl by train on 21 March 1941, swiftly followed by another 181 men the following day. By early April the company strength had increased to around 260, and intensive physical training was undertaken as well as route marches, coastal mine-laying, hutment construction and sandbag filling. A lot of work on the construction of pillboxes was completed, though the exact location of these defensive works is not clear from the *War Diary*. However, in July, an initial 15 pillboxes were under construction in the Neath Valley and, as the months rolled by, a number of pillboxes were completed along the Blackpill to Gowerton stop line, while the company itself relocated to a site in Llandarcy. The Blackpill-Gowerton stop line was a string of defensive positions that was intended to contain within Gower an enemy who had landed on its beaches. Detachments worked on various projects in Mumbles, Penclawdd, Aberaeron, Wonaston (Monmouthshire) and Margam. Taken in the round, the Royal Engineer companies in and around Swansea might have been involved in a huge amount of largely unglamorous work, but it was certainly of prime importance as Britain prepared to resist a possible invasion.[15]

After its initial issue, the 1941 Swansea defence plan was regularly updated so as to reflect changes that needed to be made. While it no doubt appeared to be an efficient mode of operation, it did lead to Lieutenant Gilmour, assistant adjutant of the 14 Defence Regiment (Royal Artillery) in Swansea, to caustically remark:

> 2 i/c [second in command] is trying to consolidate all
> important points arising from the many defence 'schemes'
> affecting this unit. There are five of these defence schemes,
> all of them having been amended to such an extent as to be
> almost unintelligible. Operational instructions contained in
> them and concerning this unit are as complicated as possible
> and tend to be contradictory. It is forseen [*sic*] that unless
> something is done to clarify the position, the advent of an
> emergency would result in complete chaos and confusion.[16]

As 1942 dawned, there was still a risk, even if of a lesser magnitude, of a German invasion or limited attack on Britain. Germany had deployed parachutists in its successful invasion of Crete in May 1941, though the losses sustained during that operation had been heavy. It was still not possible to rule out a relatively simple surprise raid on important infrastructure targets around Swansea, such as the oil refinery in Llandarcy and the docks in Swansea. Even hit-and-run raids by parachutists or glider- or water-borne troops could help German aims by blowing up industrial installations. And the docks would present a tempting target to the enemy; in 1940 no less than 329,000 tons of processed oil had left the port of Swansea and, as the demand for all sorts of oil-based fuels and lubricants rose in support of the war effort, the annual export figure out of Swansea had reached almost 1,000,000 tons by the end of 1944.

It was also possible that if the anticipated German 1942 summer offensive on the Eastern Front achieved a major success, it might free up enemy units for deployment back to the coastal ports of France in preparation for a cross-Channel invasion. Given that risk, anti-invasion planning remained a priority in Britain. Assuming that during 1942 an enemy invading force, or at least the remnants of it, could actually reach the Swansea shoreline, despite the best efforts of the town's guns and the RAF and the Royal Navy to destroy it at sea, further obstacles were gradually put in place on the ground to delay or prevent it from establishing a secure foothold. A new and expanded defence plan was issued in January 1942 by Lieutenant Colonel V L S Cowley, then the Swansea garrison commander, to take account of changes in the units available for the defence of the town as well as the extensive fortification measures that had been undertaken over the preceding year as men and materials had finally become available for their completion.

Certain beaches around Swansea and Gower were considered suitable for the landing of enemy troops, and by January 1942 no less than 14 of those beaches had been given the protection of a minefield or would soon receive one. These included Port Eynon (which had 363 mines sown across it), as well as Blackpill (180), Oxwich Bay (282), Llanmadoc (242), Three Cliffs' Bay (100) and Rhossili (34 – a surprisingly small number given the length of beach, though the terrain made leaving the beach there a problem in its own right). Even the beach at little Nicholaston Burrows 'benefitted' from 22 mines, while Pobbles Bay was provided with a mere 20, a small number but nevertheless enough to at least slow down an enemy advance.

Designated Home Guard units were responsible for supervising many of the minefields, and they were required to ensure that mines which had become exposed by the weather or other circumstances were promptly reported to headquarters for expert remedial attention. On no account were Home Guard soldiers to enter a minefield, and special wiring was to be erected so that farm or domestic animals were kept out, thus preventing an explosion. In the event of an invasion, Home Guard members would remove the red warning notices from the perimeter of the minefields upon receipt of an order from the garrison commander. Unmarked minefields would hopefully give an invader several nasty surprises.[17]

Dorothy Thomas was a teenager during the war and, after experiencing the terror of bombing raids, moved with her family to a remote house on Gower. She remembered soldiers arriving and placing what looked like upright pit props in the sand of a nearby beach, obviously intended to impede the landing craft of an invader, though, within a few days, they had all been dislodged and washed away by the tide. Although the area was meant to be out of bounds to civilians, it did not prevent the young Dorothy from occasionally approaching the barbed wire around the dunes (which had been mined) to watch friendly aircraft trailing targets across the bay for unseen gunners to fire at for training purposes. Sea mines occasionally floated in on the tide and provided handy rifle practice for the local coastguard, whose men attempted to detonate them from a safe distance.[18]

Also deployed on the roads around Gower and the west of Swansea were Canadian pipe mines, also known as McNaughton tubes, after their inventor, Lieutenant General Andrew McNaughton, a senior Canadian Army officer. The pipes, which were hollow and packed with explosives, were of a 3-inch diameter and had a length of around 55 feet. They could be pushed into the ground at a narrow angle by using a hydraulic jack so that, while one end of the pipe remained close to the surface, its other end could be buried as much as 15 feet deep.

The visible portion of a pipe could be camouflaged so as to render it almost invisible, certainly from the air, so that while friendly forces could move along a road which had the tubes already in place beneath its surface without any ill-effect, an unsuspecting enemy unit could be given a nasty and, indeed, potentially deadly surprise by the sudden detonation of the devices from a distance by unseen hands. It also allowed, for example, for an airfield to be used by friendly forces until the last possible moment before the detonation of the pre-laid tubes damaged the runway and prevented its immediate use by an advancing enemy. A pipe explosive charge could be set off remotely via wire leads by concealed friendly forces, and the resulting explosion could typically produce a crater that was about 28 feet wide and eight feet deep, sufficient to destroy or prevent the easy passage of enemy units, including tanks and other armoured vehicles.

The 179th Tunnelling Company was involved in laying pipes in the Swansea area (other units might also have played a part). During 1941 it had been based in Scarborough from where it had completed work on the Scatsta Aerodrome on the Shetland Isles. Work was underway on pipe laying in Swansea during November 1941, even if getting the town's commanding officer to accept responsibility for the future control of the tubes proved to be difficult until representations were made further up the chain of command to resolve the issue. Tube-laying work was underway or had been completed at locations that included Parkmill, Dunvant, Langland Bay, Porthcawl and Limpert Bay near Aberthaw. Pipes were eventually buried at around 30 locations around Swansea as well as on Gower, including sites at Oxwich, Port Eynon, Blackpill, Gowerton, Parkmill, Llanrhidian, Bishopston, Dunvant and Killay. In Killay, during December 1941, it was stated that 27 tubes had been buried, forming a formidable tank trap. However, it seems that those tubes had been deployed some time earlier and they had not at that time been filled with explosives. It became apparent that water had seeped into the tubes so they would need to be removed for drying out before the explosives could be inserted and the ends sealed before being reburied.[19]

Another defensive measure that was deployed at several Swansea and Gower locations was that of the flame fougasse. This was a relatively simple device that nevertheless could have a devastating effect on any enemy unit that was unfortunate enough to be on the receiving end of it. It consisted of a 40-gallon steel drum, one end of which had an explosive charge, while the drum itself was typically filled with a mixture of petrol and gas oil. Drums were usually buried at the side of important roads and orientated to point towards the desired target area. Detonation was achieved by passing an electrical charge through the 100-yard-long wire leads to the explosive charge, with the resulting explosion rupturing the drum casing and sending a ten-foot-wide jet of flame over a distance of about 30 yards. This would engulf any enemy soldiers or vehicles, unlucky enough to be in its path, in a veritable ball of flame.

In Swansea, flame fougasse devices were placed at the sides of several important roads, such as those in Fforestfach, Killay, Blackpill, Pentrechwyth, Morriston, Mumbles and Three Crosses. Detonation would be effected at the appropriate time by designated members of various Home Guard units. In all, there were 12 flame fougasse sites as well as a small, mobile unit that consisted of ten or so Home Guard members who had access to a car and a lorry as well as ten flame fougasse barrels, plus the necessary charges, batteries and fuse wire. This unit would be required to react to the prevailing circumstances following an invasion and, when needed, to quickly deploy the devices along currently unprotected roads down which an enemy was seen to be advancing.

Those units that were responsible for firing McNaughton tubes and flame fougasse devices were only to do so in the immediate presence of the enemy, while anti-tank and shrapnel mines were not to be laid until after an 'action stations' order had been issued, since those devices were prone to deterioration if placed in the ground for lengthy periods before any invasion actually took place. The sites where these portable mines were to be laid would be determined in advance and, once laid, the locations would be made known to all nearby troops as well as the local civilian population and fleeing refugees.

If the enemy succeeded in getting off the beaches and into the surrounding countryside, the 1942 defence plan envisaged that:

The basis of defence is a net work [*sic*] of defended localities
by which the enemy is bound to be contacted no matter in
what direction he may seek to advance, so that whichever way
he turns he will be met by small arms fire, flame throwers,
bombs, tank traps, booby traps and the like from every
direction.

To meet that aim, provision was made to slow up the
advance by the use of individual strong-points that were dotted
across the town and its surrounding districts. In 1942, these
strong-points were far more prevalent than had been the case
in 1941, and that enabled a number of 'defended localities' to
be established across the borough. Indeed, at least 119 pillbox
defensive structures were built, excluding those that were
within the docks area or on the Gower peninsula. Each pillbox
was usually supported by a network of trenches, earth banks or
even local houses from which supporting troops could prevent
the enemy from closing in on the structure's 'blind spots', those
areas not able to be covered by gunfire from its embrasures.
Pillboxes were typically sited in positions that allowed them to
exercise control over important roads, railway lines and other
infrastructure, and they were usually manned by a few men
with support from perhaps ten or so comrades. There were,
for example, three pillboxes in Llansamlet square, three on
the Ynysforgan viaduct, four at the Elba works in Gowerton,
four in Dunvant, seven in Killay, three in Ravenhill, four
around Danygraig cemetery and nine in Blackpill, with dozens
of others being scattered around the borough. The weapons
available for pillbox defence purposes were primarily rifles,
but might also include a machine gun, a Lewis gun (a light
machine-gun-type weapon), a Blacker Bombard (also called
a Spigot Mortar and capable of being used against men or
tanks, depending on the ammunition selected), Tommy guns
(much beloved by American prohibition-era gangsters) and
self-igniting phosphorous grenades.

The plan noted that the availability of pillboxes formed

only a part of the defence of a locality. During action, no more than two or three men should remain in them at any one time and the others should take up positions in nearby houses, in slit trenches or behind earth banks. Enemy soldiers sheltering in ground that could not be fired upon by the occupants of a pillbox should be fired at by those who had taken up defensive positions nearby. In a situation where enemy paratroopers had landed, it was incumbent on each defended locality to immediately send out patrols to engage and dispose of the attackers. Home Guard members were to patrol constantly between defended localities so that an enemy would find it impossible to approach a position without being detected. When observed, small parties of the enemy were to be ambushed, while larger groups should be fired on at long range so as to disrupt their plans for deployment. Under the 1942 plan, outposts were no longer to be defended on a 'to the last man and last round' basis but, rather, when a strong-point became hard-pressed by the enemy, its defenders should try and retire onto other defensive works in their rear. Any defenders who unavoidably found themselves in the rear of an advancing enemy were to emerge from their hiding places at an appropriate moment and attempt to engage the enemy and disrupt its plans.

The docks area would be a key target for an invading force since, if the dock facilities could be captured largely intact, it would make the subsequent docking and unloading of the enemy's follow-up troops and equipment easier than if they had to be offloaded onto a sandy beach, thus being much more subject to the vagaries of tide and weather. For defence purposes, the docks area was split into the Eastern and South Dock sectors, with the River Tawe broadly marking the boundary between the two, and with the Jersey Marine and Oystermouth roads forming the northern boundary. To restrict access if an enemy were to attack from the landward side, roadblocks were to be established at Port Tennant Road (at two locations), the Burrows Inn and Burrows Place, the main docks entrance, Gloucester Place, York Street, Wind Street, Cambrian Place, Pier Street, Somerset Place and the Queen's Dock entrance.

The force available to defend the two docks sectors was assembled from a veritable hotchpotch of units and, as regards the Eastern sector in early 1942, it included men from the 194th Company of the Royal Pioneers, anti-aircraft gun crews, barrage balloon operatives, several Home Guard contingents, and a mere ten men from the South Wales Borderers. Altogether, it amounted to around 700 souls though, somewhat alarmingly, there were still deficiencies in the number of weapons available. For example, although the Great Western Railway company Home Guard unit could provide 154 men as a reserve force, they came along with only 56 weapons. As noted, this was not a major issue when all was relatively quiet and only a portion of the men were on guard duty at any one time. Rifle-sharing when an enemy was at the lock gates was, of course, a quite different proposition, but given the general military equipment shortages in Britain at the time it was simply a case of soldiering on and hoping for the best. For the smaller South Dock sector, there were around 250 defenders but only 137 rifles, 13 Tommy guns and seven machine guns. Additionally, the officer in overall command of the docks area had a reserve available to him that consisted of 51 men of the Royal Marine Light Infantry as well as 144 members of the Movement Control force.

Some of the defending forces were assigned to act as a garrison for the static defensive structures that were spread around the docks area. On the Eastern Sector (comprised largely of the King's, Queen's and Prince of Wales Docks with their surrounding infrastructure), there were 21 pillboxes of conventional construction as well as two of the Allan-Williams type – a fairly small, partially-buried metal dome that could rotate 360 degrees while manned by one (possibly two) incredibly plucky soldiers, and from which could be fired a range of light weapons. In an invasion situation, the pillboxes plus a few sandbagged posts would be garrisoned by a mix of South Wales Borderers, RAF personnel, plus Home Guard members from the Great Western Railway company and the Magnesium Metals Corporation. This would amount to around 150 men, some of whom could be armed with a mix of rifles and heavy or light machine guns. In the South Dock sector there were nine pillboxes and two Allan-Williams domes, as well as some sandbagged positions, strengthened buildings and a bricked trench. The number of defenders assigned to those positions amounted to 77 men with the usual mix of weaponry.

The aim was to prevent the enemy gaining access to the docks area by land or by sea so that its facilities remained under friendly control. If it proved necessary to take drastic measures in the light of a deteriorating military situation, then Great Western Railway employees would be instructed by the military, via the naval officer in charge in Swansea, to take steps to damage those dock facilities that would prove useful to an enemy, assisted by any men who did not have a personal weapon to hand and thus could not contribute to active defence duties. The work would consist of the dismantling and removal of specific machinery parts, as well as the opening of bridges and the blocking of lock gates.

The Gower sector of Swansea was that area west of a line that ran roughly from Blackpill to Gowerton. Once again, the force allotted to the defence of this area in 1942 was of a mix and match nature, given the scarcity of better suited units. It included the 15th Home Guard Battalion as well as around 50 men from the 12th Home Guard Battalion. Additionally, the Tyneside Scottish (the Black Watch) provided a company of men, while the 194th Company of the Pioneer Corps supplied a detachment. The 14th Defence Regiment of the Royal Artillery also weighed in with a troop of four guns of 75mm calibre. The defenders were required to defend the approaches to Fairwood Airport as well as any of the Gower beaches that might be used by the enemy in an attempted invasion. As regards the airfield, defence of the area within its perimeter was the responsibility of the RAF personnel based there, while elements of the other units would take up fixed positions on the approaches to the base and engage an attacker from whatever shelter could be found.

A mobile column would also be formed which could rapidly move to any Gower locality that was under serious threat. Various detachments of Home Guard members would, when an invasion seemed imminent, patrol the exits from beaches, engaging the enemy as required. D Company of the 30th Battalion, the South Wales Borderers, was charged with the defence of the National Oil Refinery in Llandarcy, as well as that of Kilvey Hill where the possibility of a landing by paratroopers was thought possible. A platoon of about 30 men was available to the Swansea garrison commander as a reserve force, and that force was likely to be deployed at Jersey Marine until relieved by a Home Guard unit during an emergency.

Under the 1942 Swansea Defence Scheme, it was left to the individual units of heavy, light and anti-aircraft guns (as well as the 'Z'-type rocket batteries that were located around the town) and searchlight batteries to make their own arrangements for the protection of their equipment and personnel. That would involve fortifying the gun positions and sending out regular patrols so as to quickly spot any approaching enemy formations. Naturally, Home Guard or other units would offer assistance where it became necessary in a developing situation.

The issue of roadblocks was particularly difficult since, while it was essential to hamper the easy movement by road of an enemy force, it was also vital that defenders, reinforcements and even refugees were not unnecessarily delayed in their movements into or out of a contested area. The Swansea defence plan deemed the Neath-Lonlas-Morriston-Llangyfelach route an important 'red route', where the roads comprising it were only to be completely blocked on the order of the garrison commander, while a designated 'yellow route' ran from Morriston to Clydach and was intended for the use of refugee traffic. Initially, other roads would be blocked so as to allow the passage of one-way traffic only, until orders were received to complete the block. That would be achieved by using rails or concrete cylinders that were to be kept close at hand, ensuring the speedy obstruction of a road during a crisis. The borough police would be responsible for traffic control at roadblocks, while the credentials of anyone looking to pass through them would be checked by the Home Guard or other military personnel.

A number of 'vulnerable points' were identified in the defence scheme plan and each of these locations required a dedicated guard to be mounted, depending on the apparent seriousness of the situation. The telephone exchanges in the docks area and that at the High Street Railway Station were thought of as vulnerable points, as were the telephone facilities of the London, Midland and Scottish Railway Company in Swansea's Victoria Railway Station. Additionally, the railway tunnels at Cockett, Lonlas, Ynysforgan and Penllergaer were each to be patrolled by two-man teams, while the Landore viaduct and a number of important signal boxes would also be protected by guards. The possibility of sabotage attacks was not ruled out, and guards were assigned to a number of important industrial concerns, including the Tir John Power Station, Unit Superheaters, the Cwmfelin Tinplate Works, the Dyffryn, Upper Fforest and Morriston Tinplate Works, and the Baldwins steel plant among others.[20]

The scheme also tackled the surprisingly thorny issue of the ringing of church bells. Since June 1940, the Ministry of Home Security, in consultation with ecclesiastical authorities, had stated that in future church bells should only be rung in a situation where enemy paratroopers or glider-borne infantry were seen to be descending. Church bells throughout the country therefore remained silent throughout each week and, in the event that they were heard, it would clearly signify to the public that an invasion was underway. In the early part of September 1940, it had seemed to the British chiefs of staff that favourable weather conditions and reports about enemy troop and shipping movements in France suggested that an invasion might well be imminent. On the evening of 7 September the codeword 'Cromwell' was issued by the general headquarters of the Home Forces to the eastern and southern commands, requiring them to ready their units for 'immediate action'. In itself, this did not mean that an invasion was underway but, rather, that a high level of vigilance was required and units should be prepared for action at short notice.[21] Some local Home Guard commanders apparently misunderstood the meaning of 'immediate action' and arranged the sounding of church bells in their areas, indicating that an invasion was actually taking place.[22] Swansea was one such area, and a Mumbles air raid warden, Laurie Latchford, later noted in his diary that he was awoken by his wife, who had heard the bell of St Peter's Church ringing at nearby Newton at 3.15am on the morning of 8 September. Dressing quickly, he set off to establish just what was happening, though he was soon advised to return home for the moment and to listen for the sound of the siren that would tell him if his presence was actually required.

The bell had eventually stopped ringing and all seemed normal, though Latchford spent an anxious half an hour peering into the blackness out to sea from an upstairs window in his home before the bell commenced its ringing again. Now dressed in his full warden's kit – lacking a rifle but rather optimistically carrying an Indian club that he used for exercise purposes – he set off to investigate the situation further. He was promptly challenged by several young Home Guardsmen who pointed their rifles rather nervously in his direction before telling him that over 200 fully-armed men were present and ready to defend the Mumbles area against an invasion, with many more on the way. The bell soon stopped ringing again and the affair fizzled out. It had merely been a false alarm.[23]

In an effort to avoid this type of confusion arising again, the Swansea Defence Scheme addressed the matter directly. The ringing of church bells would indeed denote the landing of enemy airborne forces, though just who could order the church sextons to perform the bell-ringing task was carefully set out. In the urban areas, the order to sound the bells could only be given by someone who held the rank of battalion commander, and then only after any report of enemy airborne landings had been carefully verified. Such an order could be given in person or by a written order over the officer's signature, while in the case of rural Gower, the order to ring the bells at Bishopston, Pennard, Penclawdd and several other locations could only be given by designated officers of the 15th Battalion, Glamorgan Home Guard.

One of the final matters considered in the Swansea Defence Scheme was the issue of prisoners of war. Assuming it was still a practical proposition following an invasion, the collecting point for captured enemy personnel was, unsurprisingly, to be His Majesty's Prison on Oystermouth Road. Once enemy personnel were imprisoned there, additional guards would be provided by members of the Swansea constabulary and the Corps of Military Police in numbers equal to the scale of the task. 'Fifth columnists', who might be clad in British uniforms or civilian clothing, who were suspected of being involved in plans for espionage or sabotage, would usually be handed over to the police for questioning in the first instance. Uniformed members of the enemy's forces who had been captured would be relieved of all weapons and equipment, except for identity tokens, cash or valuables, metal helmets, gas masks, badges of rank, and military decorations, while enemy officers were to be segregated from their men. Other documents and effects which were not personal to the captive were to be collected and placed in sandbags and labelled with the prisoner's name, unit, date and place of capture. The prisoner could then be interrogated on matters that were relevant to local tactical issues before being taken from the prison under escort to a holding cage in Port Talbot.[24]

A final element in the arrangements for defending Britain concerned opportunities to attack the enemy after it had established a foothold in the invasion area and forced defenders to retreat. The organisation involved was so secret that it simply did not appear in the Swansea defence plan at all. Indeed, even today, over 80 years later, archival information relating to what would have possibly been the defenders of Swansea's final attempt to hinder the enemy remains hard to find. In 1940, with the threat of invasion looming, Peter Fleming (the brother of James Bond creator, Ian) was working within MI(R) – Military Intelligence (Research) – an office that was tasked with the creation of small, self-contained units that would stay behind in concealed hideouts in areas that were newly occupied by the enemy before emerging at night to harass the invader and destroy his stores and equipment, while generally making a nuisance of themselves. They were referred to as Auxiliary Units, a suitably vague term that gave no clear indication of what their role actually was, and they came under the control of general headquarters of the Home Forces rather than the Swansea garrison commander. By the end of August 1940, units were in place from the north coast of east Scotland down to Land's End, and along the south coast of Wales as far west as Pembroke Dock.

Auxiliary Units consisted of six or so men, led by a sergeant, each of whom had a pistol and a fighting knife, while there was also some access to rifles and sten guns as well as explosives. If the weaponry seems limited, it must be noted that the units were intended for hit-and-run operations and were not expected to normally engage the enemy in fierce fire-fights. The unit members were taught weaponry, unarmed combat, field-craft and how to use explosives to best effect against the enemy and its equipment. Their operational bases (filled with bunk beds and all the equipment that they might need) were deliberately located in remote and hard to get to locations or in rugged areas which enemy troops might dismiss as being not worth closely searching. A hideout often took the form of a large metal, arched 'tube', tall enough for a man to stand up in, which would be buried in the ground at a suitable location, with a well-concealed entry point and an escape tunnel that allowed for a speedy exit.

Many recruits for the Auxiliary Units came from the local Home Guard battalions, though some specialists were transferred in from the regular Army. It was common practice for a prominent local farmer or landowner to be discreetly approached by an MI(R) officer with a view to secretly forming a local unit, often consisting of capable men that they knew and trusted and who worked on their land. Knowledge of the local terrain and its people, ideas on good hiding places as well as knowledge of safe short-cuts across the fields, were all valuable bits of information that an invader would simply not possess. Many such recruits would also have some experience in the mechanics of heavy farm machinery and thus be well placed to know just where to place explosive charges on enemy vehicles parked up for the night. It was clear that the Auxiliary Units could not drive out an invader but they could, perhaps, seriously disrupt its activities while friendly forces prepared for a counter-attack.

Given the secret nature of its role, information on the Auxiliary Units in and around Swansea in 1940 is very patchy. It seems that there were 17 patrols in Glamorgan, while Pembroke had eight, Carmarthen seven and Monmouth another eight. In the Swansea area there were patrols in

Pontardawe, Skewen and Hendy, though there appear to be none in locations that were closer to the town centre. This might be due simply to gaps in the archival record or the fact that perhaps potential base locations near to the town – even in fairly rural areas – were considered too busy for the placement of a unit. It is known that the Pontardawe patrol was led by Thomas John Williams of Rhos, Pontardawe, an underground haulier. Under his command were two other men who worked in mining, a grocery shop assistant, an apprentice motor coach builder, a pharmaceutical student and a sheet metal worker. The buried operational base of the patrol still survives (though now flooded) in woodland at Cilybebyll and, happily, as the feared invasion never came, its willing recruits never had to live a semi-subterranean life, fraught with danger, as the enemy paced back and forth above their heads.[25]

Beyond the mainly land-orientated Swansea defence plan, there was one more area where the town received protection from the attentions of the enemy. Though it had little direct impact on the day-to-day lives of most of the citizens of Swansea, it was necessary to try and protect the shipping and sailors that regularly departed from or arrived at its port from enemy mines and submarines. For military purposes, the waters around Swansea came under the Royal Navy's western approaches command, and in June 1940 the area was under the command of Vice Admiral Wilfred Tomkinson, an officer who had the notable distinction of having been the first commanding officer of the famous battlecruiser HMS *Hood*, in 1920. He had control of two anti-submarine trawlers and three yachts in Swansea, as well as three mine-detector ships, nine trawlers and three drifters for use in detecting and destroying mines in the local coastal waters. The onshore naval base in Swansea, HMS Lucifer, was housed in the old Guildhall on Somerset Place, while minesweeping and coastal defence personnel who were moved into Swansea used the impressive (and still standing) Colonial Building on the Strand for billeting purposes.

The Germans developed several types of naval mines for use in the Second World War which could be deployed by ship, submarine or aircraft. Detonation was achieved by direct contact with the mine, by interference with its magnetic field due to the close passing of a metal ship, or by way of an acoustic trigger that was activated by the noise of a ship's propellors. Minesweeping was dangerous work that was often performed in difficult weather, and in among the many successes there were the unavoidable failures. As early as 5 October 1939, the steamship *Marwarri* was damaged by a German submarine-laid mine about three miles from the *Scarweather* light-vessel in the Bristol Channel. The area of sea that she was damaged in had previously been swept by a minesweeper, and it was concluded that the enemy must have deployed magnetic mines at that location and they had not been detonated in the normal manner. The *Marwarri* was deliberately run aground near to Mumbles before being towed to Swansea, where she underwent repairs. There had been two fatalities in the incident. Similarly, the steamship *Protesilaus* struck a mine off Rotherslade Bay on 5 December 1939, resulting in her being towed to Swansea for repairs, though the ship was later declared to be a total loss given the extent of the damage.[26]

In the autumn of 1940, the enemy was busy mine-laying (by aircraft and E-boat) across the east coast of Britain as well as in the English Channel and the south coast ports. Mines were laid off Swansea during this operation, and in December 1940 the minesweeping whaler *Southern Chief* detonated four acoustic mines within a few minutes of exiting the port of Swansea, before the fifth explosion damaged the vessel itself. It wasn't just the actions of the enemy that had to be endured: in January 1942 Her Majesty's Trawler (and minesweeper) *Rosette*, a requisitioned ship that was working out of Swansea, managed to run down and sink the *Scarweather* light-vessel, which was moored off Sker Point in the Bristol Channel. Happily, there seem to have been no casualties.

On a brighter note, in October 1940 officers of the western approaches command played an important role in recovering an acoustic mine that had been washed ashore at the mouth of the River Ogmore, near Porthcawl in the Vale of Glamorgan. A detailed examination of the device allowed the development of what was called the 'Kango vibrating hammer' (or SA – sweep acoustic), a device that could be fitted in the bows of a sweeping vessel or streamed outboard from it, allowing the detonation of acoustic mines at a safe distance. It was an important breakthrough in the battle against enemy mines.[27]

While efforts were being made to keep friendly sailors out of the water, in the unhappy event that they should nevertheless find themselves floating in the sea off Swansea and its adjacent coastline, there was one more service that could be depended on to come to their aid. Swansea had had a lifeboat station since 1835 and, in 1863, the Royal National Lifeboat Institution (RNLI) took over the operation of the voluntary service. The service still operated during the war, though the consent of the Admiralty, via the naval base in the town, had to be obtained before launching. Lifeboat crew member Tom Ace recalled that in the war years the lifeboat was called out on 23 occasions, and often undertook very dangerous rescues, saving 137 lives. Notable rescues include 37 crew members of the SS *Eldonpark* which ran onto the rocks at Port Eynon in February 1940. When Her Majesty's Canadian Ship, the frigate *Chebogue*, was torpedoed in October 1944, she was taken in tow and, after a journey of 1,000 miles, reached Port Talbot before being released, due to the stormy weather posing a danger to both the towing and towed vessels. Despite dropping anchor, the *Chebogue* was soon dragged onto the rocks. In Mumbles, Tom Ace found that members of the regular crew could not be quickly contacted due to the storm damaging telephone lines.

Undaunted, he quickly visited several local clubs to 'pick up the old stagers', experienced men who were readily available. Although two of them were over 70 years of age and two more were in their 60s, they were made of stern stuff and, despite the prospect of setting out to sea in gale-force winds, they did not hesitate to help. Coxswain William J Gammon approached the *Chebogue* around a dozen times – the sea rising and falling rapidly – and each time he did so several of the crew jumped onto the lifeboat, one man breaking a leg in the process. The entire crew of 42 men were saved and Gammon was subsequently awarded the RNLI gold medal, while Tom Ace (bowman) and William Gilbert Davies (mechanic) received bronze awards. The naval commander in Swansea described the work of the entire crew as 'magnificent'.[28]

With the plan for the defence of Swansea updated and hopefully able to meet all eventualities, it was still important to check that each unit involved in the defence of the town knew its role and could act with vigour and assurance, should the anticipated invasion arrive. To that end, it would be necessary to run exercises that would test the unit commanders and their men under simulated battle conditions, allowing lessons to be learned that could be applied in the event of a real invasion. It soon became apparent that there was indeed much that needed attention.

CHAPTER 11

Testing the Defences

ON 5 FEBRUARY 1942, the officer commanding the German 4th Airborne Battalion issued a secret order that would have chilled the blood of the people of Swansea, had they been able to see it. It stated bluntly: 'The invasion of Britain will commence on night 7/8 February. The task of the 4th A/B [Airborne] Bn. is the capture of FAIRWOOD AERODROME on GOWER PENINSULA.' The order went on to say that a continuous aerial bombardment of the area surrounding the airfield would take place over the night of 7–8 February, as a prelude to the dropping of paratroopers at three important Gower locations (Willoxton crossroads and the Pengwern and Clyne commons) that were in close proximity to the target airstrip.

Happily, the unsuspecting Swansea population had no immediate cause for concern; the order had been issued by a Lieutenant Colonel A Von Bum, a fictional Nazi officer whose name had been dreamt up by the commander of the Swansea garrison, Lieutenant Colonel V L S Cowley, DSO, MC. It is an old military adage that no plan survives its first contact with the enemy, and Lieutenant Colonel Cowley knew that it was necessary to test Swansea's anti-invasion defences as far as was practicable, so that unexpected developments that might arise during a real invasion could be experienced and learnt from in the absence of a dangerous enemy. The plan could then be suitably adjusted in the light of experience.

The regular Army was well versed in the staging of

training exercises where perhaps 'red force' would attempt to prise an objective from the control of 'white force', or some similar concoction of fictional unit names. The 7–8 February 1942 exercise in Swansea, one of several that were staged over time, was given the rather obvious codename of 'Fairwood', and was intended to test out the aerodrome defences under simulated battle conditions, as well as assessing the efficiency of communications between units in the field and those located at headquarters. Overall, the exercise would involve various units at differing times between the hours of 9am on 7 February and 4pm the following day. The aerodrome would be defended by RAF ground forces, a company of the Tyneside Scottish, an artillery unit and elements of the 15th Battalion of the Glamorgan Home Guard. Acting as the invading Nazis would be a contingent of the South Wales Borderers, backed up by seven platoons (around 200 men) of the 12th, 14th and 18th battalions of the Glamorgan Home Guard and one platoon of its 15th Battalion. It was anticipated that units of the RAF would provide plenty of noise and distractions by performing dummy bomb runs and the dropping of parachutes (without the requisite soldiers attached to them) to simulate an aerial invasion.

After the scene had been set for both the attacking and defending units, a number of military umpires would be present to give advice on the scenario's developing situation, much of which would be outside of the immediate knowledge of the participating units, thus helping to create the 'fog of war', which required quick decision-making when the full picture was not clear. At certain times the arrival of enemy soldiers would be suddenly announced by an umpire, and the defending troops would be expected to be speedily redeployed by their officers to best meet the new challenge. The umpires were all military men, with many of them having had experience during the 1914–18 conflict. Indeed, the senior umpire was Lieutenant Colonel O S Portsmouth, a Swansea architect who had served in the Middle East during the First World War.

Efforts were made to make the 'battle' as realistic as possible. For example, where reserve ammunition was not currently available for particular weapons at a location, then those weapons could not be deployed in the exercise, thus simulating the supply difficulties that might arise in a real-world situation. Similarly, pre-set explosive devices or booby traps could not be triggered if the men who were designated to operate them had been unable to reach their locations in the confusion and disruption caused by an 'invasion'. Additionally, the invading 'paratroopers' would be expected to allow for some delay in assembly at their landing points, so as to simulate the chaos often experienced after a hasty descent by parachute into enemy-occupied terrain. As well as the 'enemy paratroopers', the exercise also allowed for 40 seaborne 'Germans' to struggle ashore at Brandy Cove, while another 400 would be reported as having landed in Llanelli before advancing on Loughor.

The outcome of the exercise sadly left a lot to be desired, as the serious intent of the event had apparently not been impressed enough on certain unit commanders. One Home Guard detachment had been delayed in reaching its deployment point because its men had apparently been first required to attend a Sunday church parade. Others were detained for the laying of earthen sods, unimportant tasks when compared to their defensive roles in an invasion exercise. One officer had found himself hampered by the non-appearance of a radio transmitter, an obviously essential item for the job of sending and receiving instructions. He had contented himself by sitting down and merely wringing his hands, while it was later stated by those in authority that he should have found out what was going on in the surrounding area as there was no place for procrastination in a crisis. A number of men had been at a loss to know just what was expected of them at particular phases, and they had consequently spent a lot of time merely wandering aimlessly around the exercise area to no real effect.

Even the umpires themselves came in for criticism. They were there to make the exercise a success, and to devise situations that tested both attacker and defender. In practice, some of them had made decisions which immediately put out of action a large number of participants. While this may well have reflected the possible situation on the ground during a real attack, it did little to give those taking part in the exercise a prolonged chance to experience a fast-changing battle situation when they were prematurely deemed, by an over-zealous umpire, to be 'dead' or 'captured'. Even the 'dead' were occasionally prone to getting up and walking around (probably due to boredom) to add to the general confusion.

Despite the problems experienced, a number of lessons were learned. There was a lack of spare parts for the machine guns that were deployed in defence of the aerodrome, meaning that they were likely to fail after prolonged use early on in any real engagement. A number of men were required to move towards the Fairwood Aerodrome to aid its defence in the event of an attack, and it was apparent that, once they arrived at their assigned area, they had little idea of what else was required of them.

The transmission of information between units had proven to be poor and that needed immediate steps to be taken to improve things for the future, while headquarters units needed to identify and set up alternative locations that they could quickly move to if their present position was at risk of being overrun by the enemy. A wood near to the aerodrome had given some of the invaders an easy route for attacking along, and it was important that in a real incident the wood was mined before the enemy had a chance to enter it. It was recognised that the exercise needed to be re-run in the near future with a view to achieving improvements in the performance of the units taking part.

Perhaps in the light of the disappointing performance seen during the Fairwood exercise, another dummy invasion was staged over the 21–22 February 1942, and it was an altogether more ambitious affair. It had the codename of 'Duckling', and no doubt its organisers hoped that it would turn out to be not too ugly in the standard of performance of those taking part. The scenario assumed that the Germans had managed to stabilise matters on the Russian Front, so freeing up units for deployment to the West. These newly available forces enabled the invasion of Britain to be undertaken, and the indefatigable Lieutenant Colonel Von Bum was again assigned the task of annoying the defenders of Swansea. He planned to use his airborne force to attack the defended areas of Blackpill, Killay, Dunvant and Gowerton, while the guns on Mumbles Head would also be assaulted. It was intended that Swansea Docks would be secured intact to allow for the arrival of reinforcement-carrying German troopships.

The scenario contained no less than 36 pre-set incidents that were designed to test the defenders to the limit. They included enemy paratroopers landing on Rhossili and Fairwood, a land attack on Mumbles Head, six fast troop-landing craft attempting to reach the docks, as well as poison gas attacks at several locations across Swansea. Once again, a mixed bag of defending units were involved in the defence of the threatened areas. Live ammunition was not carried by attackers or defenders, though there was an abundant use of thunder flashes and smoke gas generators to add to the realism of a simulated battle. Roadblocks (covering one half of a road so that important traffic could still pass through during the exercise) would be in place, and 'fifth columnists', civilians who would try to assist the invader, would also be deployed to add to the confusion. Even the treatment of casualties was simulated, with local boy scouts being used as wounded soldiers, all needing to be safely evacuated and adding to the administrative headaches of the hard-pressed unit commanders. The exercise was expected to provide important information on how well the units involved with coastal defence around Swansea worked together in a crisis, and also their likely effectiveness in protecting the town and the Gower peninsula against invasion.

Once again, though the exercise produced much useful information to help inform the improvement of the defence plans, there were still a number of concerns. It was apparent that the Mumbles area was inadequately guarded, and any determined attack by an enemy was almost bound to succeed, a worrying prospect since the guns on the Mumbles headland were an important aspect of the seaward defence of the town. The guns were also vulnerable to attack from the air, and a lack of effective dugouts or other defensive structures near to them meant that they were likely to be rendered impotent when their crews understandably sought shelter during an air raid.

The defences at Gowerton were noted as being especially weak (though further training of its defenders would help), while Clyne Woods provided an enemy with plenty of concealment opportunities to shield an advance, though the placing of anti-personnel mines and barbed wire would assist in that area. There was also a noticeable gap in the defence line between Cockett and Swansea that could be quickly filled by the deployment of a normally static unit supported by a mobile force. Communications between units had again been poor, while those involved in the exercise had tended to focus only on what was in front of them, paying little attention to what was happening on their right or left. Indeed, several units had been bypassed by the enemy without even realising it.

On the brighter side, it was reported that, unlike in the earlier 'Fairwood' exercise, on this occasion there was hardly a man who did not play a useful part in the engagement. Every attacker or defender found himself fully involved and the men went away with the feeling that a worthwhile exercise had been undertaken and their time had not been wasted.[1]

Several members of the GPO Home Guard seemed to have vigorously taken part in this exercise (some blood was inadvertently shed), and a GPO staff newsletter issued in March 1942 (one of a series published at the request of the Swansea Telephone Area War Comforts Committee), noted:

> Our big 'Field Day' as Home Guards went off very much according to plan, and many tales of hair breadth escapes, prodigious numbers of prisoners, dead who 'wouldn't lie down' are the order of the day. Some had all the excitement, while others languished in the backwaters bringing down troop carriers and dive bombers with an AA gun fashioned from a cable trailer and a length of asbestos duct for the gun barrel… Some were in a melee where hand-to-hand fighting resulted in 'Tapped claret', illustrating that the old spirit is still there and that many stout hearts beat beneath a battledress blouse. With wise and courageous direction there is little doubt that, in spite of many 'wise cracks', the Home Guard is a force to be reckoned with when the testing time comes.[2]

It was not only the military who had their plans tested by way of staged exercises during 1942. Over the weekend of 7–8 March, a civil defence exercise was organised in conjunction with yet another invasion scenario. Under the codename 'Gower', this ambitious project sought to stretch and test the civil defence arrangements and their coordination with the military in the aftermath of a theoretical air raid. Swansea, of course, already had the dubious benefit of having been subjected to heavy attacks from the air during 1941, and a new exercise in 1942 would provide an opportunity to see if any changes already made to the defence plans in the light of earlier experience would actually work in practice.

The Gower exercise was planned to take place between 8pm

on Saturday, 7 March, and 6pm on Sunday, 8 March 1942. The military element of the exercise commenced on the evening of 7 March, and assumed that the enemy had succeeded in landing in a number of areas across the south of England, and Swansea was about to be bombed as part of the ongoing enemy actions. Among the tasks to be performed in Swansea was the theoretical immobilisation of equipment at the docks so as to render some of its facilities, at least temporarily, useless for the purposes of the enemy.

The civil defence scenario commenced with mock dive-bombing attacks on the town and the docks for a 45-minute period, commencing on the morning of 8 March. The impact of the fake attacks was accentuated by the use of thunder flash explosions and it was a given, that, for the purpose of the exercise, a number of roads (ten in total) had been made impassable to traffic by bomb damage. These included Orchard Street, St Helen's Road, Walter Road and Queens Road, Mumbles, among others. At pre-set time intervals during the morning, the exercise also simulated that the control and report centre at the Guildhall had been damaged with a consequential severing of telephone cables. That development required the urgent relocation of the staff affected to Sketty Hall, while presumed bomb damage to the main telephone exchange in Swansea would result in a total failure of the town's telephone system. Communication for civil defence purposes would henceforth need to be completed by using the civil defence messenger service. The various 'incidents' that were reported to the control centre involved trapped people, damaged houses, broken water mains and gas pipes, blocked roads and damage to elements of the civil defence infrastructure that included a direct hit on the town's fire station. The effects of an enemy attack using poisonous gas were also simulated, with both people and equipment being contaminated and needing specialised attention.

The list of civil defence organisation units involved in the

236

exercise scenarios illustrates the extensive and specialised arrangements that had evolved for handling war-related emergencies. Naturally, the police, fire service and air raid wardens would all play significant roles in any incident, but there were also decontamination squads, mobile cleansing units, a mobile first aid post, gas identification officers and parties that dealt with the rescue of people and the demolition of dangerous structures. There was also a need for work parties to complete urgent repairs to roads, railway transport, electricity and water systems, as well as first aid personnel, messengers, a mortuary van, ambulances and also cars for those injured people who were classified as 'sitting cases' and did not need an ambulance to spirit them away for treatment. The exercise was designed to present the commanders of the various teams with urgent and often conflicting requests, so that they would have to take some tough decisions as to the real priorities, some of them of a simulated 'life or death' nature, among a welter of demands.

Regrettably, no obvious analysis of the results of the civil defence element of the exercise seems to be available, though the military did comment on the efficiency of the liaison between itself and the civil defence authorities – and it was not a happy picture. Information from the civil defence teams indicating that certain roads were impassable due to rubble or gas was simply not passed on to those who might need to know, hampering the movements of local military units as well as arriving reinforcements. In contrast, it was noted that members of the police force frequently provided timely and important information, and that a proactive attitude needed to be reflected in the wider civil defence organisation during a real emergency. Even a bland periodic report that all was well in a particular location had a value, since it prevented a military commander from fretting about an area simply because no information from it had been forthcoming. If all was indeed well and had been properly reported, a commander would be free to devote his energies to those locations where things were proving to be rather more problematic.

On the military side of things, once again communication from individual units to the various headquarters had proven to be poor, and the forced evacuation of headquarters staff to a new location was not organised efficiently, meaning that reports were often sent to the location that was no longer in use, resulting in delay at a time of staged crisis. It was noted that defenders once again tended to face in the direction from which an attack was expected, and some were caught out when the 'invaders' arrived from unanticipated directions or advanced towards unexpected objectives. During the exercise, though some units were notionally firing their weapons for prolonged periods, no requests were made for a resupply of ammunition, a matter that could not be addressed at short notice in the event of an invasion. On the plus side, the use of Home Guard cadets as runners to carry messages proved to be a success.[3]

Even the higher echelons of the civil and military defence organisation in Swansea were not immune from having to take part in simulated invasion situations. On 30 August 1942, H L Lang-Coath, the ARP Controller for Swansea, supported by the commander of the Swansea garrison, the deputy Chief Constable and several other high-ranking officials, directed the discussions of eight syndicate groups in what was essentially a desk-based exercise regarding the defence of the town. Each syndicate consisted of eight individuals representing a broad cross-section of the Swansea civil and military defence set-up. As well as key council officials, the groups also contained delegates from the police, fire and ambulance services, as well as representatives of numerous military units, medical and decontamination officers, food supply officers, rest centre supervisors, a billeting officer, a gas company manager, a telephone company manager and a factories nominee.

Once again, scenarios were set out in which Swansea was

deemed to have been attacked and to have suffered heavy damage. There were the usual notional issues regarding bomb damage to properties and the transport infrastructure, as well as a hospital that was ablaze, a veritable flood of refugees fleeing the town, suspicious characters approaching roadblocks, injuries caused by poison gas, widespread looting by civilians, a shortage of ammunition and an enemy who was attempting to force entry into the town. It seems that each of these issues were considered by the syndicate groups, and some broad guidance for the future was developed in the light of the multi-agency discussions.

When Lang-Coath drew the syndicate discussions to a close on 30 August 1942, he would not have been aware of how developments elsewhere meant that the risk of an invasion of Britain was actually rapidly diminishing. On 23 August, just one week before the Swansea syndicate's discussions took place, the German 6th Army had reached the outskirts of Stalingrad in Soviet Russia. The resulting struggle for control of the city ended on 2 February 1943 with the catastrophic defeat of the German forces and their allies. Though Hitler would make one more attempt (in July 1943, at Kursk) to regain the initiative in Russia, the reality was that the Germans would soon no longer be able to conduct major offensive operations in the East and an invasion of Britain need not be a major concern for those charged with the defence of towns and cities across Great Britain. The lessons learned in Swansea from the various Home Guard exercises would happily never need to be tested in the face of a real invasion.[4]

CHAPTER 12

Winning the War

ALTHOUGH IT WAS not known at the time, by March 1941 the town of Swansea had already undergone its greatest trials of the war on the home front. Air raids still occurred from time to time, but none came anywhere near the disaster that had befallen the town during the Three Nights' Blitz of 19–21 February 1941. Indeed, for the remainder of 1941 to the end of 1942, no fewer than 11 air raids took place. Though only six deaths were inflicted, including three at the electricity power station located on the Strand in Swansea.

Swansea underwent its final air raid of the war during the night of 16–17 February 1943 – the sixth and final Blitz-style attack on the town. By that time Adolf Hitler regarded the military situation in the West as being largely a distraction – he continued to devote most of his thought and, indeed, most of his armed forces, to the titanic struggle with the Soviet Union on his Eastern Front. Two weeks earlier, on 2 February 1943, the German 6th Army and its associated units had surrendered in the ruins of Stalingrad at the end of a campaign that had seen Axis losses amount to around 750,000 killed, wounded or captured. It was not simply a defeat – it was a disaster. The year of 1943 would see Germany desperately trying to steady the critical situation on its Eastern Front while, at the same time, looking nervously over its shoulder in anticipation of an Allied invasion of occupied Europe.

With Nazi resources being stretched between the East and the West, the final air raid on Swansea during February 1943 was not considered by those in authority to be a major attack, though that was scant consolation for any Swansea unfortunates who happened to find themselves in its path. No less than 37 enemy aircraft took part in the raid and dropped 27 tons of bombs, of which only six tons actually hit the town, its industrial infrastructure or its suburbs. Nevertheless, even if the weight of bombs was not as great as the earlier Blitz attacks on the town, there were still 34 deaths and over 100 injuries of which 61 were serious. The main areas of the town that were affected included High Street, Sketty, the Hafod, St Thomas and Brynmill, while one high-explosive bomb fell near to the Swansea General and Eye Hospital, leading to the rapid evacuation of 300 patients as the bomb did not explode. Damage was inflicted on the Griffith Thomas Ward (which later had to be demolished), the outpatients unit, the Folland Ward, and the registration office

Mrs Annie Cleaver of Derwen Fawr Road, whose husband was away on business, had entered a brick-built domestic air raid shelter (the shelter adjoined her home and could be entered via a low door from the dining room) together with two of her neighbours, when a bomb badly damaged the house and caused the shelter walls and its concrete roof to collapse. A rescue party was soon at the scene and the women were eventually extricated, though Mrs Cleaver and Bertha Fowler were both sadly found to be dead.[1]

A 50kg-bomb fell close to a barrage balloon that was located in the yard of the Sun Fuel company. The explosion uprooted a large, reinforced concrete block that helped to tether the balloon, and knocked three members of the Women's Auxiliary Air Force (WAAF) team that was controlling it to the ground. Though no serious injuries were suffered, none of the WAAFs could remember the incident, other than the fact that they all suddenly found themselves on the ground.[2]

Also hit was the RAF base at Fairwood Common, in an incident that saw the deaths of three women of the WAAF. Irene Daisy Collett had only been serving for a short time, while Patricia Baxter's role was that of a plotter for the No. 10 Group Fighter Command, the same role as that performed by the third WAAF to lose her life at RAF Fairwood, Joan Phillis Chandler. Joan was killed while doing some ironing, while her fiancé pilot was involved in aerial combat with the enemy over Fairwood.[3]

David Gwyn Thomas had been working out of Loughor as an ambulanceman when he joined the civil defence service as a rescue party member and first aider; he had volunteered to go into Swansea as the raid developed. He was taken into the town in an ambulance that was driven by a woman, the vehicle carefully following a guide on a motor-cycle. After several diversions due to bomb damage, he observed numerous ambulancemen in Cockett, together with a large supply of coffins. He then assisted in the evacuation of patients from the bomb-damaged Swansea General and Eye Hospital, aided by nursing staff. The evacuees were taken to Neath General Hospital and some of the patients conveyed displayed differing reactions to the trauma they had experienced. One attempted to climb out of the ambulance while another simply fell asleep. After a welcome cup of tea and a biscuit in Neath, the ambulance and its crew returned to Swansea before making further trips.[4]

The final attack on Swansea had been a surprisingly brief affair. Imperial Chemical Industries (ICI) reported to the Ministry of Home Security the effect of the raid on production at its Landore and Waunarlwydd factories, noting that in Landore the 'take cover' warning had been issued to the workforce at 10.04pm on 16 February 1943, while the 'raiders passed' message was announced at 11.06pm, meaning that factory lights could be switched back on and production restarted. It was noted that:

> A short and sharp attack apparently from a small number of enemy 'planes developed on the Swansea district prior to the

sounding of the sirens. Flares, incendiary and HE bombs were dropped. A number of HE bombs were dropped in the near vicinity of the factories, causing anxiety to workpeople and affecting the services from outside.

Although the Landore factory had not been hit by bombs, a nearby gas main had been damaged resulting in a minor loss of munitions production. At the Waunarlwydd factory, damage to the incoming electricity supply meant that its production would be reduced by 25 per cent for two days. Prompt reports on such matters were required by a Ministry of Home Security that was always anxious to ensure that every possible ounce of production was squeezed out of the factories in support of the war effort, irrespective of the difficult conditions that often prevailed. It was a total war and every resource had to be deployed to its full potential.

Indeed, such was the attention to detail required by the Ministry of Home Security that each bomb dropped during the raid of 16–17 February 1943 was assigned an identifying number, and had its impact reported on by those officials who were on the spot. Thus bomb numbers 22 and 23 were noted as being 500kg bombs that had been dropped on the railway depot near Fabian Street. The damage caused to rolling stock and rail track was itemised by local railway officials, and indications were given as to what could be repaired (as regards damaged railway wagons) or simply written off (as was the case with a disused GWR water tank). Likewise, bomb number 48 was reported as having been a 500kg specimen that demolished an air raid shelter in Sketty Green, resulting in the deaths of the two women referred to previously. For the benefit of the ministry, the construction style and materials of the shelter were set out in a report, as was the effect of the explosion on it. Though classed as a 'near miss', the bomb had nevertheless demolished the structure and resulted in the fatalities.

The Ministry of Home Security was also eager to discern

any change in the style of enemy attacks, as well as the possible use of any new type of weapons. Any innovations introduced by the enemy would need to be analysed and reported on for the benefit of other areas that might soon be subject to a new method of attack or weaponry. One incoming report that was made on 17 February about the raid on Swansea certainly piqued the ministry's interest. A Mr Peddie, an official who was in Swansea stated, 'Possibility of new weapons, there may be a new type of container, details later.' It seems that the two bombs that had exploded close to the Grand Hotel on High Street had produced an unusual mix of small craters but extensive blast and fragmentation effects. At least seven people had been killed during the two explosions, including a night porter at the Grand Hotel, a bus driver and a passing Danish sailor.

Given that the bombs might have been of a new and potentially novel character, a Mr Amos was sent down from the Ministry of Home Security's research and experiments division to investigate. He found that the one bomb that had fallen at the rear of the hotel had wrecked the interiors of two old shop units. The wall of one of the shops had subsequently collapsed into the premises and that had, in turn, allowed the then unsupported slate roof to fall as well. Acting on information received from hotel staff, Amos had then interviewed a young boy who had picked up numerous pieces of metal after the explosions, a common practice among schoolboys in the town. In consultation with an experienced colleague, Amos determined that no new weapon had in fact been deployed during the raid. It was apparent that the second of the bombs had simply hit a concrete slab close to the hotel that was nine inches thick – this had produced only a small crater but a lot of metal fragments which had scarred nearby walls and killed or injured people, including the hotel night porter and the sailor. As no new weapon had been involved, the investigation therefore fizzled out, though the affair shows how seriously events at the local level were pondered over with concern by those at the centre.[5]

During the raid a high-explosive bomb had fallen near to the Swansea General and Eye Hospital on its Phillips Parade side, but had failed to explode, possibly because it was operating on a delayed-timing mechanism. The defusing of this bomb was a top priority, as the hospital had been evacuated and essentially put out of use when it was realised that the device could explode at any time. There had been numerous casualties elsewhere in the town who needed treatment, and the unavailability of this key medical facility for a lengthy period of time could not be countenanced by those involved in its administration.[6]

Lieutenant Edward J Douglass, of 16 Bomb Disposal Company, stepped in for the officer who would normally have been rostered for the defusing attempt, as that officer had been sent away to train other bomb disposal men. Douglass, aged 46, was an engineer by profession and also a Freeman of the City of London. He was driven to the scene by his driver, a man named Austin, and they saw on arrival at the hospital that there was visible damage to a wall and a large crater nearby from which the bomb protruded. It was a cold morning and, as the duo surveyed the scene, driver Austin thought that he'd better answer the call of nature before assisting in what would probably be a dangerous and lengthy procedure. Douglass indicated a wall behind which his driver could retire. While Austin was otherwise engaged, the lieutenant started his approach to the bomb. There was an immediate explosion from which Austin was luckily sheltered, and on emerging from his place of safety he could see further extensive damage to the hospital premises, but of Lieutenant Douglass there was no sign whatsoever. The size of the bomb and the ferocity of the explosion at close quarters had obliterated the unfortunate officer. Bomb disposal was always a risk-filled enterprise, and on occasion could only be performed at a very high cost, and that had been only too evident in the tragedy that took place outside the hospital.[7]

With 1942 and the beginning of 1943 being largely free of enemy air raids on Swansea, and with the Nazis suffering important defeats in North Africa and Russia, it did seem to the people of the town that perhaps the tide of war was finally turning in favour of the Allies. Indeed, from a Swansea perspective an invasion of the town was about to gather strength though, happily, it was friendly in form. As far back as 4 June 1940, Winston Churchill had entered the chamber of the House of Commons to update its members on the disastrous progress of the war against Germany in France and the Low Countries and the forced evacuation of the British Expeditionary Force from the Continent. He delivered his famous and defiant 'We shall fight in the fields and in the streets...' speech and, once he had retaken his seat, the House of Commons promptly moved on to generally uninteresting issues of parliamentary procedure, though the speech had certainly affected many of those who heard it that day, with MP Henry 'Chips' Channon noting that several Labour members had been reduced to tears by it. However, its effect on morale in Britain at the time appears to have been mixed. While the speech had ended on a defiant note, much of the content was necessarily depressing, dealing as it did with deaths, disaster, defeat and evacuation, as well as the imminent loss of an important ally in the shape of France.

Churchill had, in fact, intended the speech to also influence someone who was not even in Britain. His statement that, in time, it would be seen that 'the New World, with all its power and might, steps forth to the rescue and the liberation of the old', was a coded signal, and his target was the President of the United States of America, Franklin Delano Roosevelt. The president was attempting to provide as much aid as he could to an embattled Britain, while not inflaming the powerful lobby in America that supported isolationism and no American involvement in what it saw as a purely European war. Churchill was perplexed by America's apparent disinterest in the growing Nazi threat to the settled world order but Roosevelt, via secret communication channels, did offer him a glimmer of hope. The president indicated that he wanted a commitment that, even if Britain were defeated, she would not surrender her fleet to the enemy. Instead, it should be sent to safer parts of the Empire and Roosevelt was confident that, in such a situation, America would soon enter the war.

Britain of course did remain undefeated after 1940, so America still stood aloof from the European war until after Japan's surprise attack on its naval base at Pearl Harbor and Germany's subsequent declaration of war on the United States. That is not to say that America had, until then, stood by as a mere onlooker of course. Between March and December 1941, even while supposedly neutral, it had found itself able to provide Britain with $65 million worth of shipping and $86 million worth of munitions under the lend-lease arrangements. An additional $100 million of munitions was provided to countries of the Empire and other theatres of war.[8]

As far as Swansea was concerned, American involvement in the war became more tangibly visible when its soldiers began arriving in the town in increasing numbers during 1943 as part of Operation Bolero; the build-up of forces in preparation for the invasion of France, an operation that was originally envisaged as taking place in that year, though that eventually proved to be unduly optimistic. Construction work on a camp for arriving Americans in Singleton was begun during September 1943, and it consisted of tents erected on concrete bases as well as a few Nissen huts. Eventually, the site became the temporary home of around 1,600 men, while a further two camps were established in Mynydd Lliw, near to Pontarddulais, with a combined capacity of over 3,000 men. There were over 400 men at the Elba Works, Port Tennant, and other camps sprang up at Clase Farm (1,500 men),

Manselton (1,600), Penclawdd (1,200), Glanmor School (400) and Underhill Park (250) among several other locations.[9]

The sight of American soldiers, some of whom were black, became a regular occurrence within the town, and the local population was broadly happy to finally see representatives of its wartime ally in the flesh, ready to try and help release much of Europe from the grip of the Nazis. Prominent among the visitors to Swansea were men of the American 2nd Infantry Division, who wore a unit patch that showed the head of a Native American rendered in red and blue and wearing a feathered headdress placed within a five-pointed white star, thus giving the division its nickname of the 'Indianhead Division'. One of its constituent units, the 9th Infantry Regiment, could trace its origins as far back as 1798. The division had left America in October 1942 and stayed for a while in Northern Ireland before moving to various seaside locations in south Wales during April 1943.

Schoolboy John Sutherland had returned to Mumbles after a period as an evacuee in Llanwrtyd Wells, meaning that he was away from the town during the heavy air raids of February 1941. During 1943 he admired the clean-cut GIs stationed at several locations in and around Mumbles who strolled about in their smart winter uniforms. He also found them generous in dishing out the inevitable bubble gum as well as, occasionally, the rather more adult cigarette packets. Indeed, he once received a sharp telling off from his father after being caught with a packet of Camel cigarettes in his pocket. On a darker note, he also recalled some fights in the village between GIs and locals that sometimes resulted in minor injuries and the odd broken window.[10]

Mike Lewis of Port Tennant had been evacuated to Ystradgynlais in 1941 but was back home when American soldiers began arriving in the town, and he remembers there being great excitement at their appearance. Local families would often invite a couple of GIs in for Sunday lunch or a bath, gestures that were greatly appreciated by the new arrivals. Many Port Tennant women routinely baked their own bread at that time, and it was common for Mike to visit an American tented camp with a fresh loaf that he would swap for a small haversack of US Army rations containing dried milk and eggs, Spam and chocolate, among other items. American comic papers became popular, being passed on by GIs to local children who would collect a few and later swap them with their mates for a football or some other item.

Mike Lewis also remembers that there were fist-fights frequently between Americans, but also sometimes involving GIs and locals. Indeed, on one occasion, he remembers his uncle (a Swansea policeman) and a fellow constable arriving at his home with raw knuckles, the result of a fight with some black American soldiers. Mike's mother provided a bowl of water and Dettol to ease the pain of the injuries. He added that, back then, the police often dispensed with the 'book and pencil' approach to policing and, where it was thought appropriate, simply waded in with fists flying. The scrap had occurred in the Cuba Hotel, a well-known Swansea watering hole that was close to the docks and had a rather dubious reputation. Asked why he thought the fight had taken place, Mike replied, 'It was a foregone conclusion – everybody fought in there!'

It wasn't all fisticuffs of course and, as could be expected, the smart young men with the beguiling accents and sharply tailored uniforms soon made an impression on the local ladies both in Mumbles and the wider Swansea area. Mike recalled that the Americans built a community centre in Port Tennant and it proved a popular venue where soldiers could meet and dance with the local girls. After some of the females had covered their legs in gravy browning to simulate the look of stockings, it was young Mike's job to draw the 'seams' on with a pencil, 'All the way up to their bum!' as he remembered.[11]

Across Swansea, as the opportunities for romance between

Americans and locals increased, it wasn't too long before Miss Joan Nicholls of Sketty was getting married to Robert Besel of California, and Miss Audrey Colebrook was signing a marriage register in New York with Albert Alogna of Long Island. Though it is difficult to know the exact figures for GI marriages in and around Swansea, it seems that at least 100 or so took place during or soon after the period 1943–45.[12] Not all such relationships were destined to have happy endings, however, especially in a time of war and occasional extreme danger. Barbara Donne had met Pedro Rodón during 1943 while he was training in Swansea prior to the invasion of France. In early 1944 the couple married at the Guildhall in Swansea and enjoyed a brief honeymoon before Pedro's duties took him overseas. A son, Peter, was born in early 1945. Pedro survived the war, though, while walking on the beach at Le Havre, France, in September 1945, he unfortunately stepped on an uncleared land mine and was tragically killed in the resulting explosion. Barbara was sadly left to bring up Peter on her own, without the love and support of the man she adored. She made a good job of it and was able to enjoy the love of the family that her son Peter subsequently built around her.[13]

The Americans weren't in Swansea to merely fraternise with the locals of course. They were there to eventually take part in the largest sea-borne invasion in history, an incredibly dangerous mission that the fate of the peoples of Nazi-occupied Europe depended upon. As training continued around the Swansea area into 1944, and the probable date of invasion grew closer, the military camps became breeding grounds for ideas of all kinds regarding the future disposition of the American 2nd (Indianhead) Infantry Division. In May 1944, the security officer of the division's 9th Infantry Regiment compiled a report for his regimental commander, in which he stated:

All personnel have a feeling that something definite is in the wind for them and, as a result, their morale has jumped to a peek [*sic*] which will probably be maintained, if not slightly increased, until we actually get into combat. Although every conceivable idea has been 'bulled' over by the men, no one seems to have tried to start false rumors [*sic*] about the date or place, which shows that orders must have reached everyone.[14]

If the rumour mill was, for security reasons, notably discreet about the precise date and target of an invasion, nevertheless, some of the thoughts that were discussed included the idea that a June invasion of France seemed likely, while others wondered whether the regiment would end up in Egypt, Italy, or somewhat inexplicably, India. The possibility that the Germans might deploy poison gas was prominent in the minds of many, while others envisaged the regiment being utilised in an airborne operation of some sort, possibly on German soil.

These rumours were largely inaccurate of course, and as June 1944 arrived the men of the various American units in Swansea and elsewhere in south Wales began to board ships in preparation for the Channel crossings that would announce that D-Day had finally arrived. Various elements of the American 2nd Infantry Division embarked onto ships that were moored at the King's Dock in Swansea in the first few days of June 1944, and they were landed on 7 June (D+1) on Omaha Beach, near the town of Saint-Laurent-sur-Mer, where the division established its headquarters. Swansea had been the port of embarkation for around 13,000 Americans and over 700 vehicles. In total, over 23,000 men and over 3,000 vehicles of the 2nd Infantry Division were transported to Normandy from Swansea and the other Bristol Channel ports.[15] Between the Normandy invasion and the end of the war, the American 2nd Infantry Division suffered just over 3,000 men killed in action, a great many of whom would have been familiar faces to the people of Swansea. Freedom from Nazi oppression for the peoples of Europe came at a high cost and the Normandy invasion was an important step on that long and painful journey. Germany was now embattled on both its Eastern and Western fronts and, though there would be occasional setbacks for the Allied powers, final victory was only a matter of time.

It is striking to note that, although the weight of 'ballast' exported through the port of Swansea during the years 1936 to 1942 amounted to precisely nothing, in 1943 the figure was a modest 12,000 tons, while between 1944 and 1945 the total 'ballast' exported was almost 500,000 tons. Although no definite confirmation has yet been identified in the archival records, modern-day experts on the history of the port think that it's possible that the authorities were accounting for military material leaving the port by describing it simply as 'ballast' in any published trading reports, in an attempt to keep the enemy guessing. It is certainly true that, after the end of the war, the 'ballast' trade in Swansea declined as quickly as it had grown. In 1947 it was down to only 39,000 tons and by 1952 it no longer appeared in the trade reports.

What is known is that in the run-up to D-Day, the docks in Swansea received a wide range of military material and equipment of both British and American design. This included tanks, half-tracked vehicles, armoured cars, ammunition of various types, including land mines, artillery pieces, aircraft of several designs (some of which were packed in crates), and even locomotive engines. The N Shed at the docks was built specifically for the storage of bombs, some of which used Torpex as the explosive material. It was used in the 10,000kg-Grand Slam bombs that were stored at the docks, and it was 50 per cent more powerful that TNT by mass.[16]

Hospital provision in Swansea came into sharp focus in 1944 as the invasion of Nazi-occupied Europe loomed large in the mind of the Allies' military planners. It was, of course, impossible to predict the level of casualties, though it was thought that they could be heavy and the town's medical facilities were likely to be much in demand. The Swansea General and Eye Hospital on St Helen's Road had opened its doors in 1869, and was funded largely by subscriptions from wealthy benefactors, friendly societies and individual subscribers. In 1939 it had been the town's principal medical centre and, as such, would clearly be heavily impacted by the war. Indeed, once the Emergency Medical Service had been established by the government to manage and coordinate the country's hospital bed capacity in wartime, the Swansea hospital had soon been placed in Class 1A as an important resource for the treatment of primarily military casualties. It was agreed that 100 beds would rapidly be made available in wartime for military use, with an unavoidable knock-on effect on the hospital's potential civilian patients.[17]

To try and minimise this problem, the hospital had taken over the workingmen's club and institute in Langland Bay, an action that provided 137 additional beds for civilian patients displaced from the Swansea General and Eye Hospital by incoming military cases. As noted, the hospital did suffer damage during the 1941 and 1943 raids, and, as a result, some patients were evacuated to other medical units in Carmarthen and the Amman Valley. Furthermore, as a result of those heavy air raids, it proved necessary to arrange the transfer of 70 cases from Cefn Coed Hospital to the psychiatric hospital in Bridgend. The beds made available at Cefn Coed by this measure were soon filled with military cases though, over time, almost 200 civilian victims of the air raids were also dealt with. Patient shuffling between hospitals became a regular occurrence.

As the anticipated invasion of occupied Europe approached during 1944, confidential plans were made to restrict the number of civilian admissions to the Swansea General and Eye Hospital so as to keep free as many beds as possible for military use. In the event, civilian cases were also transferred to Swansea from London hospitals, a game of medical musical chairs that helped release beds in hospitals near to the south coast ports of England, where military casualties were often first brought ashore.

In August 1944 a contingent of almost 60 military casualties did arrive at the hospital and, by early 1945, with the war developing in a more encouraging manner, it was made clear that the reservation of beds in Swansea for military cases was no longer considered necessary. The attention of the hospital management then turned to tackling the waiting list of civilian cases which had unavoidably grown during the disruption of the previous few years. The hospital's relationship with the workingmen's club premises in Langland ended in November 1945, as did the association with the intrepid members of the Swansea Volunteer Stretcher Bearer Corps, a body that had provided excellent service in ferrying patients to waiting transport in a war-ravaged Swansea.

The long-established Swansea General and Eye Hospital was not the only significant medical provision in the town during the war years. As early as 16 April 1940, a meeting had been held between Town Clerk H L Lang-Coath, his senior officials and representatives of the Welsh Board of Health and His Majesty's Office of Works. The Office of Works was considering erecting a new Emergency Medical Service hospital on council land, possibly at what was referred to as 'Sketty Park Hall', though other areas were to be considered if deemed more suitable. By August 1940, the focus had switched to the Maesgwernen Hall estate land (Maesgwernen is also rendered as Maesygwernen in some sources) adjacent to Llanllienwen Road in Morriston. The estate had been the property of the late William Williams, a Swansea tinplate manufacturer who had twice been mayor of Swansea as well as MP for the district before his death in 1904.[18]

That site proved to be suitable and, given the urgency with which the matter was viewed, the Minister of Health acquired the land and buildings in February 1941 using the extensive wartime powers of requisition granted to him under the Civil Defence Act (Defence General Regulations), 1939. So hasty was the process followed that the property changed hands before a contract of sale had been drawn up, without the title to the land being investigated. The legal niceties between the interested parties could be dealt with later and, if necessary, by arbitration, as actually happened in due course.[19]

After certain preparatory works had been completed, construction work on the site began. With an eye to the future, the council was keen to be involved in the running of the new hospital as, once the war was over, it would surely become available to provide much-needed additional medical capacity to the people of Swansea and its surrounding areas. In November 1941 it was agreed that the council would indeed act as the agent for the Welsh Board of Health in running the hospital, while also being responsible for all staff appointments other than those of the most senior positions. Happily, the Welsh Board of Health would meet all construction, equipment and ongoing maintenance costs in what was a favourable deal for the council. It was initially planned that the hospital would be for the exclusive reception and treatment of war casualties, though, as it transpired, this condition was on occasion relaxed so that other classes of patient could be treated, as and when bed spaces permitted.

Understandably, given the date of its construction and the shortages of all sorts of materials during wartime, the hospital wards were rudimentary by today's standards. Thus it was that, 'Electric cables were left uncovered and were supported by wooden cleats bolted to the ceilings. Walls were unplastered; the bare brickwork was coated with paint. Ward floors were concrete, covered with tarmacadam. Windows had frames of galvanised iron.' Ward heating was provided by stoves of a vintage that was so old that, when they were seen by a Canadian nursing sister, she was taken aback as she had only seen the design previously in remote parts of her homeland and had long thought it obsolete.[20]

On 28 March 1943, the newly-built hospital was opened, under the direction of its medical superintendent, Dr Duncan Davies. It had a peacetime capacity of around 400 beds, but given the demands as the expected Allied invasion of occupied Europe drew nearer, tighter spacing of the beds meant that 600 patients could in fact be squeezed in. However, with the planned invasion still sometime in the future, the opportunity was taken to admit a number of long-term patients from the Welsh National Memorial Association as well as providing beds to help reduce the treatment waiting list that had built up at the hard-pressed Swansea General and Eye Hospital. After almost nine months of service, during 1943 the new hospital had treated almost 3,500 cases on an in-patient basis, while a further 4,000 patients had been seen in the out-patient department. Over 1,300 patients had been given physiotherapy treatments, while almost 2,000 operations of varying types had been performed and 11,500 X-rays had been taken. It was already clearly playing an important role in improving the health of the townspeople despite the wartime pressures.[21]

The run-up to and arrival of D-Day inevitably resulted in increased activity at the Morriston hospital and, over the course of 1944, almost 4,200 cases were admitted, of which 3,417 were military personnel, including Merchant Navy sailors, most of whom had been wounded following the Normandy invasion. Between 4 July 1944 and 17 April 1945, at least 24 ambulance trains brought patients who had initially been treated at the Royal Victoria Hospital, Netley, to Morriston and, as an example of the scale and intensity of the operation, over a two-week period in July 1944, 610 patients arrived from Netley via the railway station at Shrivenham. The constant flow of new casualties from France to the southern ports of Britain meant that a process of dispersal had to be performed, moving the injured to more distant hospitals like Morriston and thus clearing space for even more new arrivals in the hospitals of south-east England.

The casualties that were dispersed to Morriston by train were unloaded at the Great Western Railway station at Clase Road, Morriston, often during the blackout, before being transferred to ambulances by a convoy of stretcher bearers and then taken to the new hospital. Some of the wounded were still clad in their often mud- and blood-spattered uniforms, so rapid had been their evacuation from the battle zone. Some of the hasty, though well-intentioned, medical work that had been carried out near to the front line had the unfortunate effect of often enclosing contaminated soil and foliage within bandages and plaster casts, resulting in a high incidence of subsequent, and sometimes serious, infections. This problem was alleviated somewhat by the use of penicillin, the new wonder drug for treating infections which more than halved the mortality rate from septic wounds in post-D-Day casualties.[22]

Naturally, not all medical care in Swansea was centred on caring for the casualties of war. During 1940, the Medical Officer for Health, Dr H R Tighe, reported that there had been an unprecedented prevalence of diphtheria in the town, with numerous cases of the most severe type. This came against a backdrop of a preventive programme that had earlier seen a good number of local children immunised against the disease. Tighe thought that the unavoidable mixing of the general population in stuffy, poorly ventilated air raid shelters made the spread of the disease hard to control, given the number of potential contacts. During the year, 514 children under the age of five had nevertheless been fully immunised against diphtheria, while almost 1,000 in the five-to-15 age bracket also received the full course of medication. On the debit side, the 1940 outbreak saw a total of 1,146 cases of the disease in children under the age of 15. On a happier note, there had been no significant outbreaks of other types of infections that might have been expected to flourish under wartime conditions, though meningococcal meningitis and measles were present as usual. By 1942, the considered opinion of Dr Tighe was that the war:

> … has had no marked effect on the physical or mental welfare of the children. Diminished parental control which has been a feature of modern times, appears in exaggerated form during wartime, owing to the absence in many cases of the father on military service, and the frequent engagement of the mother in vocations or avocations associated with war conditions. This results in increased juvenile delinquency or in other forms of juvenile demoralization.

Tighe's view on the possible longer-term effects of the war on children who witnessed its horrors seems to be quite blunt and unsympathetic. Despite many of the children living through the sound of exploding bombs, the thunderous roar of the anti-aircraft guns, the crash of falling masonry and the sound of shattering glass, he thought that they were:

> … nearer to the savage state than is the adult, as may be seen by observing the games of little boys. Provided they personally are untouched by war's tragedies and sufferings, children are not likely to be ill-effected by the noises or alarms of battle, unless disturbed by adult example.[23]

This view seems possibly a little hard-nosed and it was actually the case that, by late 1943, a number of child evacuees in Swansea were receiving psychological help at a clinic in Walter Road, their previously routine lives having been upended by danger and the unsettling experience of evacuation away from their families and familiar surroundings.[24]

There were probably other, largely unrecorded effects on the children of Swansea as they tried to live as normal a life as possible in the bomb-damaged town. Alan Osborn had not reached the age of nine years when war was declared and, after the bombing raids commenced, he encountered a number of blood-stained stretchers propped up against the wall of an ambulance station. Similarly, when a bomb exploded near to the railway station on High Street, on passing the site sometime later he observed a wall that was splattered with blood and small pieces of human flesh. Happily, a bomb crater that he at first thought was filled with human blood turned out to be the result of a rather gory escape of fluid from the Dyfatty slaughterhouse. The young Osborn seems to have made the best of the situation and was able to distract himself in schoolboy pursuits in among the blood and mayhem. Bombed-out buildings proved to be freely available adventure playgrounds, while a healthy market in the sale or swapping of expended bullets and other ordnance was operating in the school yard.[25]

The Swansea Port Health Authority also played a part in keeping the people of Swansea (and elsewhere) healthy during the war. Its remit ran from the Mumbles Point to the south-eastern extremity of the port at Nash Point, covering the local authority areas of Swansea, Port Talbot, Neath, Porthcawl, Bridgend and Cowbridge. Its powers extended to all 'docks, basins, harbours, creeks, rivers, channels, roads, bays and streams…' within its area, as well as to ships that were directed to moor at particular places to prevent or limit the spread of disease.

A key element of its work was the detection of infectious diseases among visiting seamen, and arrangements were in hand to send such cases to the Hill House Isolation Hospital in Swansea. The Swansea General and Eye Hospital could deal with cases of venereal disease, while skin infections such as scabies could be sent to the hospital in Tawe Lodge, formerly the infirmary of what had been the Swansea Workhouse. Commonly encountered diseases in those arriving in the town by sea included diphtheria, malaria, typhoid fever, scarlet fever and chicken pox. It was vital that these diseases were kept out of the working population, many of whom were engaged in important work for the war economy. During 1940, nine cases of diphtheria and two of malaria were discovered and dealt with, helping in some instances to prevent further cases developing on shore and adding to the burden of a hospital system that was already creaking under the strain of wartime conditions. Also in 1940, onboard inspections of visiting ships resulted in the destruction of almost 500 beds which were found to be verminous and dirty. A never-ending war was waged against rats, both on board ships and in the wharves and warehouses of the port. Indeed, almost 400 rats were destroyed on vessels, while over 1,700 were killed in and around the port where they were often the cause of the spoiling of precious stored foodstuffs.

The food supply was a matter of great concern throughout the war and Swansea and its neighbouring ports all played a part in bringing in to the country the food that was so desperately needed. In Swansea that included beef, beans, biscuits, butter, fish, pork, tomatoes, veal and wheat, among other items. Although these were much-needed, it nevertheless proved necessary for the port health inspectors to condemn those foodstuffs that simply proved to be unfit for human consumption after their journey across the sea. During 1943 this included 153 tons of butter, 174 tons of flour and 20 tons of wheat. Not huge amounts in the grand scheme of feeding Britain in wartime, but still an unhappy loss to the dining tables of the country.[26]

With Allied forces eventually fighting their way into Nazi Germany and the end of the war in sight, on 30 April 1945 the Ministry of Health in Whitehall wrote to all local authorities in response to enquiries regarding the form that any celebrations to mark the end of the war in Europe should take. The ministry advised that it was permissible for local authorities to provide modest funding for events in celebrating the surrender of Germany, though, in the event of any later challenges as regards the legality of specific items of expenditure, it would come down to the decision of the district auditor on what was considered reasonable. Given that Germany was only days away from unconditional surrender, the lateness of the advice proffered by the ministry probably contributed to some fairly low-key celebrations in Swansea and, indeed, across much of Wales.[27]

On 8 May, designated 'Victory in Europe Day' and a public holiday (two other days were also later designated as holidays to mark the event), a well-attended drum-head service for the military units that were present in the town was held on the forecourt of the old Guildhall (now the Dylan Thomas Centre). The service was conducted by the Rev. A W Jayne, RN, the senior chaplain for the Bristol Channel area, and thanks were given to God, 'our fellow subjects beyond the seas', the King and Queen, the 'sacrifice of the whole people' and for 'the mighty help of the United States of America and Russia' in gaining victory.[28]

Many Swansea citizens simply visited the local beaches or parks for a day of relaxation and, no doubt, some solemn contemplation of what they, their families and friends, as well as the town itself, had endured over recent years. Church bells were rung to happily signal victory rather than the feared invasion of Britain, while ships in the docks loudly sounded their hooters to mark the momentous occasion. Many churches were opened and services of thanksgiving were held, while some streets were festooned with coloured bunting and impromptu street parties were staged, with tables being set up in the middle of the road. In a mocking reference to Hitler's Siegfried Line and the well-known popular song that was associated with it, a number of streets strung washing lines from upstairs windows and decorated them with what were described as 'more intimate items of wearing apparel', giving a clear 'Knickers to Hitler!' message. The overall impression was that the celebrations, while being joyfully happy, were nevertheless 'decorous' and well conducted.[29]

It seems that the later approach of the end of the war with Japan did not arrive for officials in Swansea quite as unexpectedly as had that with Germany. As the Japanese attempted to negotiate better terms of surrender following the devastating detonation of atomic bombs at Hiroshima and Nagasaki on 6 and 9 August 1945, it was possible for Swansea Council and other local organisations to plan for what would be Victory over Japan Day.

Back in Swansea, as the war ended with both Germany and Japan being defeated, it was decided to stage a 'final victory' parade in the town, on a yet to be determined Sunday that would closely follow the news of the Japanese surrender. As Japan reluctantly surrendered on Wednesday, 15 August, the parade took place on Sunday, 19 August 1945. The government had hoped that 'local authorities may be able to organise victory parades, or other celebrations, either in connection with local services of thanksgiving and prayer, or, later in the day, to include as many aspects as possible of the national effort, in addition to such representation of the armed forces as can be arranged with the local commanders.'

The Swansea parade took place on the afternoon of 19 August and was arranged by Chief Constable D V Turner who had succeeded F J May on his recent retirement. The route taken was Northampton Place, St Helen's Road, Guildhall South Road and Mumbles Road, with the parade finally entering the St Helen's Sports Ground. No less than 26 contingents took part, representing the armed forces (including the Home Guard) and units of the civil defence organisation as well as the British Legion, the RNLI, the WVS, the Red Cross, St John's Ambulance, the Women's Land Army and members of the boy scouts and girl guides. After the service of thanksgiving, the parade marched past a saluting base that had been placed in front of the cenotaph on the Swansea foreshore, where the salute was taken by the mayor of Swansea, Alderman T W Watkins, JP, and representatives of the military.[30]

The townspeople marked the day by carrying on with their celebrations until the early hours of the following morning, and included a late-night gathering outside the floodlit Guildhall where a brief service was held before community singing and dancing to music that was relayed over loudspeakers. The streets in numerous areas of the town were taken over for parties, with fireworks and bonfires much in evidence. It was reported with satisfaction that, despite the displays of great exuberance during the celebrations, there were subsequently no charges brought in respect of drunkenness.[31]

The end of the war did not arrive without its difficulties. Peace brought with it a gradual redeployment and demobilisation of Britain's armed forces and, in common with many other parts of the United Kingdom, by 1946 a number of hutted encampments in Swansea had been vacated by their military tenants as units were relocated or even disbanded. The town still displayed the scars of the conflict, with a large portion of its centre lying in ruins, while in other parts of the town domestic housing had been destroyed or subjected to varying degrees of damage. A sizeable number of civilians and demobbed service personnel found it impossible to return to their former homes, or only did so with some difficulty, frequently due to the widespread damage caused to their property by war operations. Others found themselves lodging with comparative strangers in cramped and unsatisfactory dwellings, often coupled with a distinct lack of privacy.

During 1946, squatting in abandoned military camps became evident in all parts of Britain, undermining the efforts of the local authorities to manage their housing waiting lists with regard to need rather than the simple illegal possession of a vacant property. Officials at the Ministry of Health suggested that, while it was not necessarily unsympathetic to the plight of the families involved, it was important that the facilities within those former military camps that had been occupied without authority were up to standard, and that some assessment of need was used in deciding who should be housed within them in the short term.[32]

In Swansea it was reported that on 17 August 1946 no less than 20 families had moved into a number of brick-built buildings off Mumbles Road, while other sites at Derwen Fawr Road, Sway Road and a location in Manselton had also been occupied by squatters. Within a few days eight former military camps in Swansea were filled with squatters. Eventually, squatter communities appeared in Thistleboon, Caswell, Bracelet Bay, Carmarthen Road, land adjoining Mynydd Newydd colliery, Sway Road, Heol Las, Sketty Lane, Cwm Farm, Ashleigh Road and the Manselton Racecourse. On 18 September 1946, these 11 camps contained a total of 118 families, some 407 people. At Thistleboon there was only one family, consisting of five people, while the camp in Mynydd Newydd colliery contained 95 people in 25 families. The Medical Officer of Health, Dr H R Tighe, was of the opinion that the accommodation at almost all of the sites could be brought up to an acceptable standard at a reasonable cost, though there were hurdles to be overcome in the short term. The method of hut construction varied across the camps, including some built in brick and some in wood, while others were of the Nissen hut variety, constructed from prefabricated steel. Many of the huts were leaking in several places and broken or missing window glass was a common feature. At most of the camps hut lighting was provided by oil lamps or candles, while in Thistleboon the electricity supply had been rather unkindly cut off by the military who were probably anxious to avoid being saddled with ongoing bills. The Sway Road camp had the benefit of an ablution hut in its centre, though it was noted that only two of the nine water closets were in working order. At Sketty Lane there were no water closets on site as the block that had previously housed them had been demolished. The Summerland site and that at Bracelet Bay had no water closet provision whatsoever, and required families to defecate into metal pails which then had to be emptied into cesspools.

In October 1946 an agreement was reached between the council and the Ministry of Health which meant that it would act as an agent for the ministry in managing the camps. With simple eviction being seen as a political non-runner, it was decided that, on any particular site, vacant but unoccupied huts could be cannibalised to provide materials that could be used to repair other existing but defective huts. Where a family vacated a hut that was in a reasonable state of repair, then a family living in a hut that was in a more dilapidated condition could be moved into it and their original hut dismantled to provide spare materials for repairs and to prevent a new occupancy from taking place. No tenancy rights were to accrue to the squatters, though the council could request a modest weekly contribution from each family based on a rateable value assessment of a hut, even if the sums due might prove hard to collect.

Though the families squatting at the various camps had to endure poor housing conditions, it was, nevertheless, the fact that this accommodation did reduce pressure on the council's housing waiting list. As such, it made sense for the council to carry out minor repairs to those huts in order that they remained fit for human habitation, even if they did not provide much in the way of comfort. In accepting the situation as it was, the council nevertheless did not wish to see it get any worse. In late 1946, when Polish troops vacated a well-maintained camp at Singleton Park, swift action was taken to move families from dilapidated huts at other camps into the park. The vacated huts were then promptly demolished before any new families could illegally move in.

Even then, the police had to assist in preventing an

invasion of squatters intent on grabbing a newly-vacated hut in Singleton Park. Watchmen had to be employed day and night in controlling access to the Singleton Park camp and also another camp at Tregernydd near Mynydd Newydd. The council spent the period 26 October 1947 to 4 January 1948 moving families from inferior to better huts, while keeping out any unauthorised arrivals. Indeed, during that period it spent £558 on wages for almost 6,000 hours of staff time. The men were involved in demolishing huts that were no longer up to standard, as well as a number that were adjudged to be close to collapse. Any items of salvage from the demolished properties were removed and stored for future use, while the cost of haulage in removing families and their furniture to a hut in a different camp amounted to almost £300. Eventually, 65 huts were demolished or made uninhabitable and 52 families were moved elsewhere.

By March 1949 the camps at Singleton Park and Tregernydd were still in operation, though not without some difficulties. In Singleton, 25 huts were accommodating 48 adults and 54 children, though eight of the huts could not be made suitable for longer-term occupation without excessive expenditure. The problems at Tregernydd were even greater, though it seems this was due to the character of the people who had been placed there rather than the standard of accommodation. There were 19 huts and 75 people at the camp, and five of the huts had no internal sanitary facilities but relied instead on a central ablution building. For some reason, the ablution block toilets had been vandalised on two occasions and a third attempt at repairs had been abandoned when the newly installed plumbing was yet again wantonly damaged. The Borough Estate Agent, D Ivor Saunders, decided that enough was enough and ordered the cessation of repairs, leaving the occupiers of five of the huts to make their own toilet arrangements. His considered opinion was that the potential users of the central ablution block were the perpetrators of the damage and were of a character type that was not fit to be placed in 'decent houses'.

After this time the issue seemed to fade in importance. Defective huts were improved in a number of relatively inexpensive ways, some families moved out voluntarily, having found better options elsewhere, while others slowly climbed to the top of the council's housing waiting list. Though the timeline is not clear, it seems that properties were gradually vacated and eventually the camps were emptied and closed with little controversy.[33]

CHAPTER 13

Journey's End

IT HAS BECOME commonplace today, especially in the media, to describe the ebbs and flows of someone's lived experience as a 'journey', with perhaps a celebrity of some description inviting their television audience to 'join me on my journey', whether it be in learning a new skill, undergoing a novel experience or perhaps exploring a challenging environment. The people of Swansea certainly undertook a journey during 1939–45 and it was surely one that they would rather have avoided at almost any cost. Indeed, for several hundred of the town's inhabitants the war marked the end of their final journey as they sadly fell victim to the Nazi bombing campaign.

In late October 1944, with the war in Europe progressing satisfactorily and the threat of air raids on Swansea becoming ever more unlikely, the council published the previously confidential information on the casualties suffered in the town to date. The figures revealed that 387 people had been recorded as killed in Swansea due to enemy action. Before the information was made public, it seems that many in the town – viewing the devastated town centre on a daily basis – believed the likely casualty list to be considerably longer than proved to be the case. The detail provided by the ARP Controller in Swansea, Town Clerk T B Bowen, who had succeeded Lang-Coath on his retirement in June 1943, revealed that the total dead consisted of 217 men, 113 women and 57 children. A further 412 people were seriously injured, while 439 were slightly injured. It was noted that between June 1940 and

February 1943, a total of 40 raids had taken place on the town, resulting in 1,785 'occurrences' or incidents. It was thought that 1,459 high-explosive bombs had hit the town and its suburbs, together with just four parachute mines (one contemporary Swansea record shows 1,434 high-explosive bombs being dropped). The air raid alert warning was instigated on no less than 534 occasions, and the time spent under alert by the population totalled some 623 hours.

Due to circumstances totally outside of its control, Swansea had the misfortune to 'top' a table of deaths recorded in Welsh towns and cities due to enemy action, as its 387 deaths exceeded the 355 suffered by Cardiff and the 51 lost in Newport. Total deaths in Wales amounted to around 1,000, meaning that Swansea's grim tally was almost 40 per cent of the total casualties in Wales. The *South Wales Evening Post* took an unusual reporting angle and noted that, while around 1,000 deaths due to enemy action had indeed occurred in Wales to date, in the first five years of the conflict road deaths in the country amounted to 1,900. This comparison seemed to imply that the losses had not been of great significance, but ignored the fact that most of the war-related deaths were concentrated in the large urban areas such as those of Swansea, Cardiff and Newport, while road traffic casualties often took place across the whole of Wales including some areas that never saw a bomb drop. Indeed, the press report undermined its stance somewhat when it stated that, while Swansea had suffered 387 deaths due to enemy action, the wartime road fatalities in and around the town amounted to only 122.[1]

During the war, Swansea Council, in common with similar local authorities throughout Britain, had been required to compile a register of civilian deaths due to enemy action. In the register created in Swansea, the cause of death of each casualty was recorded at a simple level by typically stating 'Bomb-blast due to enemy air raid', though occasional mention was made of 'falling masonry', 'shrapnel' or 'splinters' among other descriptions. For unknown reasons, the Swansea register of civilian deaths also includes a number of non-civilian casualties, often consisting of the bodies of military personnel whose bodies happened to be washed ashore in or near Swansea. In these cases, the cause of death was usually given as being due to 'war operations'. Additionally, a small number of military personnel who were killed during bombing raids are also recorded in the register, and that includes a number of Army sappers who sadly lost their lives while attempting to defuse bombs in the town.

The civilian death record forms were completed when a casualty was brought to a mortuary, and list in most cases the personal effects that were found on the body. The details often provide poignant insights into those whose lives were so abruptly brought to an end. One male body, aged 48, was recovered along with a 'pair [of] trousers and mutilated clothes', his death having resulted from bomb shrapnel in July 1940. A lad of 15, killed on 21 February 1941, had on his person three handkerchiefs, two pencils, a pencil eraser, a tie, two fountain pens, a scout belt, pocket knife and diary, among other minor items. A March 1941 casualty had about him several keys, a pocket knife, corkscrew, two collar studs, cufflinks, two rings, a billiard chalk, comb, cigarette case and cigarettes, matches, a pair of mittens, a handkerchief and a purse containing a small amount of cash. The belongings of a boy of 12 were recorded as being a striped shirt, a cotton vest, one brown shoe (the other presumably being not found), a pair of fawn stockings, a dark blue waistcoat and, indicative of his youth, a pair of short trousers. His death had resulted from him being struck by falling masonry. One record even goes so far as to list the effects of a 21-year-old woman as 'silk stockings, knickers, vest, petticoat, brassiere, black frock...' and a gold locket.

Though it may not be an entirely accurate assessment, it is possible to roughly gauge the level of sacrifice made by those engaged in civil defence work in the town. An examination of the Commonwealth War Graves Commission records indicates that at least 23 fire-watchers were killed in Swansea during the war, of whom five were working in Castle Street and three in Teilo Crescent during the raids of February 1941. Six air raid wardens and four members of the air raid rescue teams were killed, three of them at incidents in Corrymore Mansions on the night of 19–20 February 1941. Over a dozen fire-fighters also paid the ultimate price, while five members of the air raid precautions messenger service lost their lives, the oldest being 18 and the youngest only 15.[2]

Having carefully recorded the details of those who had so far died in the town as a result of enemy action, the question arose as to who was to respectfully dispose of the bodies by burial. Government departments had expended a lot of effort in the pre-war years in planning for large numbers of civilian dead in the aftermath of heavy attacks from the air. With the infrastructure of a town or city being badly damaged following a raid, and even routine business activities being difficult to perform, it was thought that funeral directors and municipal or parish grave diggers would possibly be overwhelmed by demand for their services in the aftermath of a raid. It was anticipated that, following the possible heavy loss of life in a single attack, there might be a need for mass graves to be prepared, into which the bodies of numerous unrelated victims could speedily be placed by the local council.

Given the likely speed that would be required in disposing of potentially large numbers of dead, the routine system of unusual deaths being investigated by the local coroner, so that foul play could be ruled out, was suspended in some respects during the war. A Ministry of Health circular (No. 1,779) was issued in February 1939 and it allowed for such bodies to be buried without further ado, provided that the local mortuary superintendent was entirely satisfied that the death had been caused by war operations. In the case of Swansea, the final word was left to Town Clerk and ARP Controller, Howell L Lang-Coath, at the outbreak of the conflict and, after his mid-war retirement, by his successor T B Bowen. It was they who essentially certified each civilian death as having resulted from war operations without involving the coroner.

That said, at least one wartime case did involve the Swansea coroner and that was the presumed death of Ronald George Allen, a 17-year-old lad from Tanymarian Road in Swansea. Ronald had been active during the February 1941 raids in helping to put out incendiary bombs that had fallen near to his home. He was seen, acting on an air raid warden's instructions, getting into an Auxiliary Fire Service vehicle in order to guide the driver to Teilo Crescent on the night of 20 February. The crescent was subsequently heavily bombed and Ronald was never seen again. His father had later visited all the mortuaries in the town but had failed to find any trace of his son, and it was grimly noted that some charred bodies and body parts had been recovered from the scene but none could be identified as having any definite link to the missing youngster. The coroner could only record that Ronald had died as a result of war operations. As it was not possible to take his body to a mortuary, his name does not appear in the council's register of civilian war dead.[3]

Another question that exercised the minds of Whitehall officials in the run-up to war was that of who would pay for the burials of civilian war dead. It was easy to imagine (albeit with a sense of horror) an entire family being wiped out as the result of a direct hit by a high-explosive bomb on a house or domestic air raid shelter. In that situation, it was hard to imagine the surviving relatives (who might be financially stretched themselves) being able to pick up the bill for several funerals all at once. The early thinking, however, was that no government grants to cover family funeral expenses should be provided since, in all probability, most civilians killed as a result of enemy actions would be speedily interred by the local authority, often by mass burial, with the cost later being reclaimed from government funds (in Coventry, on 20 November 1940, after more than 500 fatalities in a single attack, 172 people had been buried in mass graves. There were several such funerals.). Where a family did request the return of a body so as to provide a private funeral, then it would be for the family to meet the funeral costs and no grant would be payable. By the time that the first serious air raids commenced in 1940, the matter had moved on somewhat in governmental circles and the families of civil defence volunteers killed in the course of their duties were able to claim a funeral grant of £7 10s., while the dependents of civilians who were killed in this way were eligible for a modest pension, though no funeral grant. This payment of pensions to the dependents of civilians killed by enemy action resulted in an annual expenditure of only £14,000 in 1940, though, given the later heavy casualty figures, it had risen to £2,752,000 per year during 1945.[4]

As regards the provision of emergency mortuaries for the reception of the bodies of air raid casualties, the council had used the existing mortuaries at the Oystermouth, Danygraig and Morriston cemeteries, as well as those on the Strand and at the Swansea General and Cefn Coed hospitals. Recognising that even those facilities might not be enough in the wake of heavy raids, arrangements were also made to utilise the Wycliffe schoolroom on Clarence Terrace, the Christ Church (St Faith's) Men's Club on St Helen's Road, and a property named Bryn-y-Môr that was situated off Eaton Crescent. To round things off, a mortuary in Tawe Lodge (the new name of what had been the Swansea Workhouse) was also brought into the equation. Staffing was set at six full-time employees, plus an additional two who would work as and when required.[5]

It was indeed Swansea Council that took care of the burial arrangements and met the expenses of most of the town's civilian casualties, with those civilian death register entries indicating that the body was 'not claimed for burial', often despite it having been identified by a family member. No doubt, any modest pension that was payable to a dependent of a civilian casualty might not arrive in time for funeral costs to be met, or perhaps it was a simple question of the financial priorities of surviving family members. After all, if the State (initially in the form of the local council) was prepared to pay the funeral expenses of a relative killed by enemy action, then why not let it? The people of Swansea were living (and in some cases dying) in exceptional times and surely normal rules no longer applied. In the event, although around 360 civilians (excluding military casualties) had been killed in Swansea during the war, only 27 bodies seem to have been reclaimed for burial by their families or friends. The others were buried by the council, which was later able to reclaim its costs from the government.

As regards the prospect of mass burials, a possibility that was viewed by some with dread as being akin to burial in a pauper's grave, it does seem that in Swansea this was largely avoided, despite there being over 200 people killed during the air raids of 19–21 February 1941 alone. It was the practice at that time for municipal cemetery graves to be dug to a depth of seven feet to accommodate three coffins, or nine feet to provide for four coffins and, for example, on 5 March 1941 the unclaimed and unrelated bodies of air raid victims Margaret Blackwell, Luther Jones and Thomas Davies were all interred in a single grave in Oystermouth Cemetery, with the grave then being regarded as 'full', so no further burials took place in it. It was somewhat different where unidentified bodies or merely body parts were concerned and, in Oystermouth Cemetery on 5 March 1941, 'seven unidentified bodies' were buried in a single grave that was nine feet deep.[6] It is probable that some of these burials consisted only of body parts contained in small caskets.

The end of the war saw a Swansea that was still heavily scarred following the 40 air raids that it had endured, with

many domestic, civic and commercial properties showing signs
of war-related damage. Naturally, even during the war, efforts
had been made to clear away the rubble so that the town's
businesses and its people could go about their daily affairs,
while longer-term plans for redevelopment of the Blitzed
areas also gradually came into view. According to the late
Charlie Thomas (a war-time docker and later a long-serving
councillor and alderman of Swansea City Council), much of
Swansea's bomb rubble was used to fill in the North Dock
which had been closed to seaborne traffic since 1930 – thus
reclaiming the land for other uses. The North Dock covered an
area of about ten acres and was over 20 feet deep and, as such,
it received a huge amount of Swansea's wartime rubble.[7] By
way of contrast, much rubble from bomb-blasted Bristol had
made its way across the Atlantic during the war in the form
of ballast in the holds of Allied shipping, as numerous return
trips were made for the conveyance of men and materials from
America to the United Kingdom. In New York, the dumping of
huge quantities of this ballast in the East River enabled land
reclamation to take place, a process that eventually saw the
creation of the Bristol Basin, so-named as it essentially stood
on Bristol's war rubble.

The question also arose as to who was to pay for buildings
that had been damaged or destroyed by enemy action. In
1941, the government had enacted the War Damage Act (4&5
George VI, Chapter 12), which allowed for the payment of
compensation to those whose property had suffered damage
due to war operations. It was payable in respect of damage
that occurred due to a deliberate or accidental act by the
enemy, as well as that caused by a 'proper authority' (typically
a local council or a unit of the military) in taking steps to
avoid further damage or danger (for example, by demolishing
unsafe structures). It was also payable in cases where a proper
authority took precautionary measures that caused damage to
buildings or land in advance of an anticipated enemy attack,

such as when trenches or anti-tank ditches were dug. As would be expected, there were a great many buildings in Swansea that were eligible for compensatory payments under the War Damages Act, and correspondence ensued between Swansea Council and a number of the town's best-known businesses, since the council often had a direct role to play in the claims process, frequently having leased out land or premises that had subsequently suffered war damage.

There was correspondence between the council and affected parties regarding damage to St Mary's Buildings on St Mary's Square, the Exchange Buildings, the Metropole Hotel and the Grand Hotel. In the case of the Grand Hotel, for damage sustained in September 1940, the claim only amounted to £11 including architects' fees.[8] In the case of the Swansea Baths (including the laundry and flats), there was a claim for war damage repairs amounting to just over £1,241, as well as a further £1,077 that had been spent on adapting an area of the building for gas decontamination purposes.[9]

Even where the council was not the land or property owner in a particular case, the War Damage Act nevertheless required those affected to initially contact their local council to register a claim, and then to be sent a claims form to submit to the district valuer for assessment. The individual claims naturally varied greatly. During the Three Nights' Blitz of February 1941, a bomb crashed through the roof of the Swansea Museum on Victoria Road and landed on the floor of the lower library without exploding. It was soon defused, though it left in its trail damage to the roof, plasterwork and windows, resulting in the closure of the building for a period of three months. As regards compensation for the damage, a payment of £899 was eventually agreed, though, given the complexity of the compensation process, the cheque did not arrive until 1948.[10]

The much-loved David Evans store had stood opposite the Ben Evans building and was comprised of premises that abutted onto Temple Street, Castle Street and Goat Street. It had been destroyed during the February 1941 attacks and, for war damage compensation purposes, the value of this large site was later assessed as being £32,000. David Evans opened a large new premises on Princess Way in 1954, despite expressing 'grave doubts' that it would be a success. Interestingly, it was noted that 'Ben Evans had decided that the cost of rebuilding was too high' and that business never operated again in Swansea on anything approaching its pre-war scale.[11]

By way of contrast, in the likely value of claims, a man from Essex Terrace told the council that in January 1941 his front window had been blown in and he wished to lodge a claim. Mr Morgan of 21 Reginald Street was somewhat unlucky by comparison, since every window in his home had been blown in and several ceilings had collapsed. The neon sign of the Castle Hotel on Oxford Street had been damaged, while Baldwins Company (metal processors) had suffered damage to a quantity of its tinplate products stored in a shed at the King's Dock. Mrs Dinah Thomas of Carn Nicholas Farm in Bonymaen advised the council that her claim was for damage primarily sustained to stables and cowsheds. The roofs of the buildings had been blown off, exposing 16 cattle and three horses to the harsh winter weather. Additionally, though the bomb concerned had exploded some 150 yards away, the pine end wall of her home had been moved almost two inches out of plumb by the force of the blast and needed repairing.[12]

The Villiers Estate had extensive land ownings in Swansea and received ground rent for numerous properties on its land. It detailed the damage that had been sustained by those properties and it was an extensive listing involving over 60 buildings. There was damage to its holdings on Vale of Neath Road, Grafog Street, Port Tennant Road, Vernon Street and Villiers Street, among other places. Almost 40 properties were listed, which included many of its houses, a chapel and a bakehouse, and some of the properties were described as being a 'total loss' with several of them having been already demolished, if not by the bombs themselves then later by design to ensure public safety.[13]

The commercial and shopping centre of the town had simply been devastated, to the extent that Swansea Market (which had housed 415 small shops and stalls) was in ruins, as were 352 other shops, 108 office buildings, 72 industrial buildings, 87 houses, 28 public houses and ten churches or chapels.[14] By June 1945 the council was intent on taking the opportunity to redevelop a large swathe of the central part of the town, and it identified an area of some 281 acres that included elements of the Castle, Victoria, Alexandra, St John's, St Thomas and Brynmelyn electoral wards that would be subject to compulsory purchase in pursuance of its scheme. The site of Swansea's preeminent pre-war shop, the impressive Ben Evans department store, was earmarked by the council for the creation of a memorial garden, much to the disappointment of the company's directors. They wrote:

> The scheme under consideration by you proposes that our valuable building [after February 1941, it was, of course, a burnt-out shell] should not be restored, but the site of the whole of the said block used as part of an extensive open space of doubtful value to the town. So far as the scheme goes, no alternative site comparable as to position, dimensions, potentialities, or value is to be offered by way of exchange or compensation… we are not only to lose our property, but to be put out of business as well.[15]

Despite the company's protestations, Castle Gardens were subsequently established on the site of the former store and soon became a much-loved feature of the reconstructed town centre. The Ben Evans company consequently opened a shop at premises on Walter Road and another at Port Talbot, but never quite recaptured the cachet of its earlier years. It seems to have ceased trading in the late 1950s or early 1960s.

Within the town there were almost 800 buildings of

various types that had either been destroyed or were so badly damaged that repairs were out of the question. As a result of the damage, the rateable value of properties within the area designated for compulsory purchase had fallen from around £250,000 to only £147,000, while across the whole of Swansea the total rateable value of properties dropped from its 1939 figure of £1,093,000 to only £995,000 in 1945, a fall of around nine per cent that represented a significant loss of income in the medium term.[16]

In trying to restore the town to its former glories, the council was hindered by disagreements with local traders as well as with the 'man from the ministry' – those officials of the government who wanted to see modern planning ideas applied to the reconstruction of bombed towns and cities, rather than simply overseeing expensive attempts to recreate what had been lost. If that was not enough to hamper and delay progress, there was also the problem that post-war government funding was insufficient to satisfy all demands across Britain in full, while a shortage of materials, including the all-important steel, meant that unofficial rationing of scarce items was the norm. Progress would therefore prove to be painstakingly slow and the eventual results, more often than not, a disappointment.[17]

During the war the Swansea authorities took numerous photographs of the bomb damage caused to the town, whether for simple record purposes or to inform the war damage compensation process. Additionally, several artists, including Will Evans, George Little and Mona Moore, painted particular scenes of the damage, adding a splash of colour to the pictorial record that contrasted markedly with the starkness of the more usual black-and-white camera images. George Little had been temporarily evacuated from the town in 1941 when still a teenager and, after pursuing a career in art tuition at various establishments in England and Wales, he returned in his work, while in his 80s, to the trauma of Swansea in 1941.

He remembered of that time, 'wherever I stood all I could see were piles of twisted girders, the remains of masonry and skeletal buildings.' He completed 35 paintings, working from his memories of the time, and exhibited the results in Swansea and Barry in 2015.[18] Mona Moore appeared on the front page of the *South Wales Evening Post* in March 1941, in an image that showed her busily sketching bomb damage on Castle Street. This artistic work was not without its often hidden dangers; Moore returned to the Castle Street site the following day to find it barricaded off following the discovery of an unexploded bomb.[19]

*

Today there are a number of popular pages on social media dedicated to photographic images of 'old Swansea' and the history associated with them. Many of the images do give tantalising glimpses of a Swansea that is now lost, not just due to the natural passage of time but also to the destructive attention of Hitler's Luftwaffe and the necessary site clearances that ensued. Looking at the images, one has to occasionally wonder what must it have been like to sip a coffee in the Kardomah Café while Dylan Thomas and his associates argued noisily in the corner? Or to enjoy a meal in the Bovega Restaurant on Castle Street where, the images tell us, fine wines and spirits were also available. Or to shop in Ben Evans's sumptuous department store in the shadow of Swansea Castle, before taking afternoon tea in the splendid Metropole Hotel, just a short walk down Wind Street. There can be no doubt that the air raids of 1940–43, and especially those of 19–21 February 1941, ripped the heart out of the centre of old Swansea. For those who did know the pre-war character of the town and subsequently mourned its loss after the bombers unleashed their deadly cargoes, perhaps Swansea poet Dylan Thomas summed it up most poignantly.

Dylan Thomas had succeeded in avoiding being conscripted into the armed forces during the war, largely due to health issues. He had found useful employment at the BBC and the Ministry of Information, and had produced numerous articles and plays throughout the war years. He had walked through the town on 22 February 1941, the morning after the third consecutive night of bombing, later recording his thoughts in the radio play, *Return Journey*. It had clearly been an emotional and heart-rending experience, perfectly illustrated in his literary depiction of a badly damaged Swansea. The play's narrator (Thomas) enquires after the fate of a favourite pub, before mention is made of what was Swansea's grandest pre-war retail establishment – the renowned but burnt-out and later demolished Ben Evans store. He takes his audience on a melancholy stroll through the empty and barren streets of his 'ugly, lovely town', recounting the well-loved businesses that had once lined its thoroughfares and been thronged with happy customers before the bombers came. Dylan did not rely on his memory in listing the many now-vanished shops – he simply obtained a list from the Borough Estate Agent. He wrote:

Narrator: What's the Three Lamps like now?

Customer: It isn't like anything. It isn't there. It's nothing mun. You remember Ben Evans's stores? It's right next door to that. Ben Evans isn't there either...

Narrator: I went out of the hotel into the snow and walked down High Street, past the flat white wastes where all the shops had been. Eddershaw Furnishers, Curry's Bicycles, Donegal Clothing Company, Doctor Scholl's, Burton Tailors, W.H. Smith, Boots Cash Chemists, Leslie's Stores, Upson's Shoes, Prince of Wales, Tucker's Fish, Stead and Simpson – all the shops bombed and vanished. Past the hole in space where Hodges & Clothiers had been, down Castle Street, past the remembered invisible shops, Price's

> Fifty Shilling, and Crouch the Jeweller, Potter Gilmore
> Gowns, Evans Jeweller, Master's Outfitters, Style and
> Mantle, Lennard's Boots, True Form, Kardomah, RE Jones,
> Dean's Tailor, David Evans, Gregory Confectioners, Bovega,
> Burton's, Lloyd's Bank, and nothing. And into Temple
> Street. There the Three Lamps had stood...

And what of the Kardomah Café, the favourite meeting place for Swansea's Bohemian crowd? It was a much-loved place where before the war the young Dylan and his artistic friends had held forth on:

> Music and poetry and painting and politics. Einstein and
> Epstein, Stravinsky and Greta Garbo, death and religion,
> Picasso and girls...
> Communism, symbolism, Bradman, Braque, the Watch
> Committee, free love, free beer, murder, Michelangelo, ping-
> pong, ambition, Sibelius, and girls...

But the Kardomah Café was sadly no more; it had been:

> ... razed to the snow, the voices of the coffee-drinkers – poets,
> painters, and musicians in their beginnings – lost in the willy-
> nilly flying of the years and the flakes...[20]

As Dylan Thomas had continued on his sorrowful journey through the battered streets of Swansea on that cold February morning in 1941, he bumped into an old friend, Bert Trick, and they surveyed the sombre scene of devastation together. Their thoughts and sadness regarding the destruction that confronted them would surely have chimed with the feelings of many other Swansea residents who had grown to know and love their home town – warts and all – and now saw its commercial centre with its much-loved shops, cafés, pubs, churches and chapels reduced to ashes and rubble. Perhaps capturing their emotions as well as his own, on parting,

Dylan, with tears in his eyes, simply told Bert, 'Our Swansea is dead...'[21]

The town would of course rise from the ashes in the coming decades, though the new and largely functional shop units that sprang up in the town centre, with little in the way of decorative embellishment, could never match the grand old buildings that had fallen victim to the Nazi onslaught. The deaths of more than 300 of their fellow townsfolk was an absolute tragedy for the people of the town and, to make matters worse, many of its familiar and much-loved landmarks had been irretrievably lost in the eyes of those who knew and remembered the fine old town as it once had been. Future generations – who are only able to compare the atmospheric and intriguing images of the town's once impressive buildings with the more mundane architecture of their 'new' Swansea – can only despair at what had so painfully been lost.

Endnotes

Abbreviations
SL – Swansea Library (Local Studies Section)
SWEP – *South Wales Evening Post*
TNA – The National Archives (Kew)
WM – *Western Mail and Echo*
WGAS – West Glamorgan Archive Service

Chapter 1: Swansea on the Eve of War
1   *SWEP*, 21 February 1941.
2   Hughes, W T Mainwaring, *Kicks and Kudos: Candid Recollections of Forty Years as a Councillor* (self-published, not dated), p.42.
3   WGAS, D 125/2.
4   WGAS, D 23/4.
5   Swansea Docks website, 3 May 2023.
6   Lloyd, Wynne Ll, *Social and Economic Survey of Swansea and District, Pamphlet No. 6, Trade and Transport – An Account of the Port of Swansea and the Transport Facilities and Industry in the District* (University of Wales Press Board, 1940).
7   *Hansard*, 19 November 1932.
8   WGAS, D 23/4.

Chapter 2: Preparing for Disaster
1   WGAS, BA 2/9.
2   Alban, J R, 'Preparations for Air Raid Precautions in Swansea, 1935–39', *Morgannwg*, Volume 28, 1984, pp.55–73 [afterwards Alban, ARP]; *SWEP*, 31 October 1940.
3   WGAS, TC 52/3726; D/D Z 956/12.
4   WGAS, D 207/9/2.
5   Ibid.
6   WGAS, TC 52/3726.

7   WGAS, D 145/4.

8   WGAS, TC 200/139.

9   WGAS, D 145.

10   Alban, ARP.

11   *SWEP*, 16 June 1939.

12   *SWEP*, 12 April 1941.

13   *SWEP*, 4 December 1939.

14   WGAS, D 42/9.

15   Hunt, W W, *To Guard My People* (published by the author, 1957), pp.84, 89 [afterwards Hunt].

16   *Statutory Rules and Orders*, 1940, No. 1677; O'Brien T H, *Civil Defence* (HMSO, 1955), p.287 [afterwards O'Brien].

17   O'Brien, pp.590–3.

18   WGAS, TC 4/Watch 19.

19   Ibid.

20   *SWEP*, 25 October 1939.

21   WGAS, D 68.

22   WGAS, TR 1/51/2; Bank of England website, 15 March 2024.

23   WGAS, BA 2/10.

Chapter 3: Arrivals

1   WhatsApp interview with the author, 9 February 2023 [afterwards Henry Foner interview].

2   Davies, Ellen, *Kerry's Children: A Jewish Childhood in Nazi Germany and Growing up in South Wales* (Seren, 2004).

3   *SWEP*, 18 May 1940.

4   *SWEP*, 3 June 1940.

5   *WM*, 30 November 1944.

Chapter 4: Blood, Toil, Tears and Sweat

1   *SWEP*, 4 & 5 September 1939.

2   *SWEP*, 7 September 1939.

3   *SWEP*, 4 September 1939.

4   *SWEP*, 1 September 1939.

5   *SWEP*, 7 September 1939.

6   *SWEP*, 5 September 1939.

7   *SWEP*, 7 September 1939.

8   *SWEP*, 8 September 1939.

9   Ibid.

10 *SWEP*, 7 October 1939.

11 *SWEP*, 18 March 1940.

12 *SWEP*, 7 April 1941.

13 *SWEP*, 16 December 1939.

14 HMSO, *The Registrar General's Statistical Review of England and Wales; Tables Part II, Civil* (annual reports for the years 1939–45) [afterwards GRO].

15 Information from Jessica Madge, email 25 April 2023.

16 WGAS, files D/D Con/S 2/7/3 to D/D Con/S 2/7/9 contain the annual reports of the Chief Constable of Swansea for 1939–45 [afterwards Police Reports].

17 *SWEP*, 15 March 1944 & 7 January 1944.

18 Hunt, p.84.

19 Howlett, Peter, *Fighting With Figures* (HMSO, Central Statistical Office, 1995), p.26 [afterwards Howlett].

20 *SWEP*, 16 September 1940.

21 *SWEP*, 23 September 1940.

22 *SWEP*, 3 September 1940.

23 Ibid.

24 *SWEP*, 7 September 1944.

25 *SWEP*, 27 February 1941.

26 *SWEP*, 24 August 1944.

27 *SWEP*, 24 May 1944.

28 National Service (Armed Forces) Act, (2&3 Geo. 6, c.81).

29 O'Brien, pp.150–1.

30 WGAS BE 1/1/10.

31 Ibid.

32 Parker, H M D, *Manpower – A Study of War-Time Policy and Administration* (HMSO, History of the Second World War, 1957), p.157.

33 O'Brien, p.156.

34 *SWEP*, 20 June 1940.

35 *SWEP*, 21 June 1940.

36 *SWEP*, 29 June 1940.

37 *SWEP*, 17 October 1940.

38 Ibid.

39 *WM*, 23 August 1940.

40 WGAS, D/D WAW 9/1-3.

41 *SWEP*, 6 June 1940; Verrill-Rhys, Leigh, & Beddoe, Dierdre (eds), *Parachutes and Petticoats – Welsh Women Writing on the Second World War* (Honno Autobiography, 2003 reprint), pp.119–21 [Afterwards Petticoats].

42 *WM*, 24 August 1940.

43 *SWEP*, 24 May 1940.

44 *SWEP*, 23 January 1940.

45 *SWEP*, 14 February 1941.

46 *SWEP*, 14 June 1940.

47 *SWEP*, 30 July 1940.

48 *WM*, 16 May 1941.

49 *SWEP*, 21 May 1940.

50 *SWEP*, 11 July 1940.

51 *SWEP*, 12 September 1939.

52 *SWEP*, 16 September 1939.

53 *SWEP*, 16 & 27 September 1939.

54 Hammond, R J, *Food – Volume I: The Growth of Policy* (HMSO, History of the Second World War, 1951), pp.392–3 [afterwards Hammond]. During the period 1940–1944 Britain still imported an average of over 13,000,000 tons of food and animal feed each year.

55 *WM*, 9 March 1944.

56 *SWEP*, 9 June 1944.

57 Hammond, pp.111–15.

58 WGAS, HE 1/16-16C, HE 1/17, HE 1/18/18A.

59 Hammond, p.176.

60 *SWEP*, 14 February 1941.

61 Henry Foner interview.

62 *SWEP*, 12 February 1941.

63 *SWEP*, 3 May 1944.

64 *SWEP*, 13 April 1943.

65 *SWEP*, 3 June 1944.

66 *SWEP*, 30 October 1941.

67 *SWEP*, 2 June 1944.

68 *SWEP*, 16 March 1940.

69 *SWEP*, 18 November 1940.

70 *SWEP*, 24 July 1940.

71 National Registration Act 1939 (2&3 Geo. 6. c.91).

72 O'Brien, p.279.

73 HMSO, *The Registrar General's Statistical Review of England and Wales for the Six Years 1940–45*, pp.146–7.

74 National Service (No. 2) Act 1941, (5&6 Geo. 6. c.4).

75 O'Brien, p.287.

76 *SWEP*, 12 June 1942.

77 WGAS, HE/1/16-18.

78 Howlett, pp.39, 46–7, 56.

79 *SWEP*, 12 February 1941.

80 Kidwell, Elaine, *From Air Raid Warden to Landgirl: A true account of the 1939–1945 war through the eyes of a teenage girl* (Swansea Library Service, 2005).

81 WGAS, D/D WAW 15/3/31.

82 WGAS, D/D Z 349/8/1-52.

83 *WM*, 22 October 1942.

84 *WM*, 10 September 1942.

85 WGAS, D 8/2/26, D 8/2/40, D 8/1/33-39.

86 WGAS, D/D GUI/W 31/9.

87 WGAS, EA 60/1-2.

88 WGAS, TC 200/61, WGAS, TH 71; Titmuss, p.334.

89 WGAS, TC 200/140.

90 WGAS, D/D SB16/494-95.

91 TNA, WO/166/2014.

92 *WM*, 18 September 1940.

93 *SWEP*, 12 February 1941.

94 *WM*, 25 October 1941.

95 *WM*, 28 July 1941.

96 *WM*, 22 October 1943.

97 *SWEP*, 2 May 1944.

98 *WM*, 3 October 1944.

99 *WM*, 29 January 1943.

100 Howlett, p.114; these measures saved 0.5 million cubic feet of wood per year and several thousand tons of shipping space.

Chapter 5: Defending the People

1   TNA, HO 396 series; Ancestry.co.uk, enemy alien records.

2   *SWEP*, 11 June 1940.

3   *SWEP*, 12 June 1940.

4   WGAS, BE 1/2/48.

5   WGAS, BE 1/1/8.

6   WGAS, TC 52/3975.

7   *SWEP*, 18 July 1940.

8   *SWEP*, 11 July 1940.

9   WGAS, BE 1/2/32.

10   WGAS, BE 1/2/35.

11   WGAS, BE 1/1/8.

12   Ibid.

13   Ibid.

14   Ibid.

15   WGAS, D 8/2/40.

16   WGAS, BE 1/1/10.

17   WGAS, BE 1/1/8.

18   McLelland, Tim, *Action Stations Revisited, Volume 5, Wales and the Midlands* (Crécy Publishing Ltd, 2012), p.165.

19   Ibid., p.100.

20   HMSO, *Roof Over Britain – The Official Story of the A.A. Defences, 1939–1942* (facsimile – The Stationery Office, 2001), p.72; TNA, WO/166/1356.

21   TNA, AIR 13/63.

22   Collier, Basil, *The Defence of the United Kingdom* (HMSO, History of the Second World War, 1957), p.448 [Afterwards Collier].

23   Morgan, Pamela, 'The Woolwich Arsenal at Cwmfelin Tinplate Works, Cwmbwrla, Swansea in World War Two' (*Swansea History Journal: Minerva*, No. 31, 2023/24), pp.108–114.

Chapter 6: Under Attack: The Early Raids

1   Collier, p.448.

2   WGAS, D 258/1.

3   Alban, J R, *The Three Nights' Blitz – Select Contemporary Reports relating to Swansea's Air Raids of February 1941* (Swansea City Council, 1994), pp.38–9 [Afterwards Alban, Blitz].

[4] TNA, AIR 13/63.

[5] WGAS, D 258/1.

[6] TNA, WO/166/2370.

[7] *SWEP*, 12 August 1940.

[8] WGAS, D/D Z 126/1; Collier, p.208.

[9] *London Gazette*, 17 September 1940.

[10] *SWEP*, 3 September 1940; Hunt, pp.85–6.

[11] WGAS, D 32/1-4.

[12] *SWEP*, 20 March 1941 & 24 April 1940.

[13] WGAS, D 68.

[14] Royalengineersbombdisposal-eod.org.uk/col-stuart-archer /gc/ Accessed 21 March 2024.

[15] WGAS, D/D Z 1066/1.

[16] TNA, WO/166/2370.

[17] Collier, p.322.

[18] WGAS, TH 67/1.

[19] TNA, AIR 13/63.

[20] WGAS, D 258/1.

[21] Pryer, K, *Luftwaffe Over Swansea: A History of the Air Attacks on Swansea, 1939–45* (Keith Pryer and Co., Swansea, not dated), pp.17–18; Hunt, p.86; Alban, Blitz, p.72.

[22] TNA, WO/166/2370.

[23] WGAS, D 97/25.

[24] *SWEP*, 18 January 1941.

[25] *SWEP*, 21 January 1941.

[26] WGAS, D 97/25.

[27] *SWEP*, 15 February 1941.

[28] *SWEP*, 18 January 1941.

[29] *SWEP*, 22 January 1941 & 24 January 1941.

[30] *SWEP*, 18 January 1941.

[31] TNA, HO/250/21/730C.

[32] TNA, HO/250/21/730A, HO/250/21/730B.

[33] WGAS, TH 80.

Chapter 7: Catastrophe: The Three Nights' Blitz

1 Alban, Blitz, p.43.
2 Ibid., pp.72, 74–105.
3 Collier, p.504, figures extracted from certain raids during March 1941.
4 TNA, WO/166/2194.
5 WGAS, D 97/25.
6 *SWEP*, 20 February 1941.
7 Ibid.
8 WGAS, D 97/25.
9 TNA, WO/166/2194.
10 WGAS, D 68.
11 Information from Louise Davies.
12 Information from Peter Webster.
13 Wales Online, 26 March 2018.
14 TNA, WO/166/2194.
15 Ibid.
16 WGAS, D 97/25.
17 *SWEP*, 24 February 1941.
18 WGAS, D 97/25.
19 WGAS, D/D Z 829/1.
20 *SWEP*, 28 March 1941.
21 Ibid.
22 Ibid.
23 Hunt, pp.86–7.
24 *SWEP*, 28 February 1941; *South Wales Evening Post, Memories of Swansea at War* (Archive Publications, Manchester and the *South Wales Evening Post*, 1988), p.34.
25 WGAS, TH 79.
26 WGAS, BE 1/2/22.
27 WGAS, TH 77.
28 WGAS, D 235.
29 WGAS, E/DG SEC 1.
30 WGAS, D 258/1.
31 SL, S.940.534.
32 Ibid.

33 Author's personal knowledge – Private Lewis was his father.

34 WGAS, D/D Z 126/1.

35 SL, S.940.534.

36 WGAS, TH 72.

37 Alban, Blitz, p.72; WGAS, D32/1–4; Alban puts the wounded figure as 409 (p.47)

38 *SWEP*, 24 February 1941.

39 *SWEP*, 25 February 1941.

40 TNA, WO/166/2014.

41 *SWEP*, 24 February 1941.

42 *SWEP*, 19 February 1941.

43 WGAS D 32/1-4.

44 TNA, WO/166/2370, WO/166/2194.

45 WGAS, D/D AN/23/3.

Chapter 8: The Aftermath

1   WGAS, D 125/2.

2   *SWEP*, 25 February 1941.

3   *SWEP*, 1 April 1941.

4   WGAS, D 125/2.

5   *SWEP*, 1 March 1941.

6   *SWEP*, 24 February 1941.

7   *SWEP*, 25 February 1941.

8   *SWEP*, 28 February 1941.

9   Ibid.

10 WGAS, TC 54/96.

11 *SWEP*, 1 March 1941.

12 WGAS, TH 72.

13 *SWEP*, 27 February 1941.

14 Ibid.

15 WGAS, TH 72.

16 WGAS, TC 54/296.

17 Ibid.

18 Police Reports.

19 *SWEP*, 6 March 1941.

20 *SWEP*, 17 April 1941.

21   *SWEP*, 5 March 1943.
22   WGAS, FAC/177/1.
23   Mass Observation, 1 March 1941.
24   TNA, HO/250/21/932.
25   TNA HO/250/21/934; for reasons of efficiency, a National Fire Service was formed in August 1941, bringing under a unified command hundreds of local brigades and Auxiliary Units.
26   WGAS, TC 54/1838.
27   *SWEP*, 12 April 1941.
28   *SWEP*, 24 April 1941.
29   WGAS, TC 5/14.
30   *SWEP*, 9 June 1944.
31   WGAS, TC 5/14; *SWEP*, 9 June 1944.

Chapter 9: Evacuating the Children

1   WGAS, E/S 18/1/3.
2   WGAS, E/S 15/1/3.
3   Ibid.
4   WGAS, E/S 18/1/3.
5   After the war, Henry Foner took British citizenship and completed his National Service in the Army. He achieved BSc, MPhil, and PhD qualifications and worked for the City of Leeds as well as the university. In the 1960s he emigrated to Israel with his wife, Judy.
6   WGAS, E/S 15/1/3.
7   Little's story is told in *George Little, The Ugly Lovely Landscape* by Peter Wakelin (Parthian Books, 2023) [Afterwards Wakelin].
8   WGAS, TC 54/258A.
9   Interview with the author, 15 March 2023 [Afterwards Mike Lewis].
10   WGAS, E/S 32/1/1.
11   WGAS TC 54/258A.

Chapter 10: Defending the Town

1   Collier, p.127.
2   Brooke, Field Marshal Lord Alanbrooke, *War Diaries 1939–1945* (Weidenfeld & Nicolson, Kindle Edition, 2015), diary entry for 22 July 1940.
3   Collier, pp.106–7.

4   *SWEP*, 28 May 1940.

5   *SWEP*, 5 June 1940.

6   WGAS, BE 1/1/10.

7   WGAS, D/D Z 646/1.

8   TNA, WO/166/1356.

9   WGAS, TH 67/1.

10 TNA, WO/166/2014.

11 Ibid.

12 Ibid.

13 TNA, WO/166/1356.

14 TNA, WO/166/5678.

15 TNA, WO/166/3900.

16 TNA, WO/166/2014.

17 TNA, WO/166/6880.

18 Petticoats, pp.32–3.

19 TNA, WO/166/3655, WO/166/6880.

20 TNA, WO/166/6880.

21 Ibid.

22 Collier, pp.223–4.

23 Latchford, Laurie, *The Wartime Diary of Laurie Latchford, 1940–41* (South Wales Record Society, edited by Kate Elliott Jones and Wendy Cope, 2010), pp.145–7.

24 TNA, WO/166/6880.

25 Staybehinds.com.

26 Uboat.net.

27 Information from Commodore Nick Stanley, Royal Navy (Rtd).

28 sites.google.com /site/ahistoryofmumbles/ (Tom Ace); Storyofmumbles.org.uk (article by Kate Jones); wrecksite.eu.

Chapter 11: Testing the Defences

1   TNA, WO/166/6880.

2   WGAS, D/D Z 349/8/1-52.

3   WGAS, D 42/1.

4   TNA, WO/166/6880.

Chapter 12: Winning the War

1   *SWEP*, 17 February 1943.

2   TNA, HO/192/930.

3   Pearce, R T, *Operation Wasservogel – The Story of the South Buckham Farm Bomber Crash in Dorset and the Final Raid on Swansea* (Hamblin Books, 1997), pp.69–70.

4   WGAS, TH 75.

5   TA HO/192/930.

6   Davies, T G R, *Deeds not Words – A History of the Swansea General and Eye Hospital, 1847–1948*, pp.217–18 [Afterwards Davies].

7   Strickson, Pat, *Time Stood Still in a Muddy Hole – Captain John Hannaford, One of the Last Bomb Disposal Officers of WWII* (Brown Dog Books, 2018), pp.94–6.

8   Howlett, p.225.

9   Howells, Phil, *Oxwich to Omaha – American GIs in South Wales* (Published by the author, 2021 revision), p.235 [Afterwards Howells].

10 Website sites.google.com/site/ahistoryofmumbles/home, 14 March 2023.

11 Mike Lewis pursued a career in decorative glass, acquiring the established Swansea firm of C G Toft. For many years he spoke about his wartime experiences to a succession of Swansea schoolchildren.

12 Glenn Booker, email 22 July 2023.

13 nhdpedrorodon.weebly.com.

14 Facebook page – Men of the 2nd Infantry Division, 1940–45.

15 Howells, pp.200–1.

16 Jeff Manning and Ian Rogerson, email 5 February 2024.

17 Davies, p.210.

18 WGAS, TC 53/9953.

19 Williams, Dewi G, *Morriston Hospital – The Early Years* (Morriston Hospital Golden Jubilee Fund, 1993), p.19.

20 Ibid., pp.27–8.

21 Ibid., p.191.

22 Ibid., p.84.

23 WGAS, files HE 1/16-16C, HE 1/17 and HE 1/18-18A contain the annual reports of Swansea's Medical Officer of Health, 1935–1948.

24 WGAS, TC 55/3008.

25 WGAS, TH 71.

26 WGAS, files PH 1/37 to PH 1/43 contain the annual reports of the Swansea Port Health Authority for 1939–45.

27 WGAS, TC 53/7763.

28 WGAS, D 50/44.

29 *WM*, 9 May 1945.

30 The Home Guard had officially been stood down in December 1944.

31 WGAS TC 53/7763.

32 *WM*, 13 August 1946.

33 WGAS, TC 54/1798.

Chapter 13: Journey's End

1 *SWEP*, 20, 21, 24 October 1944.

2 WGAS, TC 201/1.

3 *SWEP*, 25 September 1941.

4 Howlett, p.24.

5 WGAS, leaflet, 'Civilian Deaths due to War Operations' (online PDF file).

6 Lyndon Elsey (Registrar of Burials and Cremations, Swansea City Council), email 5 June 2023.

7 Jeff Manning and Ian Rogerson, email 5 February 2024.

8 WGAS, TC 54/11049.

9 WGAS, TC 54/11101.

10 Hallesy, Helen, 'The Museum During World War II', in Helen Hallesy & Gerald Gabb (eds) *Swansea's Royal Institution and Wales's First Museum*, pp.440–1, 450 (University of Wales Press, 2024).

11 WGAS, D/D DEC 6/1-2.

12 WGAS, TC 54/4571.

13 WGAS, D/D BF/E 404.

14 Evans, Dinah, *A new, even better, Abertawe – Rebuilding Swansea, 1941–1961* (West Glamorgan Archive Service, 2019), p.3 [Afterwards Evans].

15 WGAS, D 268/5.

16 Evans, p.88–9.

17 Ibid., p.174.

18 Wakelin, p.99.

19 *SWEP*, 18 March 1941.

20 Thomas, Dylan, 'Return Journey', in *A Dylan Thomas Treasury, Poems, Stories and Broadcasts*, Walford Davies (ed.) (Phoenix, 2001 edition), pp.171–186.

21 Ferris, Paul, *Dylan Thomas – The Biography* (Phoenix, 2000), p.196.

Appendix

List of Air Raids on Swansea – summary

** Blitz attacks

Date	Areas hit	Killed/ Serious injuries/ Light injuries	No. of high-explosive bombs/ Parachute mines
1940			
27 June	Danygraig Road, Kilvey Hill	0 / 0 / 0	6 / 0
29 June	Llansamlet, Upper Fforest Works, Morriston	0 / 0 /0	2 / 0
10 July	King's Dock	12 / 13 / 13	4 / 0
18 July	Jersey Marine South Signal Box	0 / 0 / 0	1 / 0
20 July	South Dock, Elba Crescent	0 / 0 / 0	2 / 0
22 July	Talefrewe Farm, Cockett	0 / 0 / 0	2 / 0
30 July	Banc Mawr, Cockett	0 / 0 / 0	2 / 0
2 Aug	Mumbles, Foreshore, Townhill, Mayhill, Treboeth	0 / 2 / 2	13 / 0
3 Aug	Sea off Mumbles, Waunarlwydd	0 / 0 / 0	10 / 0
10 Aug	Landore, Brynhyfryd, Singleton Park, Clyne, Ravenhill	15 / 5 / 10	30 / 0
17 Aug	Cwmbwrla, Greenhill, Treboeth, Strand	0 / 4 / 8	30 / 0
18 Aug	Gors Avenue, Greenhill, Cwmbwrla, Foxhole	1 / 2 / 1	12 / 0
24 Aug	Kilvey Hill, Port Tennant, St Thomas, Killay	0 / 0 / 0	Incendiary bombs
1–2 Sept**	Various parts of the town and borough	33 / 37 / 71	106 / 0
5 Sept	Tyrhester Farm, Llansamlet and Treboeth	0 / 0 / 0	4 / 0
11 Sept	Brynmill – Langland Terrace and Chesshyre Street	0 / 0 / 0	2 / 0
24 Sept	Town centre, South Dock	0 / 0 /0	Incendiary bombs

Date	Areas hit	Killed/ Serious injuries/ Light injuries	No. of high-explosive bombs/ Parachute mines
25 Sept	High Street, Mount Pleasant, Mayhill, Townhill, Uplands, St Thomas	0 / 0 /0	9 / 0
9 Oct	Kilvey Hill, north district of town	0 / 0 / 0	6 / 0
21 Oct	Gors Avenue, Mayhill, Llansamlet	0 / 0 / 0	15 / 0
1941			
2 Jan	Field at Ynystawe	0 / 0 / 0	2/ 0
5 Jan	Dillwyn Street, St Helen's Road, Sketty Park Estate, St Thomas	0 / 7 / 13	12/ 0
13 Jan	King's Dock	0 / 0 / 5	2 / 0
17 Jan**	Town centre, St Thomas, Bonymaen	55 / 38 / 59	178 / 0
19–21 Feb**	Town centre and surrounding streets, Townhill, Mayhill, Landore and elsewhere	230 / 260 / 137	896 / 0
3 March	Banc Mawr, Cockett	0 / 0 / 0	6 / 0
12 March	Neath Road (near Bridge Inn)	3 / 2 / 4	16 / 0
14 March	Bonymaen	0 / 0 / 0	Incendiary bombs
24 March	Danygraig Road	0 / 0 / 0	4 / 0
31 March	Strand (electricity station)	3 / 0 / 0	2 / 0
8 April	Mumbles Head, Limeslade	0 / 0 / 0	1 / 0
22 April	Frederick Place	0 / 0 / 13	0 / 2
20 May	Neath Road School, Morriston	0 / 0 / 3	1 / 0
31 May	Treboeth, Morriston	0 / 0 / 4	4 / 0
28 June	Langland Bay, Mayhill Gardens	0 / 0 / 0	4 / 0
28 Nov	Strand and Burrows, Port Tennant	1 / 7 / 13	0 / 2
1943			
16 Feb**	Brynymor Road, St Helen's Road, RAF Fairwood, St Thomas, Swansea Hospital.	34 / 61 / 50	50 / 0
(40 raids in total)		**387 / 438 / 406**	**1,434 / 4**

Select Bibliography

Alban, J R, *The Three Nights' Blitz – Select Contemporary Reports relating to Swansea's Air Raids of February 1941* (Swansea City Council, 1994).

Brooke, Field Marshal Lord Alanbrooke, *War Diaries 1939–1945* (Weidenfeld & Nicolson, Kindle Edition, 2015).

Chatterton, Andrew, *Britain's Secret Defences – Civilian Saboteurs, Spies and Assassins During the Second World War* (Casemate Publishers, 2022).

Davies, Walford, *A Dylan Thomas Treasury – Poems, Stories and Broadcasts* (Phoenix, 2001 edition).

Davis, Ellen, *Kerry's Children* (Seren, 2004).

Ethell, J L, *Janes Aircraft of World War II* (Harper Collins, 1995).

Evans, Dinah, *A new, even better, Abertawe – Rebuilding Swansea, 1941–1961* (West Glamorgan Archive Service, 2019).

Ferris, Paul, *Dylan Thomas – The Biography* (Phoenix, 2000).

Foner, Henry (Heinz Lichtwitz), *Postcards to a Little Boy* (Yad Vashem, 2013).

Hammond, R J, *Food – Volume I, The Growth of Policy* (HMSO, History of the Second World War, 1951).

HMSO, *Roof Over Britain – The Official Story of the A.A. Defences, 1939–1942* (facsimile – The Stationery Office, 2001).

Howells, Phil, *Oxwich to Omaha – American GIs in South Wales* (Published by the author, 2021 revision).

Howlett, Peter, *Fighting With Figures* (HMSO, Central Statistical Office, 1995).

Hughes, W T Mainwaring, *Swansea's Mayors and Civic Events between 1900 and 1974* (Published by the author, not dated) and *Kicks and Kudos: Candid Recollections of Forty Years as a Councillor* (Published by the author, not dated).

Hunt, W W, *To Guard My People* (Published by the author, 1957).

Jenkins, Paul, *Twenty by Fourteen, A History of the South Wales Tinplate Industry 1700–1961* (Gomer Press, 1995).

Latchford, Laurie, *The Wartime Diary of Laurie Latchford, 1940–41* (South Wales Record Society, edited by Kate Elliott Jones and Wendy Cope, 2010).

Mclelland, Tim, *Action Stations Revisited, Volume 5, Wales and the Midlands* (Crécy Publishing Ltd, 2012).

Noakes, Lucy, *Dying for the Nation – Death, Grief and Bereavement in Second World War Britain* (Manchester University Press, 2022 paperback).

O'Brien, T H, *Civil Defence* (HMSO, History of the Second World War, 1955).

Parker, H M D, *Manpower – A Study of War-time Policy and Administration* (HMSO, History of the Second World War, 1957).

Pearce, R T, *Operation Wasservogel – The Story of the South Buckham Farm Bomber Crash in Dorset and the Final Raid on Swansea* (Hamblin Books, 1997).

Pryer, K, *Luftwaffe Over Swansea: A History of the Air Attacks on Swansea, 1939–45* (Keith Pryer and Co., Swansea, not dated).

South Wales Evening Post, *Memories of Swansea at War* (Archive Publications, Manchester & the *South Wales Evening Post*, 1988).

Strickson, Pat, *Time Stood Still in a Muddy Hole – Captain John Hannaford, One of the Last Bomb Disposal Officers of WWII* (Brown Dog Books, 2018).

Toye, Richard, *The Roar of the Lion – The Untold Story of Churchill's World War II Speeches* (Oxford University Press, 2015 paperback).

Verrill-Rhys, Leigh, & Beddoe, Dierdre, *Parachutes and Petticoats – Welsh Women Writing on the Second World War* (Honno Autobiography, 2003 reprint).

Wakelin, Peter, *George Little, The Ugly Lovely Landscape* (Parthian Books, 2023).

Index

All addresses and buildings are in
Swansea unless otherwise indicated

Also from Y Lolfa:

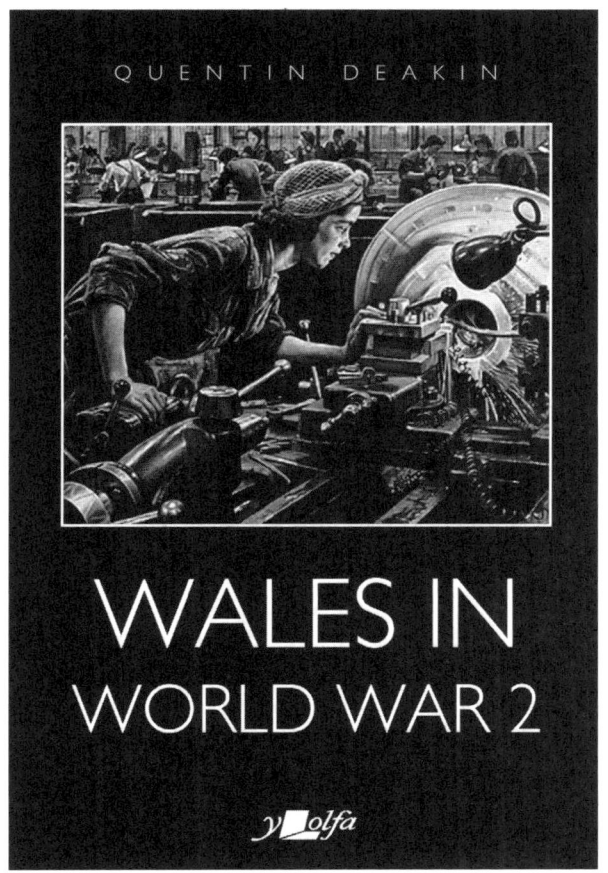

£14.99

On Dragons'
Wings

**A History of No. 614 (County of Glamorgan)
Squadron, Royal Auxiliary Air Force**

£14.99

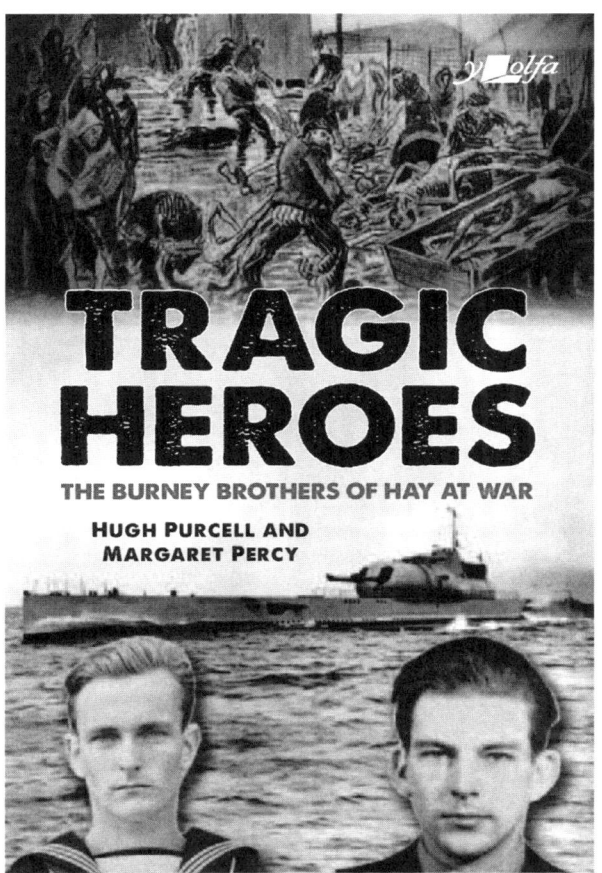

TRAGIC HEROES

THE BURNEY BROTHERS OF HAY AT WAR

**HUGH PURCELL AND
MARGARET PERCY**

£14.99

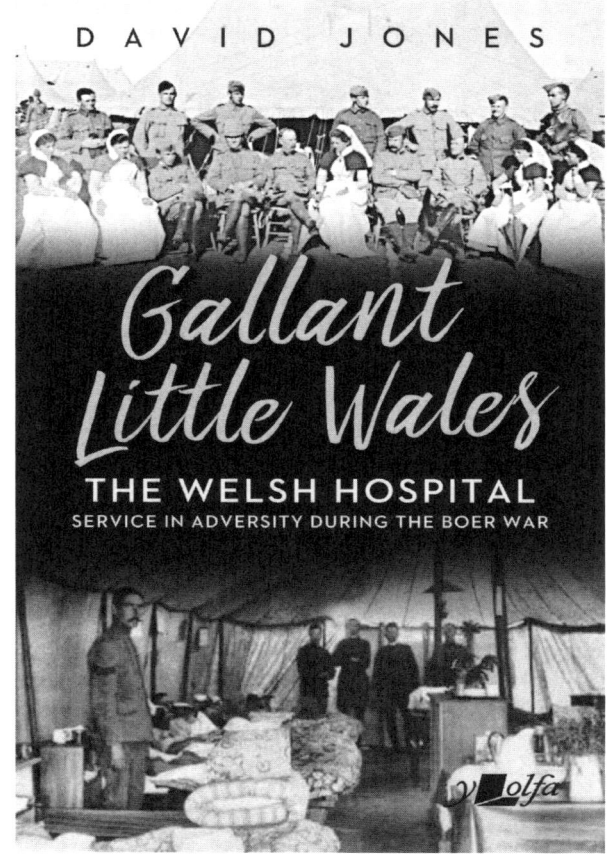

DAVID JONES

Gallant Little Wales

THE WELSH HOSPITAL

SERVICE IN ADVERSITY DURING THE BOER WAR

y olfa

£9.99

GWYN JENKINS

A WELSH COUNTY AT WAR

ESSAYS ON CEREDIGION AT THE TIME OF THE FIRST WORLD WAR

y_lolfa

£9.99